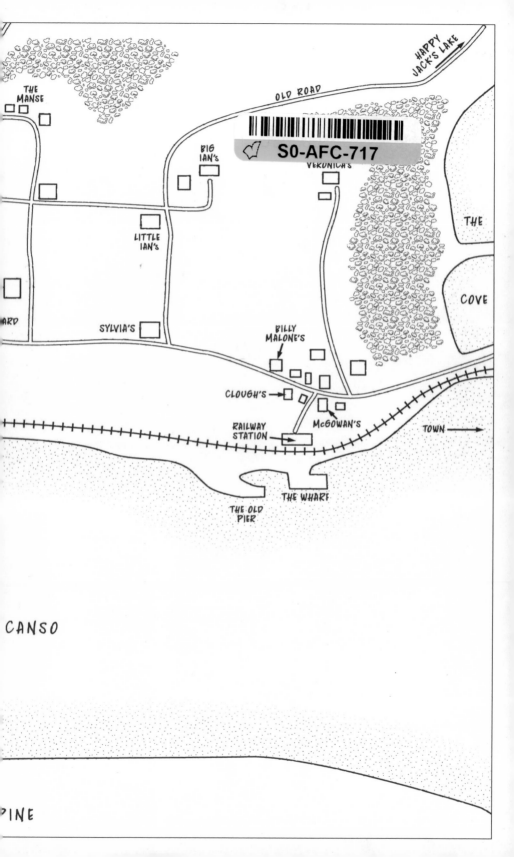

CAUSEWAY

LINDEN MacINTYRE

CAUSEWAY

A PASSAGE FROM INNOCENCE

HarperCollins*Publishers*Ltd

Published by HarperCollins Publishers Ltd

First Edition.

HarperCollins books may be purchased for
educational, business, or sales promotional
use through our Special Markets Department.

HarperCollins Publishers Ltd
2 Bloor Street East, 20th Floor
Toronto, Ontario, Canada
M4W 1A8

www.harpercollins.ca

Library and Archives Canada Cataloguing in
Publication

MacIntyre, Linden
Causeway : a passage from innocence /
Linden MacIntyre.—1st ed.

ISBN-13: 978-0-00-200724-5
ISBN-10: 0-00-200724-X

1. MacIntyre, Linden. 2. MacIntyre family.
3. Canso Causeway (N.S.)—History. 4. Cape
Breton Island (N.S.)—Social life and customs.
5. Cape Breton Island (N.S.)—Biography.
I. Title.

FC2343.25.M33A3 2006   971.6'904092
C2006-901092-7

RRD 9 8 7 6 5 4 3 2 1

Printed and bound in the United States
Design by Sharon Kish · Set in Janson
Maps by Susan MacGregor/Digital Zone

for my mother,
Alice Donohue MacIntyre

Ill fares the land, to hastening ills a prey,
Where wealth accumulates and men decay.

Oliver Goldsmith, "The Deserted Village"

CONTENTS

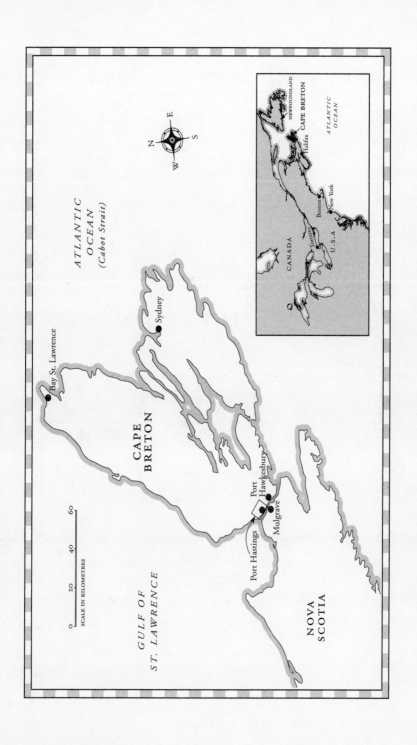

ATLANTIC
OCEAN
(*Cabot Strait*)

Bay St. Lawrence

Sydney

CAPE
BRETON

Port
Hawkesbury

Port Hastings

Mulgrave

NOVA
SCOTIA

GULF OF
ST. LAWRENCE

60

40

20

0

SCALE IN KILOMETRES

N

E

W

S

NEWFOUNDLAND

CAPE BRETON

ATLANTIC
OCEAN

Halifax

Boston

New York

CANADA

Toronto

U.S.A

IN THE FALL
OF '68

1

GETTING LOADED

It is late Saturday morning, and my mother is at the stove fishing the doughnuts out of a dangerous pot of boiling fat. My father is quietly watching her while sipping on an instant coffee and tapping his spoon on the can of Carnation evaporated milk. The top of the can is punctured by two triangular holes, and one has a collar of yellowing acrylic scum. He puts the spoon on the table and reaches past her, plucks a new doughnut from a heaping plate, rolls it around in the sugar bowl, nibbles delicately. His thinning hair is dishevelled, his eyes watery.

"Every so often a fella needs a good blowout," he says.

The reference is to last night, when we got loaded. Now he's either still half in the bag or he's getting reckless in his old age. That might be what a little bit of good luck does to a man who never had much. I'm thinking: he isn't reading the room; he isn't picking up the signals.

I'm in the rocking chair near the corner of the stove, maintaining a tactical silence.

There's the rasping rattle of spitting fat. Another plate of dough balls slides into the bubbling cauldron. I imagine the quiet invocation of spells.

I light a cigarette and, when my mother disappears briefly into the pantry, quietly propose taking our hangovers to town, where they are less likely to become a topic of conversation. The house is too warm anyway. It is November, but a fat fly is stirring on the window ledge.

The old man shrugs, drains the mug, coughs deeply, then agrees.

We'll check out the town. Postpone the reckoning.

He winks at me.

———

I hadn't seen the town for a year, not since moving the family up to Ottawa, where I have a job on Parliament Hill working for a newspaper. It was a paper I knew nobody around here ever saw because it was all business and finance. You could feel a palpable difference from before, when I was with the Halifax daily and the locals regularly followed what I wrote. It was like having a thousand editors then—every one of them with an opinion, particularly on the politics. But after I went to Ottawa in the fall of '67, it seemed I'd moved to another planet.

The trip home had been unexpected. Mid-morning the previous day I got a call from a buddy in a minister's office offering a free lift down. MacEachen and Chrétien had government business in Cape Breton on the weekend. There was a spare seat on the government plane, leaving early evening.

I called home in the middle of the afternoon. The old man promptly volunteered to meet me at the airport in Sydney, two hours away. It was Friday night, and all the liquor stores were open late.

Driving towards town, I couldn't miss all the changes. The village I grew up in, Port Hastings, and the town, Port Hawkesbury, three miles away, seemed to be in a permanent state of turmoil. Mostly stuff was being torn down to make way for new roads, by the look of it. Houses gone. Roads widened, menacing even the old stores that have been here forever, Clough's and McGowan's. Also the old Captain

MacInnis house, where my friend Billy Malone lived for a while. Even Mr. Clough's lovely old home. All landmarks, and all under the soulless shadow of progress.

It's hard to believe Mr. Clough has been dead for almost a decade—since '59. They say it was the Diefenbaker sweep of the country in '58 that did it, just two years after the Stanfield Tories snatched power from a bereft Liberal Party in Nova Scotia. It was all too much for him—two Tory victories in quick succession. Three, actually: Diefenbaker won a minority first, in '57. Then he practically exterminated the federal Grits in '58. Mr. Clough was gone a year later.

Other Liberals would scoff, of course. Mr. Clough was almost eighty, for the love of God. And he had wicked ulcers, anyway. Always optimistic about the future of the place was Mr. Clough. Yes, he'd probably have given up on the whole Western world, seeing Diefenbaker in power. But that would have just made him more determined to live and work like the patriot he was to put a quick end to that anomaly of Canadian history—a Tory majority government in Ottawa.

Who knows with politics?

Just beyond the town, in another old village called Point Tupper, there was a large Swedish wood-pulp mill, and it was about to expand into newsprint. There was talk of other big projects—an oil refinery; petrochemicals; a dock for the largest supertankers in the world; a heavy-water plant that would have something to do with nuclear power. Point Tupper was doomed, but nobody except for a few of the older people there seemed to care. Port Hastings and Port Hawkesbury were the beneficiaries.

It was becoming very exciting, but the main headline was that out of all the commotion and progress, the old man had finally scored the first dependably permanent employment he'd ever had in what he would call civilization. He was fifty years old. He was born on a mountain just out back. He grew up around here and had his own family and home here for years. But to support himself and us he'd spent most of his adult life living in wilderness camps all over the country and working as a miner, an occupation he'd begun shortly after he turned sixteen, back in what they called "the dirty thirties."

The new job, he'd explained the night before, was not exactly what he wanted to do with his life, but it was a definite improvement over the miseries of mining camps and long days blowing up rocks in the impenetrable darkness far below the surface of the earth. A steady, well-paid job in the fresh air, it was, good enough for the time being.

"Who is it again you're working for?" I asked.

"The Nova Scotia Water Resources Commission," he replied grandly, half mocking the long, vague title.

But it was good work—mostly driving around in his new Volkswagen checking out pipes and pumps and valves and keeping an eye on Landry Lake, the water resource that supplied all the new industry and the expanding town.

It all sounded very boring.

What else did we talk about?

Briefly, my newspaper work, which has to do with government policy and the balance of payments, interest rates, and a lot of abstract economic indicators that seem to reveal the future to the knowledgeable. I told him a bit of inside stuff about the Cabinet ministers on the plane. Allan MacEachen, minister of immigration, is also the local MP and, just months earlier, ran against Pierre Trudeau for the party leadership. And a relative unknown, Jean Chrétien, is in Indian Affairs, but, coming from Quebec, is a stranger hereabouts.

"Just ordinary fellows," I told my father. "Plain guys like ourselves." We'd all had a couple of drinks together coming down on the plane.

Speaking of drinks . . .

"Sure," he said.

Drinking in the car was pretty normal then, and by Kelly's Mountain the conversation was quite animated, even if not particularly meaningful. But I could clearly remember that there was a lot of talk about being your own boss, which was a dearly held dream of his from the year naught. Much like writing The Great Canadian Novel was a dearly held dream of younger fellows in the press gallery—something you talked about when you were loaded, and rarely even then.

The truth is that driving to town that Saturday morning, neither of us could remember much of what we'd talked about at all after Kelly's Mountain. I mostly remember the look of disappointment on my mother's face when she saw the condition of the pair of us coming through the door. And the artificiality of the conversation that dragged on afterwards, enlivened from time to time by sarcastic remarks from himself as he'd rise suddenly and disappear in the direction of where he'd left his coat—then come back smiling, as if he was fooling everybody.

The cheer improved when she asked about the three kids back in Ottawa. They were, I could report truthfully, great, especially the baby, born in August, who had been named after the old man. Dan.

The old fellow was known far and wide as Dan Rory.

The town was always busy on a Saturday morning. By 1968 the slump that followed the completion of the Canso Causeway thirteen years before was practically forgotten. The mud and dust and machinery of progress were everywhere again. And the noise: massive trucks loaded with sour, sticky pulpwood noisily gearing down for the congestion of cars near the new shopping mall; bulldozers digging holes for new houses, schools, and streets for all the new people they were expecting to move in.

"Somebody was saying the other day that there's going to be thirty thousand living here by 1980," he remarked as we rounded the turn at Grant's Pond.

I scoffed privately. I worked in Ottawa and talked regularly to people who knew the reality. The "limits of growth," they called it. Plus, we'd heard it all before, back when they were building the causeway.

"Thirty thousand," I echoed, trying not to sound dubious.

"Bigger than Sydney," he said.

"Where did we hear that before?" I remarked, sour memories resurfacing.

"Ah well," he said. Probably doing the math in his head: thirty thousand people plus the service businesses they'll need mean maybe ten thousand new buildings and umpteen thousand board feet of lumber that will have to come from somewhere. There are few things in the world he loves more than fresh-sawn lumber.

"Ah well," he said again. "I know what you mean."

While my father was in the drugstore, I sat drowsing in the car and watching the weekend coming and going. Vaguely familiar people rushing this way and that. Everybody more or less shaped and dressed the same. Burly, round, rumpled men wearing hard hats and vests and muddy work boots. Women in scarves and slacks with bags of groceries, and kids nagging behind them. The scene brought on, as always, a peculiar nervousness. The fear, according to Prinsky, the Dow Jones guy in Ottawa, of getting sucked by sentiment back into your own past. Prinsky and I talked a lot about that sort of thing—our ambiguous connections with home and history.

Prinsky believes home is more or less where they let you settle down, and he doesn't fully buy into the Celtic notion of belonging to a place—unless you're a Zionist. We're both mildly sympathetic to the Zionists because we can understand where they're coming from, or going—whichever.

I find a comforting symmetry in a lot of the attitudes of Jews and Celtic Catholics, especially when we're talking roots and guilt.

I saw my father, then, standing with a wino he'd grown up with out back, talking quietly while studying the ground. Eventually he dug something out of his pocket and passed it over in a pretend handshake. He's exactly twice my age, I thought.

When I'm fifty, I calculated, he'll be seventy-five. Surely by then we'll find something meaningful to discuss. He started walking towards the car. I noted that he still had the appearance of considerable physical strength. Shoulders rounded but thick, stout biceps and forearms bulging under the shirt. Hairline receding, but only because of all the years wearing the sweaty Bakelite hard hat.

I felt a brief wave of something like affection. Then he stopped again, talking to some other vaguely familiar stranger, and the ache of tedium returned. Or maybe it was just the hangover.

Prinsky is always quoting Thomas Wolfe, the author of *You Can't Go Home Again*—always talking about the incompatibility of differing generations. Maybe. But I saw last summer when the parents came up to Ottawa to visit and welcome the arrival of a new grandchild that it was a whole lot more complicated. That summer visit was when I realized that the generation gap wasn't so much from a cultural incompatibility as from a basic lack of common experience. That was our fundamental problem, my father and I—*quotidian*—a new word I just love. We lack a common quotidian experience.

I know lots of old timers in the press gallery—Norman Campbell, Dick Jackson, Charlie Lynch, John Bird, Warren Baldwin. Ancients, with lives extending long before my own. Fellow travellers through a common patch of history. We never have a problem finding things to talk about.

———

The parents had timed the trip to coincide with the due date, near the end of August. This would make three grandkids. Ellen was first. Then Darrow came—same year as Ellen. The old man was proud as anything for having come through Montreal in one piece and then finding the place in the west end of Ottawa without asking anyone for directions. The talk came easily that night, and it was all about the new arrival and whether it would be a boy or a girl. It was anybody's guess. I'd laid in beer and rye to treat the parents.

Day two we did some sightseeing. The House of Commons—you could walk right in. No hassle. The old fellow got a big kick out of sitting in Trudeau's chair in the middle of the front row on the government side. We fooled around a bit, I pretending to ask the prime minister a question from the opposition benches. Himself pretending to answer. Later we all visited a friend who worked for the Liberal Party and was vacationing in a cottage in the Gatineau Hills near a lake. The cottage had previously been owned by Lester Pearson, the Liberal prime minister before Trudeau. A very fine, down-to-earth man is Mr. Pearson, my parents were informed by our host.

My mother, who is a Tory, just raised her eyebrows.

The old man looked around the modest cabin.

"Well, well," he said.

Then things started to drag. The baby was late. Days passed, and the charms of Ottawa were soon exhausted.

We went to some of the local watering holes, but it was soon obvious he wasn't comfortable in any of them. Too much loud music in the bars in Hull. The taverns in Ottawa were either too high class or dives with wet floors and loud regulars who made a racket dragging metal chairs from table to table. Toilets smelled like piss and Creolin, with butts and chewing gum in the urinals. Maybe it reminded him too much of the mining camps.

Wilfred Gillis from home was in town at the time. An exceptional fiddle player in the Cape Breton Celtic style who also spoke quite a bit of Gaelic, Wilfred might perk things up, I thought.

But when I knocked on Wilfred's door, there was no reply.

"Chan'eil aig an taigh," said the old fellow, inadvertently lapsing into his mother tongue to acknowledge the obvious fact that Wilfred wasn't home.

We visited acquaintances of mine, but he seemed awkward among city people he didn't know. It was soon clear that he just wanted to leave, even though the baby still hadn't come.

The plan was to depart right after Mass on the Sunday. I suggested a beer before lunch. One led to another, and soon lunch was forgotten. The departure plan was amended to Monday—first thing.

We ended a long Sunday sitting out in the backyard, mostly staring at the starry sky. There was a bit of desultory discussion about the unpleasantness of mining and the difficulty of changing occupations when a lot of your life experience leaves you with serious handicaps. I kept waiting for more about the handicaps, but, as usual, he wasn't interested in elaborating. No whiner, he. I expected, at least, an updated version of the old escape strategy—the perennial scheme to give up the mining and start his own business at home. Ideally a fleet of trucks, or a sawmill. He loved trucks and sawmills, even though there was a long, unhappy history of betrayal by machinery. But there was no talk of trucks or mills that night.

Three years earlier, in the spring of 1965, we got loaded in Gander, Newfoundland, and the talk of trucks went on into the wee hours of the morning. He was working in a mine over there at the time, and I was covering a government junket of some kind and managed to get a call through to the camp.

Out of the blue he arrived at the hotel in Gander on the Saturday afternoon in great cheer. I was hanging out with Ben Ward, who works for Canadian Press, and we were in Ben's room playing cards when I heard a persistent knocking in the hallway. Finally I checked, and there he was at my door. Got a lift in to Gander with some other miner and had twenty-four hours to kill, he said. So he set up shop in the hotel bar while I did my reporter thing, which had something to do with a hydro project in Churchill Falls.

By the time we hooked up later that evening, my father was totally relaxed and uncharacteristically chatty. We got into a bit of family history. He was even asking questions about his first grandchild, my little girl who was just a few months old then. Ellen. He hadn't met her yet.

Sitting out in the backyard more than three years later, it was hard to believe he was the same guy. In Gander we talked easily about earning a livelihood—and about the difficulty of getting over the high threshold of poverty and into the place where you could consider yourself relatively secure for the long run.

"What are you making now?" he blurted that night in Gander. "If you don't mind me asking."

"Forty-eight hundred," I said, half boastfully.

"You're almost there," he announced. "Five thou' is the magic number. Once you're making fi' thou' a year, you can stop sweating the small stuff, worrying about spending a buck here or there."

It never occurred to me, that night in Gander, to ask how much *he* got for blowing up those rocks in the clammy darkness of whatever shithole he was working in at the time. How much he was being paid for putting on damp, filthy clothes and a heavy hard hat and risking his life every day by the dim illumination of a glorified flashlight stuck on the front of his head.

Maybe I didn't ask because it was clear from the reaction to my own salary that the hard-rock miner was earning less than a junior pencil pusher working on a second-rate newspaper. That would have been hard to acknowledge.

Talk wasn't the old man's strong suit at the best of times. But sitting out in that Ottawa backyard on a Sunday night in August 1968, he was quieter than usual. There was something different in the air, and it smelled a little bit like defeat.

They got away on the Monday morning.

Afterwards it occurred to me that maybe the sombre mood had something to do with an underground rockslide in Bathurst, New Brunswick, the previous autumn. He got off with a broken foot that time, but perhaps it was a message about mortality.

The baby arrived Wednesday afternoon.

———

It was obvious right away that the man who met me at the airport that Friday night in Sydney had been reborn. The new job, I figured. Finally, steady employment and living at home. Pump maintenance for the Nova Scotia Water Resources Commission seemed to be therapeutic.

"The hair of the dog."

The first words out of his mouth when he climbs back into the Volkswagen. Check out the tavern, to see who's there.

It was just after midday then. The tavern was a small, white building with green plastic plants in a large picture window on the south end of Granville Street. It was doing a booming trade. Truck drivers and construction workers and an assortment of townsmen grabbing a quick one before going home to the noon dinner.

The first went down smoothly and restored a semblance of relaxation. What to talk about? Political issues, very much on my mind, were out of the question. The old man loathed politics and considered politicians liars and opportunists. You couldn't talk much about the newspaper business because it was clear he couldn't see much point in that line of work. We'd actually worked together in the mines for a couple of summers, when I was struggling through university, but the experience didn't leave much to be discussed.

"Do you ever see . . ." and there would be half a dozen names from our common mining experience. Invariably he hadn't seen any of them for a long time—miners being like that, basically nomads. We didn't have much common experience at home to talk about because his presence there, from my point of view, had been mostly a series of visits.

It became obvious that the broken foot a year earlier had been a turning point—the point at which he'd decided to pack it in.

"How's the health otherwise?" I asked, after he explained the foot.

"Perfect," he said.

"Really?"

He later revealed that they'd made him take a complete physical before he left Bathurst. They commented on what you'd expect: wear and tear in the lungs; scar tissue and a trace of silicosis from breathing crap all those years. But there was also good news.

"They were telling me I've got the heart of a teenager. That's the main thing. Right? The old ticker."

He was stabbing himself in the chest with a thick forefinger that was calloused and stained to the knuckle.

He came home for good then and, by a rare stroke of good fortune, found himself working for the government.

Amazing luck.

I took out a package of cigarettes and offered one.

"Plus, I've quit that work," he said, leaning back in his chair defensively.

"I'm taking this up instead," he said, pulling a pipe from his coat pocket.

"Oh," I said, lighting my cigarette, trying to blow the smoke away from him. "I hadn't noticed."

"Ah well," he said, eyeing the cigarette with a sad expression. "Not used to it yet. The damn pipe is a lot of work for the little bit of pleasure it gives."

In a quick memory flash I saw him back in Tilt Cove, Newfoundland, where we worked together for a summer. He was sitting in the cookhouse, one elbow on the cluttered table, cigarette going and a look of temporary joy wreathing his face with the smoke as he stirred evaporated milk into a cup of acrid coffee.

"It smells nice," I said, trying to be kind. "I love the smell of a pipe."

"But it tastes like shit if you aren't cleaning it all the time."

And then, a stirring in the memory.

"I think Mr. Malone smoked a pipe," I said.

"Who?"

"Mr. Malone. Billy's father."

"Ah, Billy Malone," he said, smiling. "You and Billy were quite the pair, back when they were building the causeway. Do you ever hear from Billy?"

"No," I said.

"Funny about those times," he said. "Building the causeway."

The second round appeared before us and, while we were competing to pay for it, I felt a sudden pang of ecstasy. The beer? The cigarette? Or maybe just the talking.

"There," he said, as the waiter walked away. "Where were we just then?"

I was about to take us back to the causeway when a low voice from out of nowhere said, "Hello, Dan Rory." And another old acquaintance from out back was reaching for the empty chair at the table.

I recognized him, and the feeling of goodwill evaporated instantly for a number of reasons you wouldn't have wanted to get into with your father.

The new arrival studied me suspiciously as he sat down.

"This your boy?"

"That's it," he said, winking.

And the interloper instantly turned a shoulder towards me, lowered his voice, and launched into Gaelic.

The Gaelic. It was like a deep, dark forest that the old man disappeared into whenever he seemed to be around people he'd grown up with, people with whom he was comfortable. I'm suddenly remembering the long afternoon visits with his parents, out on the mountain. Dougald and Peggy, or Peigeag, as the old people knew her. A woman who could have lived comfortably in any age but the present. And I could suddenly see her as she was the last time—standing in the door of the little house on the mountain, hands tucked under an apron, a dark shawl around her skinny shoulders as my father and I drove away on the back of a truck that snowy morning.

Guilt intruded then. I must go to see her today, I thought.

That last visit to the mountain had been another of those rare moments that fell somewhere just short of intimacy with the old man— when Dougald died the year before, in 1967.

It was in April, but there had been a heavy snowfall that prevented people from driving up to his wake—a very peculiar scene that I later described in detail to Prinsky over martinis in the Press Club.

"Man, you gotta write that down," Prinsky had said, eyes wide.

"What do you mean?" I'd asked, half laughing.

And Prinsky just leaned back grinning and rolling his eyes.

"Man, you just don't get it. That's what I love about you. You're talking about another world. You have to write that down." And he just shook his head. Prinsky grew up in Montreal.

Over time I came to see what Prinsky meant. The scene on the mountain was bizarre and spiritual and completely alien to anyone who didn't have a feel for the nineteenth century and the whole Gaelic thing. And it all came back, sitting there listening to my father and his weird old pal talking in their secret language.

Here's what I told Prinsky. I was still living in Halifax and word of my grandfather's death had come as a shock. Dougald was at least ninety-five, but he'd shown no signs of frailty. He shovelled snow, split wood, walked long distances. He and Peigeag had lived near the top of the mountain in an old house without electricity or running water until they were in their late eighties. Only reluctantly did they move down a couple of miles to a little house next door to their oldest son, John Dan, who was also known as John Boy. After the first winter there, talk of moving back up the mountain gradually faded out.

Dougald died without ado on a menacing day in April of the centennial year of Canada's Confederation, just a few years shy of his own centennial.

It had been snowing heavily by the time I arrived from Halifax and picked up my father, who had also been summoned home from some-where—Bathurst, I think. We drove out the Trans-Canada Highway, which was still relatively new. The snowploughs had been busy on the main road, but it was immediately obvious that the mountain road was blocked. So we walked together from near the old Lamey place on the highway to the little house where the wake was being held. It was hard going, snow up to our knees and still falling silently. The scene was magical, but it was probably the exertion that limited conversation to the occasional monosyllable.

The snow, luminous on the broad backs of the older pine and spruce trees and deepening on the ground, seemed to magnify the shadows and the silence. My father was breathing hard when we finally arrived at the large clearing where my uncle and grandmother lived.

There were no vehicles, but both houses were packed with people from all over the district. Many of the mourners weren't much younger than the deceased. There was hardly a word of English to be heard, but that was to be expected in that time and place. The dead man was laid out in a small back room in the little house. Periodically, people would crowd around the casket to say decades of the rosary, then drift back to the kitchen or to the larger house next door, where there seemed to be an endless supply of tea and biscuits and sweets. You could hear voices in the darkness outside, behind the houses and near the barn, or in the vicinity of the lurking snowcapped woods, where men would retire for stealthy swallows from hidden bottles.

I was aching to join them, but, oddly, my father insisted that we avoid the drinkers that night. It occurred to me only later that it was probably out of fear of how Grandma would react. Peigeag, as they'd say quietly behind her back, was death on booze and had a vicious tongue when roused. She spoke hardly any English at all, so I was unfamiliar with the particulars of her wrath. But anyone who felt the sting of it even once never wanted to repeat the experience.

There were also those who maintained quite seriously that Peigeag had "special powers." I've heard she removed a cancerous growth on her face once by applying a peculiar poultice that contained, among other things, cobwebs. People with problems would, in the old days before doctors, come to her for mysterious cures. She could heal obscure ailments. Someone with, say, a tiny piece of wood or metal in his eye would come to her for help. She'd check the eye, then rinse her mouth with water—and spit out whatever had been causing the pain. People swear they saw her do it. Conversely, it was widely held that she could cause afflictions if provoked.

It was getting on towards midnight, and I was standing alone in the little room contemplating the still form of my grandfather, reflecting on the terrible serenity of death. Dougald was a gentle soul, already ancient in my first memory of him. Smiling and chuckling at the slightest pleasure, he seemed to exist in perpetual deference to his more assertive wife. He called her the Old Woman even in her presence.

It was remarked that he'd grown up hard. Lost his mother as a

18

child. Handed off while still a boy to a bachelor uncle on the mainland, where he worked like a slave but at least learned to read and write. Fled while still young into raw frontier places in the United States. There he worked hard and carried a pistol, which he still kept somewhere in their little house on the mountain.

He was probably in his thirties when he came home, met Peigeag, and married her.

I was thinking: now it's over. There he lies, unfamiliar with eyes closed, bloodless lips pressed together firmly as if to prevent his secrets from escaping back into the world of the curious. Bony hands clasped around the prayer beads on his chest.

Then, suddenly, one of the guests, an old neighbour from up the mountain, unsteady from drink, appeared in the room. He shuffled towards the casket. He started gesticulating and speaking to the corpse in Gaelic, wildly and with great confidence.

It was when he reached under his coat and removed a bottle of liquor and uncapped it right there and raised it to his lips that all hell suddenly broke out in the little room. Peigeag was all over the boozer, excoriating him with a shrill fluency that, even though I didn't know the particulars of the language, made my hair stand on end. Then she grabbed the poor old fellow, frog-marched him to an outside door, and hurled him out into the snow.

Blue eyes blazing, she wheeled and marched out of the room, back to the kitchen to resume her vigil in a rocking chair that had been strategically located close to the stove but with a sightline through a window to the outside, where she knew the drinkers were huddling.

———

The babble in the tavern completely drowned out the hushed conversation at our table. When the Gaelic interloper leaves, I told myself, I'll have to ask about Grandma. How is she getting along? Maybe we'll go out there for a visit later. But at that moment an old university pal appeared out of nowhere.

"Mac," Dennis cried enthusiastically. "When did you come home?"

"Just last night," I replied, thrilled to see a familiar face.

"What's on for the rest of the day?"

"Nothing much."

"You'll have to come by," said Dennis. "We got catching up to do."

"I will," I replied with enthusiasm.

I'd known Dennis for years and all through university. Both our mothers were schoolteachers. His mother, Dolly MacDonald, had actually been my teacher for a year, in grade seven. Both our fathers had been hard-rock miners.

Dennis had a nickname among the young fellows. The *madadh-ruadh* we called him, which means "red fox," because he had flaming red hair and was considered by young women to be sly.

The Gaelic conversation was suddenly over. My father's friend excused himself to go to the toilet. We watched as he walked away.

"Do you know who that is?" my father asked.

"Yes," I replied.

There was a long silence then as we sat, each waiting for the other to comment.

Finally he smiled and mouthed: "Q-U-E-E-R."

"I know," I said.

He recoiled in shock.

"You know?"

"Of course. Everybody knows."

"Mhoire mhathair," he said—"Holy Mother Mary"—as if he suddenly realized that I was a grown-up too.

The small details of that Saturday would remain clear in the mind for many years to come. They would often cause me to reflect on the perversity of existence, how the truly memorable experiences in life so often pass in what seems like humdrum banality. It's almost as if life has no substantial meaning except in retrospect. And that's what makes so much of life so sad—tragic even.

We went home from the tavern. We ate lightly and in silence. After the lunch I asked my father if I could borrow the Volkswagen—do a bit of visiting, if that's okay.

"No problem," he replied.

————

Dennis had obviously been to the liquor store because we were together hardly any time at all when he produced a bottle. After a couple of sips, we toured around looking up old pals from high school. The Hanley boys, Alex MacMaster, the String, whose real name was Duncan MacLellan. It being Saturday afternoon, there was no shortage of drink and talk.

Dennis was a schoolteacher, just home from Edmonton. His brother, Lewis, was a priest who taught high school in Ottawa, where I saw him frequently. Their father, a miner, had died suddenly the year before. There had been no warning. You'd never have known there was a thing wrong with him. Then one afternoon he went upstairs for a nap and never came down. We talked about that a lot—about unpredictability; about poor old Jock and all the missed opportunities.

"Dan Rory looks great, though," Dennis said.

And I agreed.

"How old was your grandfather when he went . . . When was it?"

"Last year," I said. "He was ninety-five."

"Wow. And the old lady, your grandma. I hear she's still going strong. And she must be, what?"

"Heading for ninety-five herself," I replied, strangely awed and reassured by the longevity in my family.

"Poor old Jock," Dennis said, shaking his head sadly. "He was only fifty-five. Had his birthday June 24 last year. Died in September."

"June 24," I said. "What a coincidence. My old man turned fifty June 23 just past."

"Here's to them," said Dennis.

He uncapped the bottle and passed it over.

Later Dennis wanted to know everything about working in Ottawa, on Parliament Hill. What that must be like, especially covering something as arcane as the economy.

That conversation later went off the rails when I bogged down, after too many drinks, attempting to explain the relationship between the trade deficit, inflation, and the interest rate. I recovered some of my credibility by boasting that my guest for the Press Gallery Dinner the previous spring had been the governor of the Bank of Canada, Louis J. Rasminsky—a hell of a nice down-to-earth old mandarin who loved a drink as much as the next fella.

It was around then that I noticed the deepening chill in the air and the coppery glow behind the trees and realized that the sun was going down rapidly. It was probably time to go home. Put in a little quality time with the parents, since I was around for just the weekend, and Saturday was almost gone already.

"One more little one," Dennis insisted.

Driving by the Troy trailer court I remembered hearing that my friend Jack, who was one of the four Hanley brothers, was living there and that he and his wife, Jessie, recently had their first kid—a boy. On an impulse I turned in. Just a quick visit with old Dag, which was what the boys used to call Jack at home.

Jessie was cooking supper, and they insisted I have a bite with them. After supper there were drinks and long conversations.

I met the new baby, and we compared notes about the trials of parenthood. Jessie eventually went to bed.

Jack was an electrician, a line of work no less mysterious to me than Louis J. Rasminsky's job. I couldn't have imagined, just a couple of years earlier, sitting here like this: Jack and I, a couple of working men with wives and children. And I a reporter on Parliament Hill.

"Amazing the way things turn out," Jack noted. And then he asked about my parents.

"Great," I replied.

"And I hear Dan Rory is home for good."

"He is, apparently," I said.

Home for good, I thought—again.

There were a few more drinks, and Jack wisely suggested that I have a short nap on the chesterfield before trying to drive home.

There was an ominous blue light in the room when I realized where I was. That was followed by an instant surge of self-recrimination. There was also a powerful nausea churning deep in my guts.

Mercifully they weren't up yet when I crept in.

Breakfast was silent. They understood, I reassured myself, about being young and having friends I hardly ever saw anymore now that I was married with three kids of my own and a job on Parliament Hill that was turning me into an old man before my time.

Sunday Mass was interminable, and I know I attracted curious stares when I had to leave at one point to throw up outside. The wind was damp with the probability of a storm before the end of the day. I had to be in Sydney by three, to reconnect with the travelling Cabinet ministers. I'd rarely experienced such a profound, stunning sense of misery.

I did my best to make small talk on the drive to the airport. The true menace of the weather became apparent on the top of Kelly's Mountain, where the rain thickened and turned into sleet and left treacherous ridges of slush on the pavement. The old man was driving carefully, and we discussed whether he was going to be okay on the drive back.

No problem, he assured me. He'd just take it easy. Worse comes to worst, he'd just pull over to the side. Or drop in some place. He knew people all over the island, from working underground for so long. Cape Breton is famous for coal mines, but the most renowned Cape Breton miners were the rural fellows who went off to work in hard-rock mines all over the country. All over the world, actually.

"The thing is whether that plane will take off," he said.

"They never seem to have a problem taking off," I said.

"Probably that's true."

The airport seemed empty—no sign of the politicians. One of the political assistants explained that there was a meeting going on some-where, and it was lasting longer than they expected. I suddenly felt awkward, just standing around.

"The weather is closing in," I said finally. "Maybe I'll just go on board the plane, and you can get back on the road."

"Whatever you think yourself," he said.

We stood facing each other for a moment, each probably wonder-ing what to do. A handshake would have been pompous; a hug was out of the question. So we just stood there.

"Well," I said, slightly embarrassed. "Sorry about last night—get-ting stranded like that."

"It was the wise thing to do," he said. There was no evidence of reproach in the tight little smile.

"Next time," I said. "Next time we'll . . . maybe go for a little tour together. Maybe out to the mountain. Visit Grandma."

"Sure," he said. "Lots of time for that."

"Say hello to her, will you?"

"Right on."

We were just standing in the empty airport, hands in our pockets.

"Okay, then," I said at last. "I'll be off."

And I turned and went out into the wind and the rain and dashed across the tarmac to the waiting plane.

I found a window seat and, after I was settled, looked towards the terminal building. He was still there, standing in the window. We waved at each other. After that I dozed off. Then, maybe twenty minutes later, I was wakened by a commotion at the front. The two Cabinet ministers and a posse of helpers were coming on board, complaining bitterly about one of the Indian chiefs who had, it seemed, given Chrétien a hard time.

MacEachen paused beside my seat. We exchanged some pleasantries about being home.

"Everybody well?"

"Everybody well," I replied.

MacEachen returned to resume his seat near Chrétien.

The plane engine came alive, whining. I looked again towards the terminal window. My father was still standing there, hands folded in front of him. And a sudden strange image came back to me and transformed him into someone else.

―――――

The snow continued all through the night of my grandfather's wake and, just before dawn, one of the cousins noted that the hearse would never be able to get up the mountain road. We were going to have to take Grandpa out to the highway on the back of a truck. But, even for a truck to get through, we were going to have to clear the road in places.

So my father and John Boy and a gang of the cousins and I went off with shovels and axes to break down the worst drifts between the little house and the highway and to cut spruce boughs for extra traction in the hard places. We worked like that for a couple of hours.

Then the truck, a three ton with a flatbed on back, came struggling and groaning up through the snow, and somehow fought its way into the yard between the two houses, and then backed up close to the little house where Grandma now lived alone.

They carried the casket out and heaved it up onto the back. Then my father and I and a couple of the cousins climbed up and sat on it so it wouldn't slide around on the slow slippery trip down to where the hearse was waiting, on the side of the Trans-Canada.

Driving out the lane, my father suddenly elbowed me and, when he had my attention, nodded back in the direction of the little house. No words were spoken.

Peigeag was standing there in the doorway, watching silently as we drove away with the old man in his casket. It was an image I'd never forget. The old woman just standing there, a black woollen shawl draped over her head and shoulders, bony old hands clasped before her, but hidden under an apron. Just the latest witness to a long, long history of departures.

The image came back to me with a particularly jarring effect that Sunday afternoon, staring at the old fellow who just kept standing there silently, hands folded in front of him in the window of the airport terminal. I had a sudden urge to leave the plane, go back inside, ask the questions. Who were those old people? Did Peigeag really have those special powers—the second sight, the power of the *buidseachd?* How did they and this glorified ridge we grandly call MacIntyre's Mountain escape the relentless flow of time? And who are you, born and raised there, exempted in so many ways from the progress of your century but not its pains?

Of course, by then the whine of the plane had matured into a louder, ringing roar.

I made a silent promise to myself and to my father. I was definitely going to get to the bottom of things—next time.

I leaned close to the small oval window and waved one last time. But he seemed to be distracted just at that moment, watching as two men wheeled the ramp away from the front of the aircraft.

The plane moved. And then we were gone.

CAUSEWAY

2

THE BEST THINGS IN LIFE ARE INKSPOTS

We live in a village called Port Hastings. I think I understand the difference between a village and a town. People who live in towns are more important than people who live in villages. The most important people of all live in cities.

I am told our village was supposed to be a town, which is why it seems to have streets. There is a road by our house, and it is really Field Street. The hill by MacKinnons' is Lovers' Lane. The Green Path is really Saddler Street. And the road to my Aunt Veronica's is Church Street.

I have heard there were a dozen stores here once upon a time and thirteen places where men could drink. Jack Reynolds's big old barn was once a stagecoach station.

My imagination is defeated in the effort to picture how it was. There is nothing interesting now.

There is the church, but it is not on Church Street. It is on the Victoria Line, which is a gravel road that runs up through the middle of the village, past our back door, up by Archie the Piper's, over Little Brook, and off into the woods, vanishing towards "out back." I think it meanders all the way to the other side of Cape Breton Island, but I've never gone past the side road that leads up MacIntyre's Mountain, which is thirteen miles out.

Our school is beside the church. The school has two rooms, called the Big Room and the Little Room, even though they're both exactly the same size. The Big Room is for big kids, grade six and up. Next year I will be in the Big Room.

The village has two stores. One is large, three stories high, and sells almost everything on the first two floors. The third floor is where they keep the coffins. This store is called R.J.'s because the man who owned it years ago was R.J. MacDonald. The other store belongs to Mr. Clough, and it is also the post office.

I think the merchants always ran the village, the way priests did in Catholic communities. Field Street once ran all the way across to Church Street, and poor people from out back would use it to bypass the stores on the main road if they owed the merchants money. They'd come out the Victoria Line, cross over Field Street, then sneak down Church Street and continue on to town. The merchants solved the problem by building a shed in the middle of Field Street, just past Alex MacKinnon's. Then they built fences, and what was once a street is now part of a hayfield. Now the poor people have to continue down the Victoria Line, or turn down Lovers' Lane, and take the main road through the village. Now they have no choice. They have to pass the stores.

Hardly anybody remembers R.J. anymore, and his store is now run by a quiet, sober relative who is called Ronnie the Minister because his father was a clergyman. R.J.'s store was recently bought by Mr. McGowan, who, like his name, is new and modern. Mr. McGowan, I have heard them say, has big plans for the store and for the village. Ronnie the Minister is, I hear, retiring and will be replaced by a pretty woman named Isabel Grant, who lives in Long Point, ten miles to the north.

Mr. Clough, who owns the other store, seems to be as old as the village itself and thinks the merchants are still the most important people here. Mr. Clough is a Grit. He is a very important Liberal and a Mason, which is why he has the post office and a great deal of influence over who gets jobs and contracts.

I have heard discussions when my father was away, working in a mine somewhere: Dan Rory should go see Clough.

And my mother laughing at the very idea.

But now he's home, and I hear discussions about a time, not far in the future, when our village will become a city.

I find it difficult to imagine Port Hastings as a city. We've had pavement for a few years now, but the pavement ends with a bang exactly where the village ends, in front of a house they call Hughie the Slut's. It doesn't start again until below the Catholic Church, which is on the edge of town, Port Hawkesbury. When I ask why, the answer is always the same: politics. That tells you nothing even if you're ten and already know from listening to them that politics determines many things, including where the snowplough stops and who gets jobs and pavement.

But this gap in the pavement, and the dust and potholes after you pass Hughie the Slut's and the Kennedy cabins and the MacDonalds' and the MacLeans' and the Meisners', past Grant's Pond and through Embree's Island, doesn't even make political sense. The dirt road discriminates against everybody.

I know there is pavement on the main street in town because important people live there—the lawyer and the doctor and the policeman, bankers, ministers, and the priest whose name is Father Doyle. The stores in town seem bigger than the ones at home and have more things to sell. There are places people pay to sleep and eat—the Farquhar House and the Black and White Inn, Mac's Lunch and the Cabot Grill. And there's Rocky Hazel's movie theatre. Town is also where the ferry from the mainland stops. But the pavement stops, below the Catholic Church, at the edge of town, and doesn't start again until Hughie the Slut's.

Why?

Did they stop the pavement here because this man named Hughie isn't very nice?

"Good God, no. Poor Hughie is as fine a man as ever walked the earth."

Oh.

"Why then," my sister wants to know, "is he Hughie the Slut?"

She's always asking the obvious question even when she knows there's no answer.

"You're not supposed to say that."

"What?" she asks.

"Slut," I say.

"Everybody calls him that," she insists. "Mummy. Why do they call him Hughie the Slut?"

I just look out the window of the car, annoyed at myself because I feel a tiny bit of pleasure at her audacity—using a forbidden word in an unassailable context; asking a perfectly legitimate question.

Why *is* he called Hughie the Slut?

"It's just a name," our mother sighs. "Didn't you bring your coronation scrapbook?"

Meaning: next time you ask that question there will be consequences.

"But why?" she insists.

Dan Rory pipes up diplomatically: "I think it's because he used that word, and that's what happens."

"Yes," the mother says. "A bad word will stick to you, like a burdock."

Now my sister is thinking. A troubled look darkens her face because, even though she's only eight, she knows it's true how real names get shoved aside by mockery and worse. She's probably thinking of poor John Allan Laidlaw, who innocently used the word "function," and they

34

were calling him Function behind his back for years afterward. And there's John Dan Guts. And Louie the Cat. And George the Wheeler. And Squint MacCormack.

And then there's the name they stuck on me because of something stupid I said. I don't even want to talk about it. Spruce!

She stares out the window, thinking and thinking, twirling a strand of hair on the nape of her neck. I wait. There is more to come.

"Is a *slut* the same as a *slink*?"

Dan Rory chortles, almost hitting a yawning pothole in the dirt road.

"That's enough," the mother says.

"Daddy says *slink* all the time," she says gravely.

And this too is true. He'll say: "It's a clear slink of a day out," or "I'm coming down with a slink of a cold."

And I remember that people use *slut* the same way. "I've got a slut of a headache."

"That's different," mother says.

And there are other words: I remember the barber telling the men how the Mountie came into the shop complaining about the heat last summer, and a customer said to him, "You got a prick of a job all right." And I knew by the roar of approval in the barbershop that it was about the word *prick*, a word that always seemed to get the response that is reserved for what is forbidden.

"You got a prick of a job," the man said to the Mountie. "But it suits you."

I understand how people acquire strange names, but I haven't yet got around to finding out what that one means and what makes a word like that so interesting. A prick, after all, is what happened to Grandma Donohue's finger when she was darning a sock last winter.

"I pricked my finger," she said with a shocked expression, then licked the tiny wound. Nobody laughed at that.

The Mountie has a prick of a job. I am curious about words, but there are not many people you can safely ask about a word like that. Now that I'm ten I could probably ask my father—if he stayed around long enough to permit that kind of familiarity. But that is by no means a sure thing.

And it occurs to me that pavement might make the difference. I recall that my father was around for a while a few years back when they paved the road through the village and north as far as Troy, and towards town, to where it ends now at Hughie's. My father had a truck then, and he had a job hauling small grey stones they called chips, which they mixed with tar to make the pavement. There is optimistic talk now of a paved future. The knowledge conjures up a warm feeling, riding in the truck with him, and the unfamiliar smell of the fresh tar and pavement, which is a measure of progress and civility.

"When will they pave this part?" I want to know, eyes burning in the dust that is infiltrating the car.

"When they finish the *bocan* bridge," my father says.

"The what?"

"He means the causeway," my mother says.

———

We are standing in an open field overlooking the strait, just to the north of the village. There is a chilly mist that occasionally turns to drizzle and blows away like smoke. Then you can see across to the other side where the activities are taking place, although it is impossible to see exactly what is going on there. You know the premier, Angus L. Macdonald, is over there, along with a certain Mr. Chevrier from Ottawa, and that before long they will do something significant. They will push a button or pull a lever or light a match. It is not clear in my mind. It is what happens next that is important. What happens next will "change everything," will be written down in history. But all you can see by squinting through the occasional lapses in the fog is a marshalling of large machines that vaguely look like giant dump trucks.

I've read about them in the newspaper—the forty-ton Euclids that can carry as much as a railway car in a single load. Now they're gathering around Cape Porcupine for the big job they've talked about for fifty years.

That is why we are not in school. Miss Morrison and Mrs. Gillis have told us that September 16, 1952, is a day we must experience to the full because it is a day that will affect our lives forever. It is a day we must remember in its smallest details, for what we will witness will be as important to our education as anything we will learn in books. September 16, a Tuesday. It is the day they start the causeway.

The rain diminishes and the fog returns, swift banks of mist that tease and torment the straggle of kids and adults in the field around me. We are standing near the old MacMillan house, once elegant but now sinister in its emptiness. A place for stealthy exploration. Ian and Jackie, Angus Neil and his sister Theresa are here. Also Brian Langley and Binky, whose real name is Vincent MacLellan. And, of course, Skipper, my dog.

We stand silently and wait. The murmur of adult conversation filters through the fog. I already know what they are saying because I have heard it at The Hole, where I gather most of my knowledge about the strange ways and mysterious interests of grown-ups. This opening was originally designed for a stovepipe, I think. It is near the chimney, and it allows the heat to filter up from the kitchen. The only heat in the house comes from the kitchen stove. The Hole is my connection to the larger, older world.

I sleep just above the kitchen, which is where all life happens in the house—from the porridge in the morning to the rosary in the evening. We live in the kitchen, which has a stove, table and chairs, rocking chair, visitor chairs beside the door, a refrigerator, and, on top of it, a radio. There are other rooms, but the doors are always closed, especially in the winter when the other rooms are cold as the outside.

It is just as cold upstairs, and you hate to go to bed when it is winter. My mother makes up games so we'll forget the cold. When I was smaller she walked behind me as I climbed the stairs, and she pretended that small animals were falling off my pyjamas and that she picked them up and stuck them back on, telling me to get in bed quickly to keep them warm. Of course we don't play games like that now that I am older.

The Hole in the ceiling above the kitchen stove allows the passage of heat to my bedroom when the stove is lit. It also allows the passage of sound. Sunday nights my mother listens to *Miss Brooks* and *Amos 'n Andy*. There is another one called *I Was a Communist for the FBI*, but she turns it off. For a few magical months one winter The Hole allowed the passage of extraordinary music. A young railway station agent whose name is Buddy MacMaster boarded at our house, and on special nights he played his fiddle in the kitchen with such skill you'd almost think the sound was coming from the radio. That was when I learned the value of The Hole.

Music is rare enough. But between tunes on the fiddle or the radio, or on nights when there is no music at all, the adults talk. They talk about the village and the island and the world. Or when Troy Jack is visiting, they talk about the walking, talking dead and horses that convey messages from beyond the grave. Troy Jack is a MacDonald. Sometimes when he has a little edge on, he talks about the grey ghost-dog that follows certain MacDonalds around to tell them when misfortune is about to happen, even when they don't want to know about it. He talks about the *bocan*, which means ghost, and the *buidseachd*, which is like witchcraft, and even the old house seems to listen quietly.

At The Hole I heard them talking about the blast that would

"change everything." That was last September. An explosion of dynamite that would instantly knock tens of thousands of tons of rock from the stubborn brow of Cape Porcupine. September 1952: the beginning of the change; the beginning of the future. Somehow I got the impression that this change, unlike most of the change they talk about, will bring huge improvements to our lives. The new causeway will put us on the map. With the causeway we will become a city. They talk about it the way they talk about the certain benefits that will flow from "a change of government," from getting rid of Grits in power in Halifax and Ottawa.

Grits, I've learned, are Liberals. Men like Angus L. and Mr. Chevrier, who will start the building of the causeway, which will change everything for the better.

Change is always for the better, and change always comes from away, inevitably announced by important people like Angus L. and Mr. Chevrier.

Afterwards, when the kitchen has fallen silent but for the crack of embers dying slowly in the stove, I try to imagine the improvements I would like to see. But there is only one.

———

I was only nine then, in September, when it all started. I turned ten last Friday, the 29th of May. This year the birthday feeling is lasting longer because it is close to the day we get a new Queen, Elizabeth the Second. Her father was George the Sixth, who seemed like a nice enough man. The papers have been full of news about the royal family for weeks. And on this day there are jet planes waiting at an airport in England to race across the Atlantic with the first pictures of the coronation. There will even be pictures on television, but there is no television in Port Hastings yet. That's something else I know will come with all the changes, but for now we'll huddle over newspapers, reading/ every word, examining every photograph.

Even though this day is a Tuesday, it is a public holiday. That means no school and general good cheer among the older people. There is a picnic in town, which is where we are all going, and although they have a picnic in town every year, this one is special. There's the coronation, and my father is home with a car, and a British team has just climbed to the top of the highest mountain in the world.

This last item was also in the newspaper, and I read the story very carefully while everybody else admired the coloured photograph of the new Queen Elizabeth that came free in the paper that day. They were talking about how they were going to take the picture down to Angus Walker's photography studio and get it framed for the wall in the living room. The picture of the Queen was, for them, the best thing about the paper, but I was deep into the story about the British team climbing to the top of Mount Everest. More than 29,000 feet, it said. That high up the winds howl relentlessly, and the cold is deadly, and the air has hardly any oxygen. At the very place on the planet where you have to be strongest, nature strips your strength away.

I tried to figure it out. Twenty-nine thousand feet is more than five miles. That would be more than from Port Hastings to town. More like from home to Point Tupper, which is on the other side of town.

Mount Everest, I calculate with a pencil, is about sixty times higher than Cape Porcupine, which is what I can see from our house in Port Hastings. Cape Porcupine, on the other side of the Strait of Canso, on the mainland. A high tree-covered mass where, each day, I watch from the schoolyard as giant machines dig out the rock for the new causeway that will join our island, which is called Cape Breton, to the mainland, which is called Nova Scotia.

The teacher points out that Cape Breton is already part of Nova

Scotia and, more important, Canada and the British Empire. But we never really felt a part of it before. Now we will, after the causeway.

It is already a stump projecting from the other side, like a truncated limb.

I can't imagine the causeway as a reality, but the word alone creates a shiver. The way thinking of Christmas does in October when it is close enough to be real.

"Will you be able to see past Cape Porcupine when they fill in the strait for the causeway?" somebody asked.

The teacher, Miss Morrison, just laughed.

"No. There's more than enough there for a dozen causeways. You'll hardly notice a difference in the cape at all."

That was mildly disappointing, because it would have been nice to think of seeing past Cape Porcupine for a change, into the rest of the world.

Maybe, I think to myself, you'd even be able to see Mount Everest in the distance.

My father laughed.

"It's a possibility," he said, reaching for the paper.

"How high is MacIntyre's Mountain?" I asked.

The narrow little dirt road through the pine and spruce and juniper and birch felt like a lot more than five miles, especially in the winter when, more often than not, you had to walk most of it.

But my father wasn't listening.

"Well, that's something," he said, about the British team and Mount Everest.

"A little gift to the new Queen," my mother added.

"Old Clough was telling George Fox that one of the LaFaves is with those people who were climbing Everest," my father says.

"The LaFaves? Who used to live here? On Mount Everest?"

My mother obviously didn't believe it.

"That's what he said. One of Jack LaFave's boys."

"That Clough," she said.

But that's the kind of a day it is. Men standing on the top of Everest, the British flag raised. A pretty woman on the throne of the British Empire. The whole world, embodied in the stump of a new causeway, reaching towards us. A day when you can believe anything.

———

In the group around me, I have known Ian MacKinnon the longest. We are nearly the same age. He will be ten next June, almost a month after me. He has the same birthday as my father, who is not here. My father works in Stirling, which is a hard-rock mine in a remote part of Richmond County. Ian's father is a railway engineer, which means that he drives the train that travels daily the fifty-five miles from Point Tupper to Inverness. It is called the Judique Flyer, which is a joke because travelling by train is barely faster than walking.

Because Ian's father, whose name is Alexander, works on the railroad, he can live at home. Because he works close enough to home to live there all the time, he never gets so lonely that he has to quit his job to see his family. Because he always has a job, they have a telephone at Ian's house and a bathroom with an indoor toilet. They have a furnace that heats the entire house, so all the rooms are open all year round. They always have a car.

Every evening we stand on the back verandah of MacKinnons' house and wait for Alex MacKinnon's train to leave the railway station, which is straight down below their house, near the shore of the strait. As the train leaves the station and passes through an open space, it becomes visible from the verandah. We wave frantically, and Alex MacKinnon blows the whistle just for us. Sometimes it is a long mournful howl; sometimes a bar of happy hoots. When the whistle blows, you can see a blast of steam beside the billowing smokestack, and the locomotive huffs and puffs and strains to get away with its long burden of freight and passenger cars.

We leap up and down, waving to be seen. Ian and his sister, Annie, and his little brother, Roy, who fell off the verandah one day and broke his leg. And me. I jump up and down waving with the rest of them as if I am a MacKinnon whose father works for the Canadian National Railway.

On warm summer evenings, Alex MacKinnon and other railwaymen, whose names are Howie and LV and Laidlaw, sit on the front step in their undershirts, drinking beer and talking quietly.

Alex MacKinnon's brother, whose name is Ian and who is known as Big Ian, also works for the railway, even though he owns a farm right here in the village. Big Ian never drinks beer, so you don't see him on the doorstep in his undershirt. Working on the railroad seems to be a job that runs in the MacKinnon family. Even their grandfather was a railwayman who drove a train.

Angus Neil and Theresa are also MacKinnons, and their father, Allan Joe, works on the railroad too. And Binky's father is on the railroad. Brian Langley's father works for the Department of Highways, which is just as good. Jackie Nicholson has neither father nor mother, as far as we know, but lives with his grandmother Kate, who is the keeper of the lighthouse below us on Nicholson's Point. I know that the causeway is bad news for Jackie and Mrs. Nicholson because, after it is finished, they won't need the lighthouse anymore. And the causeway will eventually land exactly where their house now sits. We don't talk about what will happen then.

Jackie Nicholson and I have this in common: absent fathers and some confusion about the nature of the improvements that will come with the causeway. It is not something that we talk about. People say that Jackie Nick is "slow."

I think I understand why my father isn't on the railway or with the Department of Highways, but the reasons seem to change with each discussion. Sometimes I believe it is because he is not a Mason. Sometimes it is because he is not a Grit. But mostly, I believe, it is because he is from out back. It is because he is from MacIntyre's Mountain and has an embarrassing secret.

The causeway, I understand, will change all that. Being a Mason or a Grit or from the mountain isn't going to matter anymore. Not after September 16, 1952. Certainly not after Coronation Day, when the causeway is already at the point where only a few people are still calling it the *bocan* bridge.

————

On Coronation Day, the town is nothing but Union Jacks and flags of Canada. The flag of Canada is a little Union Jack in the corner of a red field that also contains a symbol called a coat of arms. There are strings with plastic pennants of every imaginable colour strung above the streets and across the fronts of buildings. Everybody is out, just wandering slowly or driving around. The pennants snap and rustle in the wind, which is chilly for June. But there is bright sunshine and beaming hospitality in all the faces.

My father is home. Usually I am the only man in the house. There is my mother and, in the wintertime, her mother, whose name is Mary Donohue and who is extremely old. I have two sisters who are younger than I am. Danita is two years younger. Rosalind is the youngest and everybody's favourite. She has dimples and a mop of blonde ringlets. She is known to grown-ups as the Pup.

As we pass below the Catholic Church and feel the thump of the resumption of the pavement, Danita notices the car ferry from the mainland approaching where the dock is, just up ahead. She wants to watch it unload the cars. It is a proposal that almost everybody finds interesting.

So my father parks the car at Eddie Fougere's garage, and they start walking down. _

The car is a 1946 Mercury. It is black. I would rather have stayed inside letting the mysterious scents, collected in all the places it has been, fire the imagination. I would prefer to snuggle down into the deep, soft, cloth upholstery that is warmed by the strong late-spring sun and dream about owning a car of my own—or at least my father owning one. The car belongs to my father's brother, John Dan, who is working underground in the mine in Stirling, where my father worked until just recently.

John Dan is also talking about coming home to look for work on the causeway.

My mother and father and sisters are walking slowly down the hill to the ferry. I hang back and nobody notices. I've seen the ferry arrival many times. I've been coming to town on my own for years. Before First Holy Communion and Confirmation, I came to town alone for special instruction at the Convent School. On Saturday afternoons I often come to town alone for the movies. I will find my way to town on foot if I can't get a ride. Sometimes a bus will stop and pick me up. The driver winks and smiles, shows me where to sit. I know the bus costs money for most people, but this bus is special. Kids get on for free.

Coming home I ride the train, which is also free because the conductor is too busy between town and Port Hastings to go around collecting fares. I recently had my first real fight, not far from the movie theatre. Boys from town tried to hold me back and make me miss the train. But I beat them off. Desperation made me strong, or maybe the example of the movie heroes.

From dawn to dark, it seems, I am on the move when I'm not imprisoned in the school. There's the town, the woods, the shores of the strait, and the mysterious recesses of Plaster Cove, which used to be a quarry and was the reason for the village in the first place. And now the roar of construction, punctuated by frequent explosions, as the village gets ready for the brilliant future.

As the causeway inches towards Nicholson's Point, teams of diggers and drillers have begun to hack away at the back of the point to create a long canal that will one day allow ships to continue to traverse the strait, on their way from the Atlantic Ocean up into the Gulf of St. Lawrence and the heart of Canada.

Because I am the man of the house when my father is away, I have always had freedom of movement here. I had freedom to explore wherever my legs and curiosity, raft and rowboat, would lead me. On Sundays, when there were no trains, and before all the new construction, older boys would sometimes steal the pump-car from the railway shack. We'd travel the rails, pumping up and down at either end of a long handle that works like a see-saw. The summit of liberation—pumping slowly up and down, the little trolley car skimming over the rails silently, heading northward where we wouldn't be noticed by the railwaymen. Rumbling along the Ghost Beach, with the strait on the left and Long Pond on the right, dark and calm. Riding along with the breeze on my face, feeling like an outlaw.

I have been the man of the house, it seems, for most of my ten years. Last September I was certain that this was about to change. The causeway was begun. My father would come home. Now, on Coronation Day, he's here. But I'm not sure that he'll stay.

———

Recently I drew a map with every house and building in Port Hastings, south to north from Pleasant Hill to Mill Hill, a distance of about four miles. I want to remember it as it was before the causeway. I counted sixty-six buildings in that space, but many are abandoned. The old

Quigley house, which is next to ours; MacMillan's, near where we are standing now; Malcolm the Butcher's, up the hill from Nicholson's Point, near Angus Neil's; Captain Skinner's; the old dance hall; MacLean's old store; the forge. There's even an abandoned place that looks new, just north of here. Murdoch MacLean's new house, never lived in, now boarded up.

Once I broke into Quigleys'. I went in through a broken window, and it was dark inside. There was still furniture. It was as if the people were away and might come back at any moment. I moved quietly as if there were people sleeping there. In a kitchen cupboard there were papers—letters and bills and postcards mostly. But there was also a telegram. A telegram, I know, always brings bad news, but I looked at it anyway. This one was old. My hand was shaking as I read it. "We regret to inform you . . ." And, sure enough, it was about somebody killed in the war. I put it back carefully, wiped my hands, fearful that part of the sorrow there rubbed off—or perhaps bad luck.

The most interesting of the empty buildings is the forge. I can remember when the old blacksmith, Johnny Morrison, worked there. People from out back would bring their horses to him. He'd pick up the horse's hooves, one at a time, holding them in his leather apron, examining. The horse would just stand there, patiently, occasionally looking down watching the blacksmith's back, as if to ask how long he planned to keep him standing on three legs. Sometimes Johnny Morrison would pull out a jackknife and dig at the hoof, but the horse didn't seem to feel it. I've watched him pound nails into a horse's hoof when he's putting new shoes on, and then use a sharpened bar that is like a chisel to trim the edges of the hoof. Occasionally the horse would grunt and shiver.

Johnny Morrison was the first dead man I ever saw. I went to his funeral in the Protestant Church, which is next to the school and just below our house. I saw the crowd and just walked in and sat in the back. At the end of the service everybody got up, walked to the front, and then around past his coffin. I could see the lid was up and wondered what he looked like dead. I could see the men dropping little sprigs of spruce on top of him. He was very white and very still. His mustache, which always seemed to be all brown and yellow in the forge, now seemed to be pure white like his eyebrows and his face. The little sprigs were all over his chest, and there was also a white apron folded there.

My mother told me afterwards that the apron and the sprigs of spruce were there because Johnny Morrison was a Mason.

I asked her what they meant, but she said it was a secret—one of many secrets that only Masons knew.

I have since seen other dead people: Howard Oliver, Bill Forbes, John Archie MacDougall, and Dan Fraser. Also an old priest who was laid out in robes like a pope in the aisle of the church, with the lid of the coffin propped open.

The forge closed when the blacksmith died, and they said it never would reopen. They say blacksmiths and their forges are obsolete, as the ferry to the mainland soon will be—which means nobody needs them anymore. I still see horses on the road, clopping past, wheels crunching the gravel, or pulling sleds in winter, with the kids all running behind trying to hitch rides. But the horses too will soon be gone, like the forge and Johnny Morrison and the ferries. That's what I hear listening at The Hole in the kitchen ceiling.

There's talk now that a man from away, who is also named Morrison, might turn the blacksmith shop into a service station for cars. It is the perfect location, they say, the first place people will visit coming off the causeway. There will be gas pumps out front and, where Johnny Morrison kept his fire, there will be a pit for working under cars. Robert Morrison will make a fortune.

Most of the buildings in the village seem old, like the forge and Quigleys', and there are old people living in most of them. Dr. Christie, who is not a doctor, but a minister. Mrs. Forbes and Mrs. Annie Oliver, who are widows. Archie the Piper, who is cranky. Danny Black Dan, a bachelor we are supposed to avoid, even though he seems to like us. Danny MacIntosh, another bachelor, who was in both wars. Mr. Sinclair, a hermit who stinks of kerosene and never speaks. Harry and Rannie, two middle-aged brothers, who are not right in the head and are constantly tormented by older boys.

Harry and Rannie have one of the few new houses here because my parents bought their old one, which is where we live.

Their father was a tailor, and there are still special ironing boards in the attic. In our dining room, behind the door, are little boxes built into the wall where the tailor kept his business papers. One of the tailor's boys, John Willie, carved his initials on the kitchen wall: JWMD. The tailor is dead now and his family grown up and moved away, except for Harry and Rannie, who can't go anywhere because they're simple.

Their little house isn't far from ours. I see them every day, walking with their strange lurching motion and, from the distance, they look like twins, dressed identically in overalls and floppy tweed caps. They seem to be in charge of the church and, when they aren't around the church, they're out behind their own place sawing wood. They act as if they own the church, and you see them there every day, making sure that everything is as it should be. Then they wander through the village, gathering boards and beams from the old abandoned buildings that have started falling down.

I've been inside their house, and it is always warm, with a fire going even in the summer. There are two windows in their kitchen, one on the north side and one on the south. And every evening they sit by the windows with their caps on, rocking, and staring out, making sure that nobody goes near the church and that none of the older boys sneak up to throw things at their house.

I've been warned never to tease them because there's no harm in them at all. Not like Danny Black Dan, whom we're supposed always to keep an eye on, or some of the war veterans who become dangerous when they drink.

Because I never tease them, Harry and Rannie come to the house from time to time with bags of hard candy. They stand politely at the door of the house they grew up in, caps in hand, smiling and making barking noises that nobody seems to understand. And when they're gone, my mother takes the candy and puts it somewhere.

———

From where I stand, beside Fougere's garage, I can hear, above the snapping of the coronation flags, the rising protest of the ferry engine as it is forced suddenly to reverse. Boats don't have brakes, like cars. They stop, sluggishly, by reversing direction. Stopping always brings angry sounds of protest from the engine and a rush of water boiling around the bottom of the boat. No matter how hard they try to avoid it, there is always a gentle bump against the stout wood pilings. The cars and trucks wobble at the impact. Then the clank and thump of the ramp falling, and the ferry boat is joined to land.

Car and truck engines roar to life. The vehicles begin the slow evacuation, the slow procession up the hill, turning, at the top, to left and right, seemingly at random. Heading off, deeper into town, towards the Sydney Road, or away from it on the pavement that will end abruptly below the church.

People outside the town will note their progress by the clouds of dust. Other drivers meeting them in their groups of three or four or five will mark the sudden rush of traffic with an exclamation of the obvious: "The ferry boat is in!"

I am now ten—since last Friday. I know this already. And I know from what I've heard that everything will change with the new causeway. Words I hear a lot now: change and causeway. Words rich with promises of pavement and possibilities.

"What will happen to the ferry after there's a causeway?"

"There'll be something else," mother says.

And I know that this is true.

A new causeway is coming. A British team has achieved what no human has ever done before, somewhere far away, conquering a frozen mountain that is more than five miles high. There is a new Queen in England—an aesthetic improvement over the ugly old kings and queens who scowl from the pages of the history books, faces hardened by the bloody business of managing a world made up of primitive and stubborn cultures in places where food grows wild and the perpetual sun cultivates laziness and indifference to progress. A Queen for change, down to earth and brand new.

I have acquired a confused ambivalence about the Queen. Her picture is everywhere. The picture of her father, George, looking slightly mystified by all his fame, still hangs in school, beside the Union Jack, which is also the flag of Canada, and the massive map of the British Empire, upon which the sun never sets. But George will soon be gone, replaced by the new colour photograph that came free with the newspaper. This new photograph will grace living-room walls all over the Commonwealth. I am still becoming accustomed to changing *His* Majesty to *Her* Majesty, the "King" to "Queen" in the "God Save Our Gracious . . ." song. Miss Ladd, who looks a little like the new Queen and who came from town to train a rhythm band for a small parade to mark the coronation, assured us it was okay to get it wrong—but only for a while.

And then we all sang "God save our gracious Queen / Long live our noble Queen," and marched through the village, banging small drums and knocking blocks of wood together, clashing cymbals and clinking triangles. Marching and marching as far as McGowan's and then back to the school.

Mr. Clough stood beaming in the doorway of his store, which is also the post office, hands deep in his pockets, fondling his money.

Grandma Donohue, who says she has some English blood in her, lives alone down north but moves to Port Hastings every winter for the electricity and running water. All winter long she's been reading and talking constantly about the royal family and following all the minor details of the coronation preparations with enthusiasm. She has, for quite some time now, stopped speaking of the cruelty of the British to the Irish, and to Irish Catholics in particular. There has been an armistice of sorts—a general amnesty for the royal family. No recent references to the hardships of the pioneers, suffered because of starvation and evictions by agents of the monarchy. Only about the prettiness of the new Queen, how handsome her husband, and how cute her children. How brave the whole lot of them, standing out on balconies while the bombs fell around them in the war.

Notwithstanding their spotty history, this detail impresses me. Their bravery and, in particular, the warm prettiness of the Queen. Someday I would like to have a wife who looks like that.

I wonder what my father thinks about the monarchy and the coronation. My mother and her sister Veronica and their mother, Grandma Donohue, are full of opinions and comments on all subjects. My father, in contrast, will read the newspaper carefully or listen intently to programs on the radio but say nothing.

He'll say "Well, well," perhaps, shaking his head sadly.

Opinions, it seems, are for women. Or maybe he's afraid of having opinions because of his secret. I prefer to think that he's just quieter than all the gabby women who surround us.

I know that the Irish side of the family are here because of some great calamity in the Old Country and that the Protestant English are to blame. And that all, or mostly all, is now forgiven because everyone is better off, no thanks to those responsible for the persecution and the starvation. We are better off thanks to hard work and the Grace of God. This I know from all the talk and the opinions of my mother and my aunt and my grandmother during their long winters talking and playing cards.

But whatever my father thinks of this or any other matter remains a mystery. We are Scottish on my father's side, and it seems to me that people who are Scottish don't have half as many opinions as people who are Irish. Or maybe they're just more careful about expressing them. Or maybe it's that men have to be more careful than women.

My father is away most winters. And even when he communicates at any length, he speaks in Gaelic to people who come from the mountain or other places out back. It was the only language my people knew when my grandfather's great-grandfather brought his family from Scotland. My sisters and I don't understand Gaelic because our mother doesn't know it, and we have spent most of our lives with her while our father was away at work.

Mother knows Gaelic expressions, such as *droighneach* (trash) or *fad air ais* (backward), which she will use with obvious disapproval when discussing certain people, many of whom live out back. And she will use words like *ton*, which means arse, and *buinneach*, which means shit, because slang is okay in Gaelic, even for us. But she will grow uneasy when people from out back show up in the kitchen looking for Dan Rory and start speaking exclusively to him in quiet waves of impenetrable Gaelic.

My father has never encouraged an interest in learning Gaelic. "It will get you nowhere," he says, as if Nowhere is a real place that is the opposite of Somewhere. Sometimes I think the real reason is that it is a private place for him—a private, secret hiding place.

I will sometimes say to my father, "Ciamar a tha thu," which sounds like "Kimmera-how" and means "How are you?"

But, instead of replying "Gle mhath," which sounds like "Clay-vah" and means "Very well," he will just smile and answer "Clay pipe"—which means "Leave me alone."

I've noticed that Gaelic conversations are always conducted in a soft monotone that would be difficult to follow, even if I could understand the words—like flies buzzing on a warm, sleepy afternoon. And that my father changes noticeably when he speaks Gaelic—that he relaxes and that his face takes on a faraway expression, eyes squinted, the corners of his mouth turned down. Inevitably, before I have time to catch the rhythm and the meaning of it, they take their conversation outside and it continues near the well or behind the corner of the house.

———

There is no obvious reason why anybody would have wanted to locate a town on our particular hill. But Mr. Clough told me that it was because of the cove, which is just to the south, below my Aunt Veronica's. Now the cove is just a place to swim in the summer and fish smelt when they run in dense packs in the late fall. But Mr. Clough explained that it was once called Plaster Cove because there is gypsum behind it and there used to be a quarry there. Ships would sail right into the cove, load up with the gypsum, and sail away.

Later, there were large piers and shipping wharves on the shore of the strait, down below Mr. Clough's store and just across from the railway station. Coal trains from Inverness would be unloaded there. Boats from everywhere would come and take it all away.

My blood races with excitement at the images. Boats and people from afar. Change and possibility sailing in on every boat. New people with new voices and stories from away. Barrooms clamouring, and a dozen stores packed with prosperous people shopping. The roads busy with commerce, and fields and woods loud with children. There is even a story that a MacIntyre from the Old Country arrived on a boat once, trying to find the people who had left.

After that he went away, probably disappointed by what he found here, because he was never heard from again.

There is a story they never talk about. That once upon a time, back in the Old Country, the MacIntyres were Protestants. But after one of them married a Catholic, they were kicked off their land by the Protestant landlord because the Catholic wife, who was Irish, insisted that the kids be baptized Catholics. When they were leaving for the New World, the priest told them that the MacIntyres could only prosper there because, by going into exile, they were making a great sacrifice for the Faith.

I would have asked the mysterious visitor from the Old Country whether any of this is true, but of course that was long ago, long before my time.

They say that nothing much has happened in the village for nearly forty years. There are hardly any children, and it's because of the wars, they say. And then there was the Depression. People were too busy fighting and coping to be having children. There was rationing in the last world war, limits on the liquor and the gasoline and food and also, I presume, on babies. So now there is me and Ian and Brian and Angus Neil and Jackie Nick. And of course the dog. Everybody else is older, from before the war, or at least before they got too busy with the war.

Mr. Clough says the whole village was once named Plaster Cove. It was official. Then they changed it to Port Hastings after an important government official whose name was Sir Hastings Doyle. That was a big mistake, he says. That was when everything went to hell. Changing the name of a place brings bad luck.

The village looks like a place with bad luck. It is now neither cove nor port. The cove is blocked from the strait by roads and railway tracks and is slowly filling up with muck. The only evidence of quarrying is the bare white rock that is visible through the trees at the back end. The coal piers have been abandoned: the larger one torn down entirely, leaving only a small projection of rock and pilings; the smaller one intact but useless, except for risky games. In summer we swim there and use the chutes for diving boards.

I understand that soon there will be even fewer kids my age. Binky's father is being transferred to Inverness; Angus Neil's to Sydney. Brian's father is getting a bigger job with the Highways Department, and they will move to town. And that will leave just Ian and Jackie Nick and me. But then, I know, from listening at The Hole, that the place will grow. The causeway will be like a giant pipeline, pumping new life and new people in, removing, at last, the curse that came with the new name: Port Hastings. Maybe even making jobs for people from out back who are neither Grit nor Mason—people with secrets in their childhood.

––––––

The cars from the ferry are now coming slowly up the hill, and most of them are turning right. Mostly people from the mainland town of Mulgrave, which is where the ferry leaves from, or further down the Guysborough shore. People coming to Port Hawkesbury for the celebration of the coronation.

I went to Mulgrave once, when I was much younger. My Aunt Veronica used to be the housekeeper for the priest in Mulgrave, and I went with my mother to visit her. We went by train. From Port Hastings through the town to Point Tupper, which is where the train ferry docks. I remember the black, menacing locomotive and the metallic steam and sulphurous billowing smoke. It never seemed to go far without stopping and backing up, and starting forward again in jerking motions—huffing and puffing. And there was something terribly precarious about riding on a train that was riding on a boat.

I also remember the chilly silence in the large Glebe house over there in Mulgrave, and staying close to my mother and my aunt because I was afraid of someone they called Alex the Devil, who, I learned later, was really the priest in a nearby parish—Father MacDonald. Father Alex the Devil.

Like Hughie the Slut, the name was beyond understanding. But it was somehow appropriate in this odd little town, which was the beginning of the rest of the world.

Mulgrave had a fish-processing plant that constantly gave off a reeking, billowing mist. My mother, even though her father was a fisherman, hates the smell of fish and held a hanky to her nose as she walked by. Mulgrave also had the asylum, a place of horror signified by the universal reluctance to talk about it, except in low, cryptic expressions that mostly avoided, if at all possible, the use of the word "asylum" or the names of the people lost inside. "The poor dizzy people," as they were sometimes called.

"That fellow should be in Mulgrave" or "They put her in Mulgrave" were expressions that conveyed menace or despair without need for any further elaboration. When a child was acting foolishly came the threat, "You'll end up in Mulgrave."

I know there was an asylum in Mabou, to the north. It burned down one night, and many people died—including a close relative who is never mentioned.

You can see the Mulgrave Asylum plainly from where I'm standing near Eddie Fougere's garage. It is a small, white building, just beyond the edge of the town, across the water at the beginning and end of everything else that is.

Now I see them coming up the hill. The two little girls each have a parent by the hand. There is Danita Mary with our mother, and Rosalind Veronica with our father. I am Linden. My second name, Joseph, is lost behind the overwhelming strangeness of the Linden. At Confirmation I added Peter, hoping it would make a difference. But it didn't.

I have asked my mother where the name is from. She says she doesn't know, but I don't quite believe her. Because the name is her fault, I am reluctant to confess to her the pain it causes me. The burden of a name unmotivated by tradition or blood would be incomprehensible to her. She is Alice, a plain, sensible name that runs like a unifying thread through her entire personal history. Grandma Donohue, whose name is Mary, has a sister, Alice.

My father is Dan, a name that resonates through many generations with such frequency that all the Dans alive must have identifying modifiers. Dan L., Dan B., Dan Alex, Dan Joe, Dan Archie, Dan Rory.

"Linden is a tree," she said.

"A *tree?*"

"The lovely linden tree."

My heart sinks. It is already bad enough that it sounds like the name of a girl.

They named me for a tree. I have also heard that there was a detective on a radio program and his name was Linden Wade, but that is a small source of consolation. I know that I cannot go through my whole life explaining that I am named after an imaginary detective on the radio any more than I can hope for comfort explaining that mine is also the name of a tree.

I have considered changing it to Joe, my second name, which is also the name of my uncle Joe Donohue, who is a powerful little Irishman with a booming foghorn voice and an accent straight from County Cork. I admire Uncle Joe, but the prospect of adopting his name is too complicated. Where do you begin? I realize it is a solution I should have thought of before I started school. But before I started school it didn't matter. It was only after I started school that I discovered the strangeness and the painful burden of being different. School was all Ian and Angus and Jack and Patrick and William and George.

When Phemie, my first teacher, whose name was actually Miss Euphemia MacKinnon, called my name, as if pronouncing some exotic food discovery, all the heads turned. The smirks and smiles announced the birth of cruel plans for after school—in the yard, on the road home.

Mercifully, home isn't far from the school.

Just once, years before, I tried to change it. The result was a disaster. That it is how I ended up with a nickname as bad as Hughie the Slut or John Dan Guts. It was after one of the big MacNeil boys set himself on fire playing with matches around gasoline, and the Mountie came to investigate on a motorcycle.

I remember clearly. I was in the MacNeils' apple tree when I heard a sudden clatter in the lane. Then I saw the motorcycle. The grand machine swept past below the tree and stopped with the front wheel practically against the MacNeils' doorstep. The Mountie was wearing his brown tunic, the tight navy trousers with the yellow stripe, and great shining knee-high boots. He sat there astride the idling motorcycle, asking the little girls if any of the boys was around.

Their mother, Marie, came out, drying her hands on her apron. The Mountie got off the bike, and they went around the corner to talk.

Afterwards, I asked the Mountie what his name was.

He seemed surprised by my boldness. Then he smiled and held out a gloved hand. "It's Bruce MacKinnon," he said.

Even though I didn't hear it right, it sounded better than my own: Spruce MacKinnon.

"I'm going to become a Mountie and change my name to Spruce," I announced, when the motorcycle was gone and we were all watching the suddenly quiet lane.

Spruce?

The error dawned on me too late.

"Hey, Spruce," they'd start. "Where's your motorcycle?"

Now I have two embarrassing names—both trees: Linden; Spruce.

All my mother could say was "Just don't pay any attention to them. They'll get over it."

Of course they didn't, and they never will.

My cousins on the mountain have normal names: Donald and Archie, Marybelle and Margaret, John Dougald and Johnnie. Later there will be an Annie and a Gerald. There was also a Gabriel, but nobody seemed to think there was anything unusual about it. Gabriel, after all, was a very important archangel, prominent in the Bible, in the book of Daniel. Gabriel is different, but normal. But then, on the mountain, nobody seems to find the name Linden unusual either.

In fact, my grandmother, who lives there, utters my name with a breathless reverence.

"Lindy," she'll say. "M'eudail a'ghaol, Lindy."

Affectionately. And she pronounces it in a way that gives the name a kind of dignified destiny. She seems to say, just in the pronunciation: You have important things in store. "My treasure, my dear treasure," she's saying.

But I think, afterwards: what does Grandma MacIntyre know about anything? She can't even speak English. She doesn't have a clue what the name means. A tree that sounds like a girl.

———

The rain is steady now. From where we're standing in MacMillan's field, you can see across the strait—slow, antlike movement on the side of the cape. I imagine I can actually see people working there. Jackie is grumbling. What is taking them so long? Angus Neil believes they're waiting for the fog to lift entirely so we can all see what happens and remember it forever. It will be like a bomb going off, he said. Thousands and thousands of tons of dynamite in little caves dug into the side of the cape exploding in one gigantic blast. They call the little caves "coyote holes."

Theresa MacKinnon wants to know why it's called Cape Porcupine, and Binky tries to convince her that it's shaped like one.

"When did you ever see a porcupine?" she asks.

And he is stumped because we all know there are no porcupines on Cape Breton Island. No porcupines and no skunks.

"I was over there once," he brags. "I saw a dead one on the road."

There are no porcupines on Cape Breton Island, according to what I have heard, because the Indians once tortured a missionary priest by locking him in a cage with a skunk and a porcupine. God's punishment was to eliminate them from the island. And what about the Indians? They sure weren't eliminated, though you have only to look at them and their poverty to know they got punished too.

I consider telling the story of the priest and his tormentors but decide not to, because Ian and Brian are Protestants.

My dog is sitting by my foot with his head pressed against my leg. This is his way of staying at least partly dry. Skipper is a clever dog, and I suppose if I was forced to admit it, I would have to say he is my best friend here. When we got him, they said that everybody owned him—mother, father, me, the two girls. Skipper is everybody's dog, but he and I both know that he is mine.

He is part boxer, with a broad chest and no tail. He belonged, briefly, to my uncle Francis Donohue, and we got him because Francis planned to shoot him. The reason Francis was going to kill him was because Skipper killed a hen. My uncle said that once he started that work, he'd be more trouble than any dog was worth. "An eye for an eye and a tooth for a tooth," he said.

They were having an unscheduled chicken dinner when my mother pointed out how unfair it would be to kill the dog who made the dinner possible. There was considerable discussion then about fairness and crime and justice, and they finally agreed that killing the dog who made the lovely chicken dinner possible was, perhaps, a punishment too cruel and final. Maybe the more appropriate penalty was banishment. Give the dog away to someone who has no hens. We have no hens, and so we got the dog.

My father seems to like Skipper even more than I do. Whenever he's leaving home, you'll see him sitting on the doorstep playing with the dog, talking to him or just sitting with his arm around him, rubbing at his neck and ears, looking and sounding as though he doesn't want to go. And Skipper seems to be asking the question nobody asks: "Why? Why do you not live at home like everybody else?"

The dog knows when my father is about to leave and becomes very quiet. And he also seems to know exactly when he's coming home and becomes noisy and hyperactive long before we see him. The dog will suddenly run to the top of the hill in the field below the house near Harry and Rannie's, or right down to the main road below the church, prancing nervously, looking up and down the road. That is often how we know when my father is arriving.

If he was working close to home, he'd come for weekends when he could get a ride or if he wasn't working Saturdays. He'd come strolling up the Victoria Line on a Friday evening with the dog running in circles around him, bumping his feet and almost knocking him down. Sometimes I'd run to meet him. Before Stirling, when he'd be far away in another province, we'd see him only at Christmas or maybe in the summer. Once he was home for part of a winter, but he couldn't do much here because he had a cast on his body from waist to neck, like a plaster undershirt. He'd let us knock on it, pretending he was a door. When the cast came off, he went away again.

When he's working in another province, Quebec or Newfoundland, we write letters. He writes short, funny letters, and though he doesn't bother with things like punctuation and capital letters, the spelling is perfect and the words are exactly like his voice.

This, I guess I should admit, is my father's secret. He never went to school. He learned to read and write from his father, Grandpa Dougald.

My mother taught him how to do arithmetic, and now he knows it well enough to be a captain in a hard-rock mine, working with engineers and geologists and bosses. My mother always says my father could have been anything in the world if he'd had a chance. He never got a chance because he never went to school, which should be a lesson for us all.

I ask why he never went to school, but nobody ever answers— except to say he wasn't well enough. He was sick when he was a boy and nearly died, which is another secret.

I know he had a brother and a sister who died when they were children. And that there was a time when he was small when epidemics passed through here like forest fires. And that people living out back, in places like MacIntyre's Mountain, rarely ever got to see a doctor.

But we don't talk about things like that. Not yet, anyway.

———

I know all about the causeway and all that it will do because I listen at The Hole in the floor of my bedroom and read the newspapers that come in the mail. I read the *Sydney Post Record* and the *Victoria-Inverness Bulletin*. We also get the *Star Weekly* from Toronto and the *Free Press Weekly*, which is from out west. We get the *Standard*, which comes from Montreal and is folded into the *Post* on Saturdays. And also the *Casket*, which is a Catholic newspaper that has news only about religion and the church.

Binky and I had our names in the *Bulletin* once for pulling Brian Langley out of the strait after he fell off the pier. We suddenly realized, after he kept sinking out of sight, that he couldn't swim. All we did was pull him out and take him home, but somebody put it in the paper and spelled all our names wrong.

It is in the *Post* and the *Bulletin* that I get the news about the causeway. At The Hole I discover what it means.

First it was supposed to be a bridge. Then some engineers pointed out that a bridge wouldn't last a single winter. I could have told them that. From my bedroom window in the winter I can see the drift ice sailing past like swift ghost ships on the racing tide. First it travels south; then, a few hours later, north—reversing constantly with the tide. At least once a winter it comes through in massive packs that carry off the ferries, shouldering them off course and shoving them all the way down into the open waters of Chedabucto Bay, where they have to wait for the tide to change and the ice to reverse direction. Anybody here could have told them what that ice would do to the pillars of a bridge, especially as the pillars would have to be hundreds of feet in length to reach the bottom of the strait.

But they were desperate for something. There is a steel plant in Sydney and big coal mines in Glace Bay and New Waterford and Sydney Mines. Crossing on ferries is a nuisance for them. Besides all the coal and steel, more than a hundred thousand passenger cars have to cross the strait each year. Now that Newfoundland is part of Canada, they're saying there will be even more and that the Newfoundlanders are demanding better access to the country they didn't want to join in 1949.

They say the causeway will cost twenty-two million dollars and will have a road and a railway track and a sidewalk for pedestrians.

Of course I know the biggest reason for it happening is Angus L. I know this from listening at The Hole. Angus L. is the premier of Nova Scotia and is famous all over Canada because he was a war hero in World War One and built the Royal Canadian Navy in World War Two. They say when Angus L. became the minister of the navy in

Ottawa, there were only six ships and two thousand men. In a flash he built it up to five hundred ships and ninety thousand men and women, and they helped to win the war. My uncle Francis Donohue was one of the people in Angus L.'s navy. But, most important of all, Angus L. is from here. He grew up poor like everybody else, in Dunvegan, which is near Inverness.

Angus L. is a great man, and it's a shame that he's a Grit, they say. He even speaks perfect Gaelic.

Here is *my* secret, something I cannot tell to my mother or Grandma Donohue or my Aunt Veronica, who are all Tories, or even to my father, who is nothing: if Angus L. can really build this causeway and make jobs for men from out back who are not Grits or Masons, who almost died from sickness and have never been to school, I will become a Grit and vote for him as soon as they let me and for as long as there are men like him in charge.

––––––––

There was a time when we all lived together. When I was born, my mother and my father lived in the same little house in Newfoundland. I learned this in the attic. Access to the attic is through the ceiling in my bedroom. You could say that I learn about now and the future through a hole in my floor, but that I learn about the past through a hole in my ceiling. It was in the attic that I found a suitcase that was full of old letters and other papers.

One document in the suitcase was a small blue card, and when I brought it to the light I could see that it had my name printed on it. So I put it in my pocket.

Sitting on my bed afterwards, I examined the card and saw, written in bold black letters across the top: LANDED IMMIGRANT. Then my name and date of birth and some other information that was smudged. I seemed to have discovered something very important: I am not who they've been telling me I am. I was dizzy with excitement. I am someone else and, perhaps, I even have another name.

My mother explained it to me afterwards.

She was the schoolteacher in Troy. My father was home from working somewhere in Quebec. They met and married and moved to Newfoundland, where another mine was just beginning. It was during the war, and working in the mine in Newfoundland was the same as being in the army or the navy. The mine produced a mineral called fluorspar, which they need for making aluminum, which they use for making airplanes, which were important in the war. Anybody who was even indirectly helping them build warplanes was as good as in a uniform. I was born in Newfoundland, but Newfoundland wasn't part of Canada then. So when they brought me to Cape Breton I was, technically, an immigrant.

A DP?

Not exactly, my mother said. After Newfoundland joined the Confederation, everybody born there became Canadian—whether they wanted to or not.

But I was different anyway and went around feeling special for several days, all thanks to the blue card that said I was a landed immigrant.

My mother says we were happy then. Newfoundland was a lovely place, and the Newfoundlanders she met in St. Lawrence and Lawn and Lamaline were the kindest human beings she's ever known. Friendly and generous, bringing things to the house, even though they were so poor themselves that when she brought some oranges over from Cape Breton once, the children didn't know what they were. But I think she was lonely there because she kept coming home for long visits at Grandma Donohue's, which is at the very northern tip of Cape Breton island, in a village called Bay St. Lawrence. It was also around the time that Grandpa Donohue died of cancer.

Then we moved to Port Hastings, where my father planned to start his own business and live like everybody else—in his own house with his own wife and children and his own dog. But that didn't last for long, and eventually he was gone and we were here and I became the man of the house—until my tenth birthday.

———

The last of the cars have gone. The waiting vehicles facing down the hill towards the ferry have begun inching forward. I can hear the first of them boarding—thump, clump, over the ramp. On a sudden impulse I rush down the hill to meet the family and grab my father by his free hand. It is a large, strong hand with rough skin. He has his sleeves rolled up. On his right forearm there is a faint tattoo: DRMI. His initials—Dan Rory MacIntyre.

I have asked: "Why do you have your name on your arm?"

I would never, in a hundred years, tattoo my own miserable name on my arm or any other part of me.

"It's a long story," my father says, looking slightly uncomfortable.

What he always says when he's being evasive.

There is a brilliant parade to mark the coronation of Queen Elizabeth the Second. A coal miners' marching band from Donkin, over near Glace Bay, dressed dramatically in red and gold. The Port Hawkesbury fire brigade in crisp blue uniforms with white gloves. Brave veterans, heads high and shoulders back, medals clinking and flashing. Scores of kids from the two town schools, some in silly sailor suits and kilts. Girl Guides. We keep our position at Eddie Fougere's garage and watch as they all straggle by, then run up the steep hill to the public school, where there are speeches and kids singing "Land of Hope and Glory," directed by Miss Ladd, who looks like the Queen. I wave and try to catch her eye, but she doesn't notice me in the large crowd.

Later, at the Legion Grounds, there is a picnic. It isn't really a picnic, but that's what they call it anyway. Every year there is a picnic that isn't really a picnic in Judique, which is twenty miles to the north, and they have games there. Everybody talks about the tug-of-war and the dancing and the fist fights at the Judique picnic. And in Lower River Inhabitants, which is to the south, I once watched real boxers beating each other as they danced around on a small platform surrounded by ropes and a cheering crowd. I remember one of them was a MacIntyre from Glace Bay, a hard little man with blue scars on his face from going back to work in the coal mines too soon after the fighting. Later there was a famous boxer from here named Rockabye Ross, who beat a larger man from Sydney.

Every parish seems to have a picnic. Port Hawkesbury has no special attraction like the tug-of-war or boxing competitions, but this one is special anyway. There is a new Queen, and the highest mountain in the world has suddenly been humbled. The ferry, I have heard them say, will soon be "a thing of the past." There will be a causeway, and it will be in Port Hastings, not here. I imagine that soon Port Hastings will be the town, and the town will be a village. Perhaps our village, when a town, will have a picnic of its own. But for now, Port Hawkesbury is up for celebration anyway.

At the Legion Grounds there is a crowd of casually dressed people amid a jumble of shacks and booths, the smoke and smells of cooking meat, sounds of happy voices and mechanical music. The sense of fun is dampened only by the knowledge that everything there costs money, and money is "hard to come by." My sisters have not yet acquired an understanding of this reality and ask for everything they see.

I know that I must be selective. You can't have everything—one of the things you learn as the man of the house. One of the reasons the man of our house is a boy is that, often, the real men have to go far away and work hard for the money necessary for survival. You must not waste what is necessary for survival. I know there are people here who have more money than they need to survive. Mr. Clough and Mr. McGowan, who own stores. Mr. Gordon Walker, who owns a bank. The Langleys, who seem to own everything else. But that, I'm told, is "neither here nor there." We are who we are and we have what we have. And it isn't very much, but it's enough. There are always people who have less, and we must be thankful.

I wander through the crowd, past the open-front stands where men and women with faces that are familiar from church self-consciously cajole the passersby to part with money.

"Step right up," they say. "Try your luck."

I pause. A tall boy hurls a softball towards a stack of fake milk bottles—he misses and looks silly. His second try, propelled by anger and embarrassment, is like a stone from a slingshot. The stack of bottles explodes in a clatter.

"Hey, hey," says the man inside, laughing. "If you can do that against Petit-de-Grat this evening . . ." He hands the tall boy a yellow teddy bear, and he walks off proudly, teddy tucked securely under the bulging arm.

At night there will be a ball game against a team from Petit-de-Grat, which is in Isle Madame, where they all speak French, and, later, a chaperoned ball with Joe Murphy's Orchestra.

There is a wheel that spins. People are lined up, placing money on a piece of plastic that is like a tablecloth with crowns and anchors and other symbols that are duplicated at the wheel. A woman inside the booth spins the wheel with small yelps of enthusiasm. Round and round it goes, making a ticking sound, quickly at first, then slowing down. Where it stops, nobody knoooows.

Someone shouts "Yahoo"—and gets a prize.

I move on. I hear the crack of rifle fire and head towards the sound. There I find men lined up to fire a pretend rifle that looks like a .22 at a row of tiny mechanical birds moving along the top of a wall in a silent, resigned procession. Once hit, the metal bird flops out of sight behind the wall. I watch for a while and am tempted, but the fifty cents in my pocket suddenly feels too vulnerable. I know, when it is gone, there will be no more.

I arrive at a small cubicle, walls at least six feet high. I see in large letters on the plywood the words FISH POND. People pay money and are handed a fishing rod, flick the line over the wall, pretend to fish, then reel in prizes.

"Everybody wins!"

"How much?" I ask.

"Ten cents."

"I'll try."

After a moment I am the owner of a Union Jack.

————

The rain is cold. We are wondering what the premier and the man from Ottawa are doing on the other side. What does it take to set off an explosion?

"I think I'll go," says Theresa, who is shivering. Like Jackie Nick, Theresa MacKinnon always seems to have a cold, even in the summer.

"Suit yourself," says Angus Neil, her brother.

In school we learn there are four seasons in the year. But in Cape Breton there are only two—winter and summer. The summer usually lasts a little longer than it did this year. Sometimes it hangs on even up to Halloween. Then the winter comes in November and stays till June.

Some winter mornings you can't see through the window because of frost, but by holding your finger against it for a minute you can make a small hole and see outside. On days like that you have to be careful using the chamber pot because it often freezes over in the night. We don't have a bathroom in the house.

On winter mornings my mother gets up first and lights the stove, and when the fire is rumbling and crackling to life we rush downstairs and dress quickly, huddling close to the only source of heat in the house. I've heard them say we will soon have a floor furnace in the back hallway, and that will help. They say we are slowly making progress. When we first moved in, after Harry and Rannie left, there was no electricity. One night my little sister Rosalind tried to blow out a kerosene lamp, but the shade exploded and almost set her and the house on fire. I think it was after that we got the power.

When there is hot water ready, we wash in a pan in the pantry sink, where there is a hand pump for cold water. Some day, I have been assured, we'll have water from taps and a bathroom, instead of the outdoor toilet, which is attached to the barn.

We have a cow. My mother named her Beulah, another name without any apparent reason for it. Around the time we got the cow we also got a little pig, which she named Oriole—also completely out of the blue. Oriole and Beulah became, like Skipper, part of the family, but when the pig grew large and fat and noisy, some men came and killed her, scraped the guts out, and hung her upside down in the barn. My mother explained that that's what pigs are for. You feed them and fatten them, and then you eat them. Apparently they don't mind.

Cows are different, she assured me then. Beulah is for her milk. We would never kill Beulah.

We're supposed to be lucky because we live so close to the school and can come home to eat at noon. But I often envy the kids who stay there to eat their lunch at their desks, then run wild in and out of the schoolrooms afterward, shouting and banging on the piano and, when it's fine, playing ball.

There are about forty kids in the school. The number varies. Kids seem to start and stop for very little reason. For a while the Fraser kids from out back were coming in a horse and wagon, dropped off by their father, Angus. But then they stopped coming. Older boys just quit. People move away.

We're divided between the two rooms—up to grade five in one, six to ten in the other. I'm in grade five and can hardly wait until I move to the next room. I know that Mrs. Gillis can be cross, though she's not as cross as Miss Euphemia MacKinnon, who would beat the older boys with her own strap, which someone said was made from braided telephone wire.

I spend all day in school trying to concentrate on my own work while Miss Morrison struggles with the hopeless smaller kids, trying to teach them how to read and spell. Each day is like a month of my life.

In the morning, before school, I help my mother with the cow. I shovel the manure and pitch down hay from the scaffold above the stable. My mother milks. Milking, I am told, is women's work. Before I go to school I will fill a hod with coal in the barn and bring it in for the fire. I will also fill the woodbox.

During winter the cow lives in the barn most of the time, venturing out only to drink some water from a washtub near the well. Then she'll happily go back, even without being told. But starting in May we'll just let her wander off anywhere she wants to go. And she always seems to go to the same place, around here somewhere, near where the causeway will connect. I usually find her in one of the fields and pastures that nobody uses near the old MacMillan place.

I wonder what will happen now. With the causeway heading in this direction and plans for a big canal right down there, across the back of Nicholson's Point, it is difficult to imagine that these fields will be safe for a wandering cow anymore. Not even for an intelligent cow like Beulah who manages to take care of herself all day long.

It is my job, every evening in the summer, right after supper and the rosary, to go looking for her, though she is never hard to find.

One evening last May she didn't answer when I called, and I had to come home without her. Nobody seemed to worry. My mother just said, "Start looking again tomorrow." But I couldn't find her then, either.

I found her by accident on the third day. She was hiding in a little grove of trees in a difficult place behind the graveyard. I could see that she was lying down and assumed that she was hurt. The dog went in first, then came running back, bouncing with excitement.

The cow was lying there, staring at me with annoyance in her large brown eyes. Standing nearby was a tiny calf. When the dog went over to sniff at it, the calf tried to move away but staggered and fell down. The cow started struggling to her feet, and then I saw the great disgusting mess behind her. A great puddle of slime that I now know is called the afterbirth.

I had to go and get adults to help me take her home.

What will Beulah do, I wonder, when the causeway takes away her territory?

———

I see the family moving through the crowd at the Legion Grounds, my mother and father and sisters. Suddenly I am hungry.

"I want to buy a hot dog," I announce.

"The money is burning a hole in your pocket," my father teases.

My mother says: "Save your money. In a little while we'll go to the Cabot Grill."

A restaurant. I have never eaten in a restaurant before because my parents see no point in paying someone for food you could prepare for yourself. "Money doesn't grow on trees." Plus, "Who knows what they do to the food out in the back kitchen?"

My father says he was getting tea at Mac's Lunch one summer day and he could see a big raw T-bone steak on a plate inside the kitchen. It was crawling with flies. Then he saw the cook grab a dishtowel and kill all the flies on the steak with one whack of the rag. Then brush the dead flies away and toss the steak in a frying pan for some other customer.

When my father is away working, he eats in a cookhouse. When he comes home he always reports, among the most important details of his absence, that "the grub is great" or that "the bull cook wouldn't know how to boil water if his life depended on it."

In some places where he works, people have plotted to kill the cook—to shoot him or blow him up with dynamite.

I have heard my father and my uncle Joe Donohue talking about a lumber camp where they once worked and lived mostly on porridge and bread and molasses and got paid a dollar a day.

A dollar a day? It sounds like a lot of money when you're down to forty cents.

I understand that money is important. My Uncle John Dan tries to live without it on the mountain. John Dan rarely goes away to work. He's in the mine in Stirling now, but nobody expects that he'll stay for long. John Dan, according to Grandma Donohue, "has no ambition."

This means that John Dan and his wife, Mae, and all their kids try to live on the mountain the way the MacIntyres have lived for more than a hundred and thirty years. They plant their vegetables in the mountain's sandy soil, which is, they say, perfect for potatoes. They grow hay and store it in the barns to feed their animals—horses for the work, cows for milk and butter. For meat, they "butcher"—which means, I understand, they kill an animal.

None of this, of course, produces money, and money has become essential for survival.

———

Coming home from school, I knew there was something wrong even before I found out what was happening. The first sign was the cow, Beulah, at the barn. She was standing there bawling loudly, face up close to the front door. It was still October. Normally she wouldn't be home unless I went and got her. Normally, she'd be at the back door, the entrance to her stable.

But there she was, home early and at the wrong door. I was about to go see what her problem was when the barn door opened and there was a stranger, standing with a cigarette in one hand and a large knife in the other. There was blood on his fist and wrists and on an apron he was wearing. The cow bawled again. It wasn't her normal indifferent moo but more like a howl. The man looked at her briefly, flicked his cigarette, and went back inside and shut the door.

I went straight through the house and up to my bedroom. I just sat there for a long time, trying to shut the sound of the cow out of my mind.

Later my mother came up.

"I thought you knew," she said.

"No."

"It was a boy calf."

"So what?"

"We couldn't keep him. What would we do with a boy calf after he grew up?"

"Sell him. Give him away."

"We can't afford to feed him. Besides, we need the meat. Do you have any idea what veal costs?"

And there it was again. What things cost. Cars, clothes, houses, calves. Everything is about what things cost.

"You have a soft heart," she said after a while. "There's nothing wrong with that."

I still feel bad for the calf. His mother, Beulah, hovered around the door of the barn for days. This, I know, is how the world works. Things die so other things will live.

When I asked my father once: "Why are you always going away?"

"We have to eat," he said. "That's all you have to know."

In case I didn't understand, he said: "We eat, or we are eaten."

My father would go away because there were no jobs close to home. Not for him, the man who never went to school; the man without connections. We keep a cow for milk. We sometimes raise a pig to kill for meat. If, by some mysterious process, the cow ends up with a calf, it will be either sold or killed.

I'd ask my mother: "Why can't he stay home—like the MacKinnons and Ellis Langley and the MacLellans?"

"Some day soon," she'd say.

"There are lots of people here who don't have jobs. Harry and Rannie. Sinclair. Danny Black Dan. They survive."

"But just look at them," she'd say. "Is that how you want us to live?"

"What about the causeway?" I'd ask. "There will be lots of people working on the causeway."

"We'll see," she'd say. "Remember your father in your prayers."

———

My grandfather, Dougald, was a painter of houses and, from time to time, would leave the mountain to paint something and then return with money. Dougald's father, whom they called Alasdair Chiorstaidh, was a famous carpenter and built, they say, a hundred houses. But he never had much money because there wasn't any and, luckily, he didn't need it.

Now you need it and, because my uncle on the mountain tries to

76

live the way the old people did, John Dan's house has a dilapidated look about it. It needs paint and shingles and new foundations—things that now cost money.

After he started working in the mine in Stirling, John Dan bought a car, and he has loaned it to his only surviving sibling, his brother, Dan Rory. I know he will work there for as long as he has to, and then he will go back to the mountain and live as MacIntyres have always lived.

Even without money, the mountain is a happy place. Boisterous kids rampaging in and out of the house and hanging out the windows. Always laughing at something. You go to the mountain and you laugh all the time you're there. I have heard my father describe his brother's wife, Mae, as "a saint." And she has holy pictures and rosaries and little crosses made from Easter palm on the walls of her kitchen.

My grandparents, Dougald and Peggy, whom the old people call Peigeag, are also always smiling and laughing. And calling me Lindy *a'ghaol*.

"M'eudail Lindy a'ghaol." Being called a treasure doesn't sound so bad in Gaelic.

If John Dan had "ambition," I think, they'd probably be even happier on the mountain, because ambition, as I understand it, is a virtue. But I can't imagine a happier place or happier people.

Sometimes I just come out and say it: "Why can't we live on the mountain?"

And they just look at me.

My father told me that when he was sixteen he left the mountain and never once looked back. He was off into the world to seek his fortune, just like Dick Whittington in the story. I'm not sure what he means, but his face has the expression that tells you not to ask any more questions.

Grandma Donohue thinks Dan Rory is a dreamer.

Jackie Nick is pointing towards the strait. I can see some movement on the other side.

"Where?" asks Binky. He has very bad eyes and is always going to the doctor because of them. Ian is wiping at his glasses, suddenly alert.

Brian is the first to notice the explosion.

"Holy frig," he says.

A massive black shape gushes outward from the cape like a great, silent, rolling roil of smoke. I hear excited voices all around me.

"Holy God," says Angus Neil.

Then the earth begins to shake beneath us. I feel a sudden shortness of breath, as if the air has been punched out of my lungs.

Then Ian shouts: "Look at 'er go."

And as we watch, the distant hillside suddenly blossoms brown and lurches in our direction, cascading billows of dust. It looks like smoke—except that I can also see the surface of the strait suddenly popping and splashing as the stone rockets almost all the way across. Then, as if an afterthought, there is a rolling, rumbling roar that starts deep inside the mountain belly, breaks free, reaches across, and settles all around us. The air moves and becomes wind. High above us a hawk, balanced on a shaft of air, suddenly slips and slides downward, struggling to resume his dignity. Then he surrenders to the fear and flees, flapping furiously towards the trees.

The dog begins to bark and run in circles, dashing towards the edge of the embankment overlooking the point, then swiftly back again, trying to wrap himself around my legs.

I realize Jackie Nicholson is no longer looking at the blast. He is watching something near the lighthouse. It is his grandmother, Kate, standing there alone on the point, probably remembering the long years looking after the light they'll soon no longer need, the long chilly nights sitting bundled at the point operating the brooding foghorn. Poor old Mrs. Nicholson, redundant now, watching the beginning of the future.

––––––––

In February there was excitement in the school. I noticed after New Year's that Angus Neil MacKinnon's sister, Theresa, was missing almost every day. Theresa always seemed to have a cold. Then, in February, we heard that Theresa was in the San. The San is the Sanatorium in Point Edward, near Sydney, where they send you if you have tuberculosis.

Theresa always seemed sickly but, compared to Jackie Nicholson, she was robust. Jackie is skinny, and his nose is always running. If there is impetigo on the go, Jackie gets it first. The teacher always had her eye on Jackie for signs of illness, and you'd have bet money that if anybody had tuberculosis it would be Jackie.

But it was Theresa, and we all had to have tests. They stuck a patch on your arm, and you had to leave it there for weeks, it seemed. Everybody was looking at everybody else, wondering who else had it. Keeping a little distance from Angus Neil because he was Theresa's brother, and from Jackie Nick because he was always poking at his runny nose or wiping it on his sleeve.

But when they took the patches off, everyone was clean.

––––––––

The Cabot Grill is on the south end of the paved main street that runs through town, Granville Street. I remember being inside it once because, in a room above it, there was a doctor—Dr. Knodell. I would go to the doctor for the terrible nosebleeds I get certain times of the year. And for the infestation of plump watery hives that torment my body, usually in the spring and fall.

Recently I've been going to the new doctor who is from far away, a place called Poland. The new doctor has a name few can pronounce—Dr. Guzdziol. In the beginning they'd call him Dr. Goose-oil, mockingly. But as they get to know him and his story, and that he and his wife, Anna, fought in the war against the Nazis, they struggle to get the name right. "Doctor Goose-a-doll," they'll say. Or simply, "the Polish doctor."

The Polish doctor lives in West Bay Road, which is out back. But there is a rumour that Dr. Knodell is moving away and that the Polish doctor will replace him here in town later this year.

After visiting Dr. Knodell once, my mother and I waited in the Cabot Grill for our ride home. I, though only four or five years old, was permanently impressed by the perpetual clatter and the powerful aromas of the restaurant. It all comes back on the day of the coronation.

The place is full of people, and we are told we'll have to wait for a booth. There is loud music, and I wander towards the source, a shiny jukebox with chrome and soft lights. I recognize the song and know the singer is Hank Williams, whom everybody around here seems to love. I remember the day Hank Williams died. The older boys and girls stood around talking about it quietly, as they did when King George died the year before. It was New Year's Day and we were coasting, and when young Angus Walker brought the news, everybody stopped.

I wander off in the direction of the jukebox. Through a glass front, I can see lists of songs. I return to my mother and announce that I'd like to play a song on the jukebox.

She laughs.

"Save your money," she says.

"Money?"

"Yes, dear. It costs money to play music on the jukebox."

"Oh."

I wander back to the jukebox. And yes, I read that it costs a nickel for a selection. Five for a quarter. My fingertips caress the coins in my pocket. Forty cents, burning a hole.

I am reading carefully through the titles. "The Yellow Rose of Texas." I saw a movie with that name once. "Wheel of Fortune." "Your Cheatin' Heart" by Hank.

Then, to my astonishment, I see a song that is "free."

One song out of the dozens and dozens listed there at a nickel each, and clear as can be, it is "free."

I return to where my mother is waiting.

"Can I play the free one?"

"The free one?"

"Yes," I announce. "There's one there that's free."

"Nothing is for free," my mother says.

"Come," I say, and take her by the hand. Lead her to the jukebox and point it out.

THE BEST THINGS IN LIFE ARE
free INKSPOTS.

My mother has a puzzled frown on her face.

"Look again," I say, because it's clear she doesn't understand.

"The best things in life are inkspots. Free."

Now she is smiling broadly. I read her expression as pride, remembering that, most of the time, I am the man of the house. She places a gentle hand on the top of my head.

Then she laughs. "No, no," she says. "It's *by* the Inkspots."

The Inkspots?

"The Best Things In Life Are Free," she says. "The Inkspots are the singers."

Singers called inkspots? The best things in life? Free? It makes no sense to me. It is the opposite of what I know. The best things in life cost money. The best things in life require grown-up men to have jobs, and if they lack connections or an education they have to go away.

I am about to ask my mother for some further elaboration, but she is gone already. She is already at Dan Rory's side, whispering and laughing.

I watch a slight twitch at the corner of my father's mouth, as it grows into a smile broad as the dawn.

Later, when the sun is gone and it is dark, there are fireworks. Rockets sail into the night sky, then burst into showers. There is the noise of giant firecrackers exploding. The people in town are greatly impressed and roar out in excitement with every explosion of noise and light. It is a real celebration—for the new Queen and the conquerors of Mount Everest. But the spectacle is unimpressive compared to what we see across the Strait of Canso, almost regularly now, as they tear a mountain down to build the causeway that will bring the world to us.

3

THE MISSION

Sunday morning, riding the church bus to Mass, I couldn't take my eyes off a kerchief on the head of the woman sitting alone in front of me. It was made of silk and was bright red and green, and there was something written there in block letters, but I could see only *KOR*.

We go to Mass in Port Hawkesbury because there is no Catholic Church in Port Hastings. Most of the people who live here are Protestants and have their own little church down below our house. Sundays, in the summertime, you can hear the singing because they leave the doors open. I often go down there after I get back from Mass to listen and try to hear their sermons. I can hear the singing clearly from over beside the school, where old people from out back tie their horses to the trees. I sometimes sneak in to watch their funerals. The Protestants leave the caskets open during funerals the way we do at wakes. That way you know there's nothing dangerous about the dead.

I like the sound of the Protestant Church music and the way everybody sings along. I've seen them at the funerals with their books and their mouths wide open, singing loudly, their faces flushed and their eyes closed. The minister just talks, like a teacher. At Mass the priest has his back to us and mumbles privately in Latin. The singing is by a choir, or sometimes by a kid my age from town.

His father is Eddie Fougere, who owns the service station near the ferry terminal. The kid's name is Aloysius, and you often hear him singing by himself, his high voice ringing in the far hollows of the ceiling. He's been trained to sing by both his mother and the nuns, and he can even play the organ. I appreciate him mostly because he has the misfortune of a name as dubious as mine. Aloysius. Misery loves company, they say.

For some reason or other, Catholics never seem to want to sing along. We just stand or sit and listen.

There is a parish bus for Catholics who live in Port Hastings and Point Tupper and don't have cars. Hardly anybody has a car, it seems, unless he has a job on the railroad or with the Highways Department.

I don't know much about the differences between the Protestants and the Catholics, only that they are wrong and we are right. But then I wonder: if they are so wrong, how come they seem to have so much more? Plus their own church, right here in the village.

When I'd remember my father in my prayers, I was always careful to point out that the request was not for me. I understood why my father had to go away to find work. But I could also tell by the expression on his face when he'd be leaving that he would prefer to have stayed home. It's as simple as that. "Away" is a place of loneliness for him, much as, in some strange way, home is frequently a place of loneliness for me.

I leaned forward, studying the scarf on the head of the woman in front of me, wondering where she got it. It was pulled forward on her head, so I couldn't see her face from where I sat.

I remembered that the Syrian had been around a few days earlier. I saw him struggling up the hill, by our place, bent under the heavy load he always carries. Maybe she got the scarf from him. I'm not certain where the Syrian comes from. I've heard he has a store somewhere on the mainland, but he carries much of what he sells in the store in a large

84

leather case slung over his back. It is held shut by a wide leather strap that he grips with both hands as he trudges through the countryside. He goes from door to door, opening the case, holding up his merchandise and praising it in English that is difficult to understand—kitchen things and clothing, pills and colourful cloth, and delicate silk scarves.

The poor Syrian, I thought. This is what he has to do to eat. Walking the roads, bent double under his heavy load. And I realized there are worse things than being away, working underground by the light of the lamp on your hat.

One night he came to our house late and asked if he could stay.

"Please, Missis," he begged. "I have no place to sleep. Please, Missis, let me come in."

My mother was just standing there, looking anxious.

"I can't," she said.

"Please, Missis."

"No," she said. "There's no man here."

"Please, Missis, I have no place to sleep."

"I'm sorry," she said.

And then she shut the door. Through the window I saw him plodding up the hill like a tired old horse, until he vanished in the darkness. And I felt angry, the echo of those ugly words ringing in my ears.

"Please, Missis."

"I couldn't," she told me afterwards. "I just couldn't. Where would we put him?"

"I don't know," I said.

"We're all alone here," she said.

I could tell she thought I was feeling sorry for the Syrian, but it was only the sound of the begging that bothered me. My father says a man should never beg. Once when they were saying go see Clough about a job, he said he'd rather starve than beg. And somehow it seemed right. Praying is not the same as begging.

I remember the church bus was banging along on the rutted road, past the end of the pavement. Near Embree's Island, which isn't an island anymore, curiosity moved my hand to where the tip of the red and green silk scarf draped over the back of the seat in front of me. With one finger I touched it to see what else was written there. Her hair was shiny black and very thick. She must have felt the touch because she turned her head quickly, and I finally saw her face. Her name is Jean Larter and she lives up the hill from us, near the O'Handleys, Johnny and Mary.

She's originally from Prince Edward Island. She smiled.

I said "Excuse me," which I'm supposed to say whenever I bother an older person. I'm also supposed to tip my cap to an older lady, but I wasn't wearing one.

"That's okay," she said, believing my touch was accidental.

Jean Larter turned back, and when she did the folds concealing other letters on her kerchief flattened out and I could see the whole word now—*KOREA*. And that the design on the kerchief was actually a map of the country—one of the places we're always reading about in the papers because of the war. And I remembered that her husband, Joe, had been there.

He didn't have a job. He joined the army. He wound up in Korea.

I was thinking: maybe there are worse places than Stirling, where my father was working at the time.

Besides Korea, the only other name that I could see on Jean Larter's kerchief map was Seoul, which I know from the papers is a city near the middle of the country. That the Reds took it over early in the war, but the Allies quickly took it back, then drove them all the way to Manchuria—which was when the Chinese got involved.

For the rest of the bus ride to Mass, I studied the kerchief map that Joe had brought back for Jean, trying to imagine what Korea and its people looked like up close, head swirling with images of the war from the newspapers and a whole jumble of other times and places and their wars. I tried to imagine the rivers named Ponchon and Imjin, and a valley called Kapyong where Canadians fought heroically on Hill 677, according to the papers. Comic books and magazines are mostly pictures of Americans, but because of Joe and the Canadian stories about Hill 677, I know it wasn't just the Americans.

I suppose I could walk up the hill behind our house and ask Joe all about Korea—except that I know from Danny MacIntosh and John MacDougall and all the others that you're never supposed to ask them questions about their wars.

I know from talk at the post office that Joe Larter is working at the causeway now. Veterans, like Liberals and Masons, never seem to have a problem getting work.

———

Mr. Clough is a short, round man who wears glasses that slide down on his nose. He has a large round stomach that projects in front of him and is accentuated by wide suspenders. He complains about his stomach, and I have heard that he has ulcers. He moves slowly and makes puffing sounds.

Many people seem to be afraid of Mr. Clough. And when they go to buy their things at the larger store, which is farther along the road and which they call R.J.'s, they hurry by looking straight ahead. Going back, they walk on the other side of the road. Sometimes Mr. Clough will stand in the doorway of his store with his hands in his pockets and glare.

Everybody owes him money because he sells groceries on credit. He has two counters in the store, and behind one there is the post office. Behind the other he seems to have a little office of his own, and he keeps the bill-books there. Everybody has a bill-book, and you pay it off at the end of every month. Knowing they have a bill-book at Mr. Clough's store seems to make the older people nervous.

But there are certain things you never buy at Mr. Clough's, even if you owe him money. Meat, for instance. My mother says she doesn't trust his fridge. And she constantly complains about his bread box. It is a large wooden crate with a lid on top, and the lid is worn and chipped because men sit there when they're waiting for the mail or when they're talking business with Mr. Clough.

My mother hates the fact that men have their big rear ends so close to the bread, and she knows that some of them will fart on the bread box just for devilment. I've seen them do it—leaning gently to one side, smirking privately, and letting go.

Not that it matters to us because we never buy bread anyway. My mother makes our bread on Thursdays.

But I know all about Mr. Clough because he has sometimes caught me going by the store.

"Come here," he'll say. "What have you got there?"

I'll show him.

"You could have got that here," he'll say, frowning into the bag.

After that I'll feel guilty all the way home for somehow having betrayed the only storekeeper who lets people buy food on credit even if they're Tories and Catholics.

Sometimes if it's something like salt cod, I'll buy it at Clough's even though I'm supposed to go to R.J.'s (which we are beginning to call McGowan's because Mr. Howard McGowan owns it now). Mr. Clough keeps the salt cod in a wooden box in the back room, and I know how to pick out what we want, always selecting the white thin pieces that are less likely to have the worms.

But if I had my way I'd always go to R.J.'s because it is a much more interesting place, with clothes and equipment and ammunition and the smell of new rubber boots and leather, and coffins on the third floor.

Both Ronnie the Minister and Isabel Grant, who work for him, are friendlier than Mr. Clough, who always seems to be in pain.

Once when he looked in the bag and frowned, he said to me, "I have to make a living too."

And it stayed with me all day. Mr. Clough, who has a store and a post office and important connections, has to make a living too.

Mr. Clough is by the bread box talking to Danny MacIntosh, who is sitting on it. Danny MacIntosh was shot in World War One but went back again for World War Two anyway. Because he spent so much time in the wars, he never got a wife and he lives alone in a little old house at the foot of Church Street, the street on top of which my Aunt Veronica lives. Often Danny goes on benders, and other war veterans will be at his place telling stories. Sometimes they don't even notice if you sneak in to listen.

His house is full of interesting stuff he brought back from overseas. My favourite thing is a cane with a three-foot sword inside it.

What Danny MacIntosh and Mr. Clough have in common is their pain. Mr. Clough's is in his stomach. Danny MacIntosh's pain seems to be all over, and he wears copper bracelets that he thinks will help. He is also always eating garlic, which Mr. Clough keeps in the store just for him because it's impossible to imagine that anybody else here would ever want it. Danny MacIntosh thinks the garlic helps control his suffering. You can almost tell before you get there that he is in the store because you can smell his breath even before you're through the door.

Danny MacIntosh doesn't have to earn a living because he has a pension, from fighting in two world wars. But if he ever needed a job I don't think he'd have any problem, being a veteran and being in with Mr. Clough because of religion and politics.

Mr. Clough has power and money and a bad stomach. Some people respect him and some are afraid of him. I haven't yet been able to figure out the difference between respect and fear. The two seem to go together, at least where we live. I'm not sure what it is that makes people nervous— the power, the money, or the ulcer. My Aunt Veronica figures all three go together, and we're better off than he is with our health and our poverty. That's the way she talks, using a word like poverty that describes people living far away, in places like China and Korea. Everybody says she has a gift with words and can even make a word like poverty sound hilarious.

"Are all the people in Korea poor?" I ask.

"I'm sure the kids in Korea would be happy to trade places with you," I'm told. "So eat your supper."

Johnny Eddy MacDonald is one person I know who is not afraid of Mr. Clough. Every day he picks up the mail for out back and delivers it with his horse and wagon. He is big and fat and red-faced and always laughing. In the wintertime he uses a horse and sleigh to drive the mail, and he lets us clamber onto the back when he's passing by the school on his way out the Victoria Line. Johnny Eddy will even torment Mr. Clough about politics. He isn't a Mason because he's a Catholic, but he gets away with it because they're both Big Liberals. You know he's a Liberal because you have to be to get a job driving the mail out back.

Johnny Eddy suddenly looms in the doorway and shouts a greeting. Danny MacIntosh looks up, and Mr. Clough turns. Because the wicket is near the door, he finally seems to notice me. Johnny Eddy walks in and the store suddenly feels crowded.

Mr. Clough says something like "Poof Poof," and walks behind the post office counter, past the weigh scales and the ball of string and the big roll of wrapping paper and the large, open box of cookies that have spots of jam in the centres. We never buy the cookies either.

He fusses around the little pigeonholes where he keeps the letters, then turns and examines a pile of parcels on the floor.

Then he announces: "There's a COD from Simpsons."

My heart is beating faster as I race home with the news. I can remember another Christmas, long ago, when the talk about the Christmas COD would make you feel afraid and sad.

But it's different now. That was the Christmas when we didn't know where he was. We didn't know if he had a job or not. And people with serious faces would be coming around asking where Dan Rory was, and my mother would be saying, "Believe me, I'd like to know as much as the next person."

This Christmas he's home. For good, at last.

———

Late in November the Christmas music starts, and you get the special feeling. And going for the mail becomes a big adventure.

Christmas is particularly welcome this year because everyone is talking about prosperity and the future. Everyone is talking at the store about the jobs available for miners over on Cape Porcupine, and for trucks on both sides of the strait. Building the causeway was all about drilling and blasting and hauling rocks in trucks.

I'd been hearing the talk for years, wondering: would there be work for him here, finally? When he was in Stirling, he'd come home on a Friday night. There would be no talk about the causeway. Sunday afternoon he'd go away again, as usual. Even after the first big blast in the fall of '52. It was as if there was nothing happening here.

I'd be reading in the newspaper that comes from Sydney about thousands of miners who live in places like Glace Bay and Dominion, New Waterford and Sydney Mines, where there have been coal mines for at least a hundred years. There are more than ten thousand coal miners working. That's what the paper said when they were all threatening to go on strike.

"What's a strike?"

"It's when people who have jobs refuse to work."

"What?"

"It's complicated. It's all about belonging to a union. When you belong to a union you get to have a say in how much you work and how much you get paid. And you can stop working if you don't like what they're giving you."

"Does my father belong to a union?"

"No."

"How come?"

"It's a long story. Anyway, your father isn't a coal miner."

I can tell that coal miners live like ordinary people. They live in towns. They go to work and then come home. They go to church on Sundays and play at sports—boxing, ball, or hockey.

My father, who is a hard-rock miner, hardly ever gets to church and has never played a sport.

Once I asked: "Why can't you work in a coal mine and come home every day when you are finished working?"

He told me: "A coal mine is a death trap."

I remembered all the stories in the paper about coal miners killed in underground explosions. And I remembered that the only explosions in the hard-rock mine are the ones you make yourself to break the rock.

"You do what you have to do to make a living," he says. "Some people will work in coal mines. More power to them."

"What about the union?" I asked.

"What about the union?"

I know that coal is dangerous. We buy it from Port Hood and burn it in the stove along with wood. Every so often you'll hear a pop in the stove, and a piece of coal will snap. Sometimes you can see blue flame hissing out of a burning lump of coal.

Once a house blew up in Glace Bay, and nobody could figure why. Maybe gas leaked in from underground. They found the family just sitting there in the smoking ruins that had been their house and was now completely gone. A little girl was killed. The mother went stone blind.

Then the truth came out. The men in the house were bootleg miners, which means they earned a living digging coal illegally. They dug their own mine where the coal seam came close to the surface, not far from where they lived. To make the digging easier, they stole some dynamite from the coal company.

But the dynamite was wet and wouldn't light, so they put it in the oven of the kitchen stove to dry and forgot to tell the women it was there.

You do what you have to do to earn a living. And yes, there are worse places than Stirling, I thought.

Last spring, just before my father took a holiday for the coronation and borrowed his brother's car, one of our excursions was to Stirling, to see the mine where he'd been working.

After driving for what seemed like hours over dusty roads, we came to a cluster of buildings, like a small frontier village. There were little houses, and I wondered who lived in them. He pointed out a peculiar structure that stood tall above the others, and he told us it was the head frame, the entrance to the mine. Beneath it was a shaft that went straight down and, branching out from the shaft, there were tunnels he called drifts. Among the drifts there were other tunnels, and caverns called cross-cuts and raises and stopes. A long, low building nearby, he said, was the mill. This was where the rock they brought through the drifts and up the shaft would be ground into powder and the metals extracted. You could hear a terrible racket of roaring and crashing and crushing coming from the mill.

Then he said, "Let's take a look at the head frame."

It was freezing cold inside the building. The floor was made of concrete. There was rusty equipment everywhere. Lying on the floor were long drills my father said were used for boring holes into the rock. Some of the holes would go in twelve feet. Others would be shorter, and they'd all be drilled in a special pattern. Then they'd load the holes with dynamite. And he explained that it was freezing in the head frame because of the damp, cold air rushing up from underground. Underground is cold and wet, he said.

"That's how I got piles," he says.

It's an old joke.

"Piles of what," I say.

"Piles of money," he says. And we both laugh, every time.

Inside the entrance to the shaft I could see heavy greased cables moving silently. Up. Down. Stopping mysteriously. Taking off again. Gusts of sour mist billowing from the darkness. I wanted to go and look down, but he told me not to.

Then a sudden chatter of sound and a crash and the low swinging door blocking the shaft swung open, and there were bobbing lights and men with hard hats and dirty faces and wet rubber overalls jostling out of a metal box my father called the "cage." The cage runs up and down the shaft all day, taking the men down to their working places, then back up again, transporting the dynamite and the tools they need to do their work.

The miners all seemed to be happy to be back in the daylight and the fresh air, talking loudly and laughing. And they all knew him and shouted as they passed. He seemed embarrassed. He was one of them, but standing with us seemed to create an uncomfortable distance between him and his friends. Two worlds side by side, vast differences exposed.

You feel like that sometimes, standing with your friends and a parent shows up.

And after that he took me to the mill, and when we were leaving he gave me a Maxwell House coffee can half filled with a fine grey powder for a souvenir.

"Zinc concentrate," he said. "One of the things we find down there in all the rock."

"What's it for?"

"Well, now. You'll have to ask somebody else. Anything that zinc is in."

I sniffed the can, and the powder smelled sour and vaguely rotten, like the taste in your mouth when you have a terrible headache.

He took us to the cookhouse to eat, and the place was crowded with large, noisy men hunched over long tables, eating, arguing, drinking mugs of coffee, smoking cigarettes. And then there were the older ones, pale, grey-headed old men, sitting alone and staring into space.

"You could come home," I said. "Work in the daylight. Over on Cape Porcupine."

"We'll see," he said. "One of these days, we'll see."

Then, of course, I'm home again. And the house is, once again, half empty. And once again I pass the time with books and stories of sailing ships and the silent wind transporting you to far-off places. I stand in the window, trying to remember Stirling, which was unlike any place I'd ever seen. And there is a freighter paused almost motionless in the strait, as if contemplating this foreign presence suddenly blocking the way in front of it. The causeway, like the armoured back of a giant serpent, now more than halfway across. Taking over, soon to be master of the ancient waterway. I can imagine the men on the ship, studying their charts, puzzled by this new obstacle.

Then the ship is gone, except in the mind and in the dreams.

Stirling is soon forgotten, until I remember the men emerging from the cage, loud and strong and fearless, faces smeared from dust and sweat. Only the eyes are clear as the white teeth when they laughed at my father, standing there in his Sunday clothes with us, the people from his other world. I still see him embarrassed to be clean and dry and idle among the women and the kids.

Before we left Stirling, we stopped to see a friend of his. The friend's name was Danny Shaw. We sat in the car while he and Danny Shaw walked a short distance away and stood talking beside a large truck. Then they walked around the truck, examining it carefully. My father opened a door and climbed in and sat behind the wheel for a moment. Then he got out and seemed about to climb underneath.

Then he stood up, slapping his hands together to remove the dirt.

When he returned to the car, my mother asked: "What do you think?"

"I think that's the ticket," he said.

———

Christmas is the one time of the year when money doesn't seem to matter. Gifts and food appear as if by magic. Worries disappear.

I ran for home with news of the COD from Simpsons, the dog ahead at first but then doubling back to urge me to go faster, swinging behind me and passing me repeatedly, whirling in excitement because he knew as well as I do what Christmas means.

The COD is the conclusive sign, but the weather is always the first indicator. After Halloween the trees are bare, leaves that were red and gold and orange all through October are now congealed in soggy, rotting piles that are, on chilly mornings, covered with a furry-looking frost. Cold rains flatten the dead brown grass in ditches and in the fields. The chilly air is heavy with the smell of fermenting apples.

The week before Christmas, the dog and I will go to the woods with an axe the way we always do. Over the hill and past Jack Reynolds's, where there used to be a stagecoach depot. Past Alex MacKinnon's, where the railwaymen sit in their undershirts on the doorstep on the warm summer evenings. Past Mrs. Eva Forbes's, the widow who has plum trees in her yard and a big piano that she sometimes lets my sister Danita and her friend Annie MacKinnon play on. All the way out through Big Ian MacKinnon's back field.

We follow a track that probably was once a road, around the edge of the field, past a clearance that used to be a farm they still call LaFave's, until we are now behind the cove where they used to quarry gypsum. I pretend that the axe is a rifle and that we are Indian scouts, defending our village from all the white explorers. I would like to get a real rifle for Christmas, but I'm probably too young. The house could use a rifle, I believe, for when he isn't here.

There is a high waterfall that crashes over ice-encrusted rocks at the bottom. I go carefully around that obstacle, and then back on the path that leads to Happy Jack's Lake. Red squirrels chatter and rabbits dive for cover in bushes, with the dog darting after them.

The lake is frozen. The older boys believe it was formed by a meteor from outer space and that it has no bottom. They skate there when the ice gets thick enough. I have skates, but they don't fit me yet. They belonged to a miner who was killed in Newfoundland. My father told me I can use them just as soon as my feet are big enough to fill them. I asked him what happened to the man who owned the skates, and he says he'll tell me some day when I'm older.

Near Happy Jack's Lake, as usual, I'll find the perfect tree. The dog will bark in approval as I chop it down, feeling the glow of knowing I have done the man's work and that my mother and Grandma Donohue will rave about it.

Then we'll open the door of the dining room to let the heat in.

And one evening, when the room is warm enough, we'll stand the tree in a corner and decorate it.

On Christmas morning I will join my sisters in their bedroom, which is just above the dining room, and we'll look down through the hole in the floor of their room to see what's there, underneath the tree. It will still be dark, but we have a secret way for turning on the light that hangs on a wire in the middle of the ceiling. It was my invention, the first Christmas after we got electricity in the house: I tie a string to the chain that turns the light on, run the string down and through the rung of a chair, then back up through the hole.

Early Christmas morning we gather round the hole. I pull the string. The room is suddenly illuminated. We take turns peering down, figuring out who got what.

Then I pull the string again. The room with all its Christmas riches is lost again in darkness. We return to our beds and begin the long wait for daylight.

———

Once my father showed me a large photograph of a group of men in rubber working clothes and with lamps attached to the front of their hard hats. That was in Newfoundland, he said, where I was born.

The miners were standing in front of the head frame, everybody smiling and looking full of mischief.

"This," he said, pointing to one of the men, "is the one whose skates you inherited."

The dead man was standing beside my father with a big grin on his face and not a clue that he would soon be gone.

And now it is Christmas, and this year he won't be coming home because he's already here. He is our father again, no longer just a visitor from somewhere else.

———

My Aunt Veronica is like us. Her husband, Mickey MacNeil, had to go away for work. Mickey MacNeil is a milkman in Toronto, and obviously the people in Toronto don't pay their milkmen very much because Mickey hardly ever comes home. My aunt is always taking on hard jobs here to support herself and her two little boys, Barry and John Blaise. She works so hard that sometimes she gets sick. She used to work for priests, cleaning their houses and cooking for them. I've heard her tell stories about keeping the fires going in the big Glebe house fireplaces while the priests sat around keeping warm, drinking brandy, and discussing fine points of theology.

When she married Mickey, she thought she'd escaped all that. But now he's in Toronto delivering milk, and she survives here by scrubbing floors and pinching pennies. Some mornings when we go to school, the hardwood floors are gleaming and the room smells fresh because my aunt spent the night on her hands and knees there with a bucket and a scrubbing brush.

In my private moments, I have to admit that I'm not looking forward to this business called "making a living."

———

Everybody on the bus to Mass knows everybody else, but hardly anybody speaks. It's like being inside the church already—people studying their prayer books or their empty hands. I finished my investigation of Jean Larter's kerchief. Now that I knew about Korea, I turned my attention back to the land around me. To the right of the bus the strait was dancing and the sunlight was flashing and Mulgrave had become clearly visible, with the little white asylum standing out among the darker colours of the town. There is a man from Inverness in the asylum because he was hit on the head once by a baseball and never recovered. They say he was a great baseball player and had a brilliant future and that maybe, one day, he'd get paid for playing ball.

But instead, when he was playing the outfield in Inverness one day, he lost sight of a high fly ball because of the sun, and it changed everything. I can imagine him standing there with his hand shading his eyes, trying to see the plummeting baseball. Then everything goes black. And now he's over there, standing at a window, large and pale, staring at the water, wondering what he's doing there and when they're going to let him out.

I think of him at his window, looking towards Cape Breton, while I stand at mine at home, watching the new confusion in the strait. Two people dreaming about what they don't quite understand.

The Strait of Canso and Cape Porcupine are like the border of a strange land. Everything important seems to happen over there, across the strait and far away, beyond the hulking cape. Only the *Victoria-Inverness Bulletin* has stories from here, and they are almost all about people visiting other people. Or about the wonderful sermons by the Reverend Clark MacDonald, who is the minister for St. David's United Church in Port Hastings. They don't report what he said, just that it was wonderful—which makes it all the more mysterious. It's all part of the secret lives of Protestants.

The village is located on the side of a hill, and the strait is really all there is to look at. Behind us, beyond Archie the Piper's on the Victoria Line, is out back. You can't really see the town. My first act each morning is to look out the window of my bedroom towards the strait, and, after years doing it, I am able to guess what the weather will be like all day just by the colour of the water. A sharp blue in the winter means a bitter coldness. Northbound spittle from a grey churning reveals the stinging southeast wind, bearer of long spells of dreariness. If it is raining, I know by the mood and colour of the strait how long the rain will last. And on the best days of all, summer mornings when it is still and black, I know it will be hot all day and that the woods huddling around the village will hum with the business of nature. The spruce and pine and juniper will offer a sweet cool sanctuary, and, by early afternoon, when the rising heat stirs a light breeze, poplars and birch, beech and maple will rustle contentedly. The graveyard, up the hill, past the Piper's, will be lush with juicy raspberries. And I know that the day will end with deep orange flames consuming the horizon, promising the same again tomorrow. A gentle breeze will stir the massive silver poplars outside my bedroom window, and the whispering will start again. Wind and trees exchanging secrets in the darkness, as I drift away from here on waves of dreams.

Some days I sit on the shore and look across the water and think I will never know the world beyond except in books. And there are days when I think I'm lucky to be so removed from all the misery of the world beyond the strait. I think of Korea and Germany and Russia, Africa and China, and that maybe it isn't such a bad thing to have the cape and the strait over there, keeping the angry, hungry, tragic world I read about away from us. But then I think of the man in the asylum, going nowhere. And I think of Joe Larter in the war in Korea, and Danny MacIntosh and John MacDougall and the secrets they brought back and the mysterious knowledge in their eyes. I want to know the secrets of the world. I want to know what they have seen, even if it's bad.

And then I realize, again, the world is coming here.

Listening at the post office, everything is about before, when ships and trains and strangers were everywhere and when, the way they tell it, the world included Port Hastings. And people here felt part of the world, if only for the world's great wars.

I want to ask the older people: What was wrong with you? I want to say to Mr. Clough: You have connections, don't you? Why did you let progress stop? How could you just let everything petrify and turn into history?

But I already know the answer. Bad luck—decisions made by people far away.

He'll stand quietly for a while thinking, gazing through the rear window, behind his special chair beside the stove, studying the railway station and the strait, which are down below his store, hands deep in his pockets, eyes scrunched, remembering the giant piers and the ships from everywhere, and coal trains rolling slowly in from Inverness.

And the eye will turn to the growing scar on the face of the mountain on the other side. There is now a great, open expanse of bare rock, and people moving buglike on the side of what appears to be a cliff. Each day the trucks dumping rock into the rushing strait seem a little larger as the causeway inches closer. There are explosions closer to us now, and a constant roar as the drillers begin preparing to blast out the great trench that will sever Nicholson's Point for a canal. Survey crews are everywhere, planning new roads and railway lines.

And everybody is thinking the same thought—more decisions made by people far away, creating something called a Future.

———

A new year begins. 1954. There is nothing now but talk about the causeway.

Since September 1952 there have been many blasts. It has become part of the local atmosphere. The ground will shake, the cape will gush another mighty torrent of rock and mud and smoke. You watch in awe, half expecting that when the smoke has cleared it will all be gone, leaving a vast and unobstructed view of all the world beyond. But it's still there, hardly diminished at all.

Now you can see the huge trucks backing carefully to the end of the advancing limb and dumping the massive rocks that roll, or are pushed by bulldozers, into the swift-moving waters of the strait. You can see the water turning brown, as it snatches at the rocks.

It'll be across in no time flat, claims Mr. Clough. But my father says they're at the easy part now. Wait until they get farther out, where, he's heard, the water is hundreds of feet deep. With the currents strong as they are, the rocks they dump out near the middle will be in Point Tupper before they hit the bottom. My father speaks with the authority of one who knows all about the behaviour of rocks.

After school, sometimes, I go down to the point, and Jackie Nick and I stand by his grandmother's lighthouse and watch what's going on over on the other side. Where they dig the rock is a long way off, but I've seen the pictures in the paper of men in hard hats and rubber working clothes drilling there—men who look exactly like my father and the miners around him in the photograph.

The lighthouse has been here forever. Nicholson's Point is like a granite fist, held out threateningly, ready to punch a hole in the boat that comes too close. Just a few feet out, the water whirls and foams, and any boat caught in the turmoil will quickly disappear down one of the swirling frothy funnels.

In late summer, crowds gather here to watch herds of giant black fish passing by, a silent procession surfacing in an endless flow of arching bodies that seems, after you watch them for a while, to be a single organism. It's like one gigantic snakelike fish rippling down the thrashing strait, heading back to the ocean after a slight diversion around our island in search of food.

Near where Jackie Nick and I are standing are the graves of strangers who fell into the whirlpools just off Nicholson's Point or who got sick and died and were dropped off here for burial on the land. One of the tombstones is dated 1793—a little girl named Douce Elizabeth Balhache. A little mystery.

I try to imagine what it was like back then, when people vanished into childhood or the sea, never to be seen again. We're clearly better off today and luckier than in all those places where things don't seem to have changed much.

The place is full of stories about pirates and battle ships and immigrant strangers sailing up and down the strait looking for places to build new homes. Near Mulgrave there's a dent in the shore called Pirate's Harbour. And the pirates weren't all on the other side. One of the Fox boys, who are all older than we are, says there is buried treasure over here too, somewhere near the Ghost Beach, which is just north of Nicholson's Point.

Jackie and I talk about what we would do if we ever found the treasure.

I tell him I would use the money to go away, and he responds, "Go away where?" and I say "Everywhere." I want to see the world. Jackie retorts that there's enough of the world for him right around us—and, in any case, the world will soon be coming to us whether we like it or not.

He would use the money to buy a fast car and a new house for his grandmother and himself.

"What about the old house?" I ask.

And he tells me they're going to burn it down—the first thing they'll do when the causeway is across, he says.

"They'll put a match to it," he insists.

"They wouldn't."

"Oh yes," he says. "And before they're done they'll be burning down half the village."

Of course we all know that Jackie Nick is always making things up just to get attention. But I also know from my experience with change that every time there's something new, something old will disappear.

———

And then one Friday night he came home driving a truck. It was the truck we saw at Danny Shaw's. He had his bag of mining gear in the back.

For a celebration, I suppose, he traded with his brother on the mountain. John Dan got the truck, and we took the car again. Temporarily, of course. They announced that we were going on a trip down north, to where my mother comes from. She grew up in another village called Bay St. Lawrence, which is beyond the mountains and the National Park and the Cabot Trail, and it takes almost all day to get there. Nothing ever seems to change in Bay St. Lawrence.

Going to Bay St. Lawrence, there are long stretches of pavement where the ride goes quickly, with the car windows open and the summer breezes on your face sweet with the musk of lupines and wild roses and clover and the dark evergreens hovering beside the road.

By Creignish you know you're on a journey, when you leave the narrow strait behind, and the water beside the highway broadens out into a great flashing bay, and the mainland dissolves into hazy distant shadows until, finally, by Port Hood, it disappears entirely. In Inverness, where there is a liquor store, we stop to buy a bottle because Grandma Donohue will expect a little treat when we arrive. We already told her in a letter we were coming for a visit.

Then we stop in Chéticamp, and it is like a foreign country where everyone speaks French. There is a fish plant there, and it always smells like dinnertime on Fridays, and flocks of squawking seagulls swoop and squabble on the rooftops. The harbour is full of fishing boats of all shapes and sizes. Chéticamp has the biggest church I've ever seen, and my father tells us that his father, Dougald, painted the steeple once, long, long ago.

Just beyond Chéticamp, the pavement ends again. The northern mountains loom, and, just as we hit the first potholes on the rippled washboard road, my father always says, "Hang onto your hats . . ."

Crossing the mountains, everything slows down. The car creeps up and around the endless winding hills, my father constantly working clutch and gear shift, wrestling the wheel to avoid the larger rocks and ruts and the oncoming cars that suddenly burst out of clouds of dust. In places, your heart leaps when you look downward into nothingness just beyond the shoulder of the road, blue sea sprawling to infinity, motionless but for the gold and white spangles dancing in the distance. Cars are pulled to the side where small streams cross the road, and men with tin cans pour water into steaming radiators.

My father watches the temperature gauge nervously as every turn in the steep road reveals yet more hills to climb.

"Feel your ears pop yet?" he asks, to create a distraction.

At the top of French Mountain, we stop to let the car cool down. My mother points into the distance and describes the fire that swept through these hills a few years back, destroying vast tracts of forest, driving animals and humans from their homes. "And now look at it," she says. "Nature regenerating. New life building on the ashes of the old."

And I am looking around the little circle of ourselves, a family regenerating.

Just beyond the village of Pleasant Bay, we stop to eat our sandwiches at the Lone Sheiling. My sisters and I wander away from our parents, into the cool, green stillness of the trees, the moss damp and soft beneath our feet. We are slow and quiet in the unfamiliar place.

The tiny stone building with the straw roof is supposed to resemble the houses people lived in before they left the Old Country long ago. I stood there in the cold little hut, imagining a large family living in a single room like this one, a fire smoldering on the floor, smoke eventually escaping through a hole in the roof. Maybe eviction and exile weren't such a bad thing after all.

There is a poem on a metal plaque, and I know it off by heart.

From the lone sheiling of the misty islands,
mountains divide us and the waste of seas

yet still the blood is strong and the heart is highland
and we in dreams behold the Hebrides.

I know that, long ago, the first of our MacIntyres came from the Hebrides, but when I ask my father about it, he just smiles. To him, I believe, Scotland is just another foreign country. I wonder why. My mother says she'd kill to see the world, especially Old Ireland, where the Donohues came from. She says our people came from Cork. My father couldn't care less about faraway places. Maybe when you're away most of the time, it's hard to think of anywhere but home.

More mountains, now away from the sea, but my mother is explaining how the first European, meaning people like us, to set eyes on these hills and valleys was a man sent out by England whose name was John Cabot. I know from the history books that he was actually an Italian, but he worked for England and landed in Cape North, which is just before you get to Grandma Donohue's, and he claimed the whole territory for the English King.

Past Cape North and Sugar Loaf, the road proceeds into a narrow valley, and then, on the right, just below, there's a farm belonging to the Buchanans before the dangerous bend in the road they call Buck's Turn. My mother always mentions all the people who were killed there.

By now we are sitting up alertly, peering past the adults, waiting for the magical moment when the little valley ends. Sprawled before us, we see the flat expanse of church and hall, graveyard and houses in St. Margaret's Village and, just beyond it, Bay St. Lawrence, where Grandma Donohue lives.

My mother sighs at the sight. The ocean in the distance, the tidy fields, and the sudden mountain rising like a wall to block the wild Atlantic winds that rush across the Cabot Strait from Newfoundland. All exactly as she remembers it.

My grandmother lives alone on the lap of the mountain. She is standing in front of her house when we arrive, wiping her hands on her apron and smiling broadly. She doesn't get many visitors.

Like the houses on MacIntyre's Mountain, the old place in Bay St. Lawrence has no electricity or indoor plumbing. But it is more like the houses I'm familiar with, bright and clean, with large pictures hanging on the walls of people wearing strange clothing and uncomfortable expressions—and everybody speaking at once in English.

Like my grandfather on the mountain, Grandma Donohue spent part of her younger years working in the United States. But while Grandpa MacIntyre carried a gun and never mentions his time in the States, she talks about it all the time—about working in Boston for a fancy woman named Mrs. Wing, who paid her two dollars a week to look after the household. Then going to work for a seamstress and getting a raise of fifty cents a week, which was a lot of money back then, especially if you were a girl from the northern tip of Cape Breton Island with nothing to offer Boston but your wit and stamina.

In return, Boston gave my grandmother enough sophistication to last the rest of her life—even though she married poor Jack Donohue, a simple fisherman who worked like a slave until he died of cancer, and she spent her life living in a house with none of the conveniences of Boston.

Shortly after we arrive, my Uncle Francis and his new wife, Annie Mae, stroll up from the little house he built on Grandma Donohue's property, closer to the road. Francis was in the navy during the war, but now he works in a gypsum quarry in Dingwall, which is fifteen miles from Bay St. Lawrence. He is the youngest in the family, and boyish in the way he carries on. Uncle Joe will eventually come by, with his booming voice and Irish accent, which makes my father smile. And the bottle from Inverness will appear, and everything will get even louder.

Joe drives an oil truck for the Irvings. The men all talk about their work.

They talk about the causeway and the difference it will make, and how Uncle Francis is thinking of moving up to the strait for work because there's talk of closing down the quarry in Dingwall. I decide to climb the mountain that rises directly behind my grandmother's house and is even higher than Cape Porcupine.

It is a steep climb, through low bushes and coarse grass and thistles. It has, for several visits, become a ritual for me—climbing Grandma's mountain, a few steps farther every time. Each visit I get a little closer to the top, but I feel a strange anxiety as I rise above the village where my mother was born and spent her childhood—getting too far away from what I know, too close to the unknown. But I push on, knowing that when I reach the top I'll finally be able to see off over the Atlantic to Newfoundland, where I was born, and beyond it, to Scotland and Ireland, where all my people came from.

Below me sprawls the land in alternating patches, all in shades of green, cloud shadows moving slowly, changing green to darker shades of green, and gold to brown, mauve to black. Small boats bob in a sheltered pond. I stop and imagine the lives of my mother and her brothers and sisters, watching each other grow. People aging are the only changing feature in a vast unyielding landscape. And I remember my own village where nothing today is as it was yesterday—where it's getting hard to notice people for all the noise and mud.

From the mountainside I can see the cemetery where they buried my grandfather, Jack Donohue, who was, they always say, a saint for putting up with the cancer and the many emphatic certainties Grandma Donohue brought back from Boston—certainties about the superiority of America, the Conservative Party of Canada, and the Holy Catholic Church.

I think of this ghost-grandfather I never knew as I study the small boats below me nodding on the little pond. He was a fisherman, and I try to imagine Jack and his boys, Joe and Francis, venturing cautiously beyond the narrow entry to the pond and out into the writhing sea, looking for their livelihood. And I wonder about this vast concept— livelihood—and how men and women dedicate their lives to it. Lives spent struggling to live, while simultaneously struggling to believe there's a Better Life awaiting after this one.

Across the road from the cemetery where my grandfather has been buried for longer than I have been alive, the Catholic Church looms over the surrounding farms, like a benign sentry watching over a vulnerable community.

Once when my mother and Veronica and their older sister, Catherine, were girls, Grandma Donohue got sick and went to bed and didn't recover for, I think, two years. Nobody talks about what was wrong with her; just how it affected everybody.

The older girls, Veronica and Catherine, had to give up school to run the house. And after two years, it was too late for going back. They were women then. There was no more time for childhood or books. Learning now would come from Experience, which, in many ways, they now insist, is the only reliable source of education.

They had to go to work, but the only work available for two uneducated women from down north was looking after priests. And so, after a couple of years as Grandma's housekeepers, they both became priests' housekeepers—an honourable job, their mother thought. Looking after quality people in a quality place was the highlight of her life. And there was no quality like a priest, or better places than the church.

My mother got to stay in school because she was the youngest of the girls—too young for looking after priests.

School has become a bit more interesting. I have moved on to the Big Room—grade six. No more endless days sitting in a desk that was too small, listening to Miss Norma Morrison trying to teach the younger children how to spell.

When I learned to spell, everything was different. It was my first year of school. There was only one room then, from primary to grade ten, and one teacher for us all. There was a stove in the middle of the room and, all around it, piles of rubber boots and overshoes that became so hot they'd almost catch on fire as the day progressed. The room was full of the smells of feet and hair and burning rubber mixed with chalk and Dustbane, which is something they use to sweep the floors and makes you want to sneeze. Sometimes, for mischief, an older boy would throw a wad of gum onto the stovetop, where it would bubble and burn and fill the room with smoke that smelled like poison, while the teacher tried to persuade the culprit to confess.

"You'll be a better person for it," she'd assure, slowing tapping a yardstick against the palm of her hand as she prowled around the classroom.

The only sound in the room would be the crackling of the fire and the sizzle of the burning gum.

What is now the Big Room was the only room when I started school. There was obviously a second classroom, from the time when the village had more people, but it had been boarded up for years. Then, anticipating all the activity with the causeway, the authorities cleaned up the abandoned room for the junior grades and now it's called the Little Room. They eventually installed a furnace and indoor toilets. They tore out the wall and cloakrooms that separated the two rooms and replaced them with a new wall that was built in sections. The new wall can be taken down, so the two rooms become one large hall for concerts, dances, and other public events. The removable wall sections are then placed on blocks to become an elevated stage for speeches or performances.

The first year I went to school, Miss Euphemia MacKinnon taught us how to spell the old-fashioned way—memorizing. She spoke in a loud, careful, nasal tone that was patient, but dangerous at the same time. Enunciating the letters in the words as she walked back and forth, she held the yardstick in her hand and hid a homemade strap of braided wire in her drawer for backup. She was large for a woman, and very pale, and she seemed to have a long, thick pigtail coiled up and pinned to the back of her head. She wore long dresses and low boots, which made a slow marching sound on the wooden floor. From time to time she'd test us in a spelling bee.

I learned quickly how to read and how to spell just about everything, which was why I managed to get to grade three without grade two. I even learned to spell Euphemia, and that may have helped. Later, after they opened up the Little Room and I moved there, I'd listen in despair as Miss Norma Morrison struggled to teach my sister and the others how to spell simple words by drawing boxes around them.

You have to *visualize* the words, she'd tell them. Just as the word has a sound, it also has a shape. My younger sister, Rosalind, who is just learning how to spell, will be lucky if she even learns to spell her own name.

My last year in the Little Room was pure misery, starting with an incident just before Halloween. Mr. Sinclair, who lives alone in a filthy house next door to Angus Walker's, barged into the schoolroom that year, accusing us of setting off firecrackers on his doorstep at noon hour. Nobody knows who Mr. Sinclair is or where he came from. He is almost a hermit, though you see him shuffling along the road towards Mr. Clough's about once a week. People avoid him because he's cranky and never washes. They say the explosions across the strait are making Mr. Sinclair worse.

That noon hour he said there were explosions on his doorstep that almost caused a fire. He headed straight for the school. He just walked in huffing and puffing and making accusations. Then he spotted me.

"That devil there," he shouted. "He's the ring leader!"

Devil? Ringleader? The words stunned me. And though I wasn't anywhere near his miserable little house, nobody listened to me.

"You'll remain after school," Miss Morrison said coldly.

Part way through the afternoon I had to go to the toilet, which was still outside behind the school. When I raised my hand, Donald Cameron, who sits near the window and whose father, Finlay, is the railway station agent, signalled me a warning.

"Don't go out," he whispered. "Sinclair called the Mounties, and they're waiting to grab you when you go outside."

Eventually I pissed my pants, and when Miss Morrison asked me why I had my head down on the desk, I told her I was sick. She told me to go home. There can be no punishment worse than to piss your pants when you are ten.

When I went outside, there were no Mounties. I could see Donald Cameron waving and grinning at me from the pencil sharpener, which is screwed onto the window ledge.

That night Miss Morrison came to the house, and I listened at The Hole as they discussed the Sinclair Situation. My mother said I couldn't have been at Sinclair's because I was home at noon hour having dinner.

Miss Morrison often comes to visit, because my mother is a school-teacher too. After they were finished talking about me, they talked about my sister's problems with learning how to spell. My mother said she never in her entire life heard of such a foolish way to learn to spell as *visualizing*, drawing boxes around words.

Miss Morrison agreed, but said that's how they're supposed to do things these days. And they continued about how school is changing and everything is getting worse.

All that is ancient history now. I am in the Big Room, and it is almost Christmas. It is when we forget school and the weather for a while. There is always a concert, and some of us have parts. We take down the wall and turn the school into a hall, and the wall becomes a stage. The COD parcel somehow comes home and vanishes into one of the cold, closed rooms in the back end of the house, where nobody ever goes in wintertime. Grandma Donohue, who comes to live with us when the winter drives her out of Bay St. Lawrence, is remarking on what a change it is to have Dan Rory home.

They sit around the kitchen table playing cards and having drinks. Christmas is one time of year when there are lots of drinks for everybody, and nobody seems to mind. When my father came home at other times and had his drinks, you knew my mother wasn't pleased about it. But at Christmas even Grandma Donohue has a little glass near her elbow and remarks that the drinks are flying straight to her head. She laughs as if it's the best feeling in the world.

Grandma Donohue can be strict, but she taught me how to play all the games of cards she knows. And when we're playing, I can even get away with teasing her. Once when I was losing badly, I noticed that the kitchen had filled with a foul odour. The dog was sleeping by the stove. I saw him smile and realized he was farting silently. So I blamed Grandma, just to distract her from her game.

"You farted," I accused.

"I WHAT?" she said, blue eyes blazing.

"You farted," I said, studying my cards. "There's just the two of us and it wasn't me."

I never let on about the dog.

She put her cards down and swore that never in her life had she ever, ever broken wind.

"It's one thing I never does," she said.

That's the way she talks. She puts an *s* on the ends of words.

And I thought: it's probably the truth . . . a discipline she picked up among the quality in Boston.

But it was a weapon I knew I would use whenever she was winning at cards. It was a sure way to destroy her confidence. From what I knew of her, it was probably the *only* way to rattle her.

My Aunt Veronica, whom we all call Ronnie for short, is also at the table for the Christmas card party. All the players are shrieking, hitting the table with their fists every time they play a good one.

During the dealing or between games they'll talk about the causeway and about the changes it will make—big changes coming in the long run. My father will go quiet then.

We'll see about that, he'll say, what happens after the construction.

My Aunt Veronica knows a lot of politicians because she's a Tory and works for them during elections. She believes that everyone will be better off after there's a change of government. People like my father will never have to go away for work again. People like her will no longer have to scrub floors just to make a living.

People say she should be a politician herself, but she just laughs. With a little education, everybody says, she could be anything she wants. Education has nothing to do with it, she says.

Some of the worst people she has known were the most educated. And the best were the plainest.

She writes political letters to the editor at the Halifax newspaper, which publishes them regularly. It is amazing to see them, always giving politicians hell in a comical way and signed Mrs. Veronica MacNeil, Port Hastings. There's a Liberal named Francis Campbell who lives in Inverness, and he always answers her. Reading the letters you'd think they were enemies, but they've come to know each other, and she says she respects him because he's reasonable and fair, and he's in a wheelchair and worse off than she is. Being a Liberal, like being crippled, is a misfortune that he can't do much about, she says.

My aunt is always telling my father to go see some Tory who she thinks can help him get a permanent job at the causeway or somewhere else near home.

My father just smiles.

The Tories!

The Tories haven't been in power for years, in Halifax or Ottawa, and there's no sign that is going to change any time soon.

"This is where you're wrong," she tells him. Mr. Stanfield has just taken over the party and he's the one man who can beat Angus L. It will happen inevitably, and no doubt about it. The Tories are on the march. Last May they took six seats away from the Liberals in the provincial election. Next time, for sure, they'll form the government. A Tory government in Ottawa is also inevitable.

But my father figures that nobody alive will ever beat Angus L. Macdonald, and even if they did, the Tories wouldn't be any better. They're all the same. Promise everything to everyone, then do exactly what they want.

"Well, we'll just see about that," my aunt informs him.

I think of my father's words—eat or be eaten—but say nothing because I'm not supposed to be there.

My aunt points out that the work is already under way at the canal and the locks on this side of the strait, and that they're going to have to rearrange the railway tracks and build a lot of new roads.

And, of course, after that, there will be the Trans-Canada Highway, which has to go to Newfoundland under the terms of Confederation. To get there, it will have to pass through here. After that, there'll be factories and work for everybody because the causeway will turn the

Strait of Canso into one of the biggest, deepest ice-free harbours in the world.

"Lots of opportunities for work, if you know the right people."

Time to get involved. And did we know that they've already burned down Mrs. Nicholson's house down by the point? Just put a match to it, and the old place went up like kindling. And now Kate and poor Jackie are moving into the old place near Clough's, where the Bellefontaines used to live. A sure sign the project is moving into the final phase.

"Well, well."

They sure were pretty quiet about burning Nicholson's.

My father says no more on the subject.

———

The church bell was ringing lazily as the bus slowed to make the sharp turn onto the church hill. The turn is so sharp, my father says, you almost meet yourself coming back. The bus driver is Heck MacNeil, and he struggles with the gear shift as the old bus groans and whines and creeps up to the church. St. Joseph's looms proudly over the flashing strait. From the front steps you can clearly see across to Mulgrave and imagine people over there going into their church, St. Lawrence's. I know about the church in Mulgrave because my Aunt Veronica was the priest's housekeeper over there once upon a time and she told us about a mainland priest they all called Alex the Devil.

And she and my mother talked about the time Jack Donohue, her father, found a keg of rum on the shore and sold it, but he had to give the money to the church down north because the priest there said it was a sin for him to profit from his neighbour's weakness.

Priests are funny people, she says. And she should know, having worked for them. But she never misses Mass. The church, she says, is larger and more important than any of the little people running it.

Outside, the wind from the strait and, to the southeast, Chedabucto Bay, and beyond, from the Atlantic Ocean, was chilly. Jean Larter clutched the kerchief map to her throat and hurried inside.

St. Joseph's is vast and cluttered and full of the holy odours of varnish, candle wax, and incense. Wherever the eye settles there is something ornamental, in a sacred way, to study. Two large angels crouch prayerfully on either side of the towering altar, marble faces buried in their hands. Little Father Doyle is dwarfed by the altar, the looming angels, and the statues of Jesus and His mother as he quietly performs his rituals. He bends and kisses the altar and genuflects and raises his face and hands towards the ceiling, walking around the altar mumbling the Latin Liturgy, which I know from following in the prayer book. My favourite part is the Gospel according to St. John, where he says "et verbum caro factum est, et habitavit in nobis." You kneel briefly in the middle of it, and then there's the last blessing and you know the Mass is over. But it isn't just that. It isn't just the prospect of release from the confining ritual. There's something deep and mysterious in that gospel: "And the Word was made flesh and dwelt among us." I believe that words are miraculous, the way they make it possible for us to know things.

Father Doyle is a friendly man, always asking questions. When we were talking once, I noticed he wasn't much taller than I was. He wants to know what I will do when I grow up. I suspect he wants to hear me say that I'll grow up to be like him—a priest.

I measure my growth against the height of the pew, remembering with satisfaction that once I had to stand on the kneeler to see the sanctuary. I watch the men around me standing loosely, fingertips gently touching the wood on the top of the pews in front of them, some so tall they have to lean a bit. I stretch to my full height and note that I can now comfortably rest my elbows there.

Soon I will have to decide what to do when I'm a man, leaning with my knuckles on the back of the pew.

Because most of the people in Port Hastings are Protestants and we don't have religion in the school, most Sunday afternoons Father Doyle drives a couple of nuns from town to Art MacNamara's house, where they teach us catechism. The nuns teach us why God made us and how we are supposed to get to know Him and love Him and serve Him. They teach us about sin and the soul, which, in the catechism book, is like a milk bottle that turns black as we commit more sins.

If you die in a state of mortal sin you go to hell. But I get the impression that you'd have to be an idiot to let that happen, because God is merciful and anxious to forgive even mortal sins for anybody who genuinely asks. It would be like starving to death when you have an open invitation to eat in a restaurant free of charge. The catch, I guess, is that you have to be a Catholic to get into the restaurant.

At Mass, Father Doyle announces catechism classes and that there will be a mission soon. The mission is a special week of prayer and ser- mons, and we will attend as much of it as we can. Father Doyle says the mission will be led by a priest from the Oblates, a religious order that sends missionaries all over the world. The priest coming here has been almost everywhere, including the Holy Land. I know it is in the Holy Land that the next big war might start, according to the newspapers and Grandma Donohue.

And I know that we will get to the mission because my father is home and has a truck.

Art Mac's house, where we have catechism, is next door to the Manse, which now belongs to the retired minister Dr. Christie, who lives there with his wife and his sister Annie, who was never married.

Sometimes on Friday nights during the winter Dr. Christie will invite the younger boys from the village to go to the Manse for enter- tainment. I thought at first it was another, trickier kind of Protestant catechism, but because there isn't much to do here on a Friday night in winter, I went anyway. But there was no catechism, just games of checkers and tossing beanbags and talking.

Then there were sandwiches and sweets and tea. Mrs. Christie read to us from a large book by a French writer named Victor Hugo. One part told the story of Jean Valjean and the bishop, and you could tell he was a Catholic bishop because it all happened in France. And that didn't seem to bother anybody.

Then one Friday night Dr. Christie introduced his sister Annie. She was a large and homely woman, and I assumed he was only being polite introducing her. Then he told us that she used to be a missionary teacher in China, and I saw her as a different person entirely. She has really been to China?

She smiled, and her face came alive, and she talked about her experiences there and how she came to love the Chinese people. She clearly meant it, sitting there speaking softly, eyes shining and old hands folded in her lap. I was shocked. This simple old lady, living on the hill next door to the MacNamaras, had been to China. She talked about teaching in a place called Honan. She showed fancy needlework and small paintings that she brought home from there, and delicate wood carvings. She had loved it there, and loved the Chinese.

So why did she leave? someone asked.

She paused for a moment and sighed. "Things change," she said. "The world is changing. China has changed."

I figured if somebody from here can love the Chinese people, then clearly we can love anybody. Nothing on the planet can be stranger and more mysterious than China and the Chinese, with their stern faces and strange clothing. But Dr. Christie's sister told us about the ancient traditions of China and how the Chinese were civilized long before we were, and how young people in China respect their elders and never misbehave. How they were all polite and kind when she was there.

I wanted to ask her about the war in Korea and the stories in the comic books where the Koreans and the Chinese who were on their side were "gooks," treacherous and merciless in killing Americans (and Canadians). Could these be the same civilized people she was talking about?

But listening to her, it was as though there was no war at all, and I didn't have the heart to remind her. It occurred to me eventually that she didn't think the war or the Communists mattered in the larger scheme of things, and that the war was almost over anyway. And, before long, we'll hardly remember that we were ever at war with the wonderful Chinese people or that, if they'd had their way, they'd have killed Joe Larter, who lives next door to Johnny and Mary O'Handley, just over the road from where we were sitting.

She sighed again and, after a pause, thanked us for listening to her stories, excused herself, and left the room.

I remember going home afterward, and Jackie Nicholson talking about how boring it was and how the evening would have been better spent coasting on our sleds down the steep hill in Alex MacKinnon's field.

But that is one of Jackie's problems. You ask Jackie about where he'd like to go some day, and he asks back why would you want to go anywhere?

Jackie's notion of being an adult is more of the same, except with your own money and a fast car. Then you ask him about where he's going to get the money for the car, and he says there's lots of time to worry about that.

"The Man who made time made lots of it," Jackie always says—which is as close as he'll ever come to a religious comment.

I think it really started with the stories from Dr. Christie's sister, and the revelations about the Chinese and how clever and civilized they really were before the Communists took over. And then Father Doyle was talking about the mission and how the Oblates go everywhere, and the one who would come to preach to us had been working in the Holy Land, trying to turn Jews and Arabs into Catholics.

And I remembered that I have cousins who are priests—two brothers, Father Murdoch and Father Jimmy, who are the sons of Grandma Donohue's sister Alice MacLean. Father Jimmy joined the navy after he became a priest and got to the war in Korea, which, the way I see it, is also a kind of missionary work. When we visited Aunt Alice, when we were down north last summer, her house was full of postcards and souvenirs and photographs. Father Jimmy had even been to Ireland.

Aunt Alice had a newspaper clipping, and Father Jimmy was mentioned, helping the doctors on his ship with casualties from the fighting in Korea. You could almost see him, in a movie inside your head, wearing his Roman collar and a navy uniform, his sleeves rolled up, and blood all over his hands and arms from working on the wounded.

Until then I hadn't really thought much about my future. Once I read a book about a newspaper reporter who solved a series of murders in a travelling circus, and that seemed interesting. But I could never imagine how anyone from here would ever get a job on a newspaper—unless it was working for the *Bulletin*, though I find the *Bulletin* boring.

Then I read *Two Years before the Mast*. It was a great adventure, full of hardship and excitement. Even though I realize there are no more sailing ships, there was, for a while, no doubt in my mind about what I would do when I was old enough. I would run away to sea.

Once my father asked me, half joking, "What are you going to do with yourself when we stop feeding you?"

I didn't want to mention running away, for fear his feelings would be hurt. Like Father Doyle, he seemed to have an answer in his mind already. I think most men would like their sons to want to be like them.

So, half joking, I replied: "I'm going to follow in my father's footsteps." That is an expression I had read in books.

He didn't laugh, and I knew from the look on his face that he thought I was serious. But I couldn't tell whether he liked the idea.

"We'll see," he said.

It's always difficult to know what he really thinks, and for quite some time after that it almost seemed like a half-decent idea—working as a miner. By then there was a lot of drilling and blasting going on all around the village. I'd stand and watch the men in their hard hats and rubber clothing, covered with white dust, and listen to the roaring of compressors and the jangling clash of steel boring relentlessly through rock. The sound, I realized, of change; the sound of making something happen—consummated, in the end, by the crash of an explosion and the invincible rock shattered, making way for something new. You can go anywhere to work as a miner. I even know of men from here who work in the Congo, which is in Africa. Miners are probably in China too, if the Communists allow it.

But I wasn't sure. I remembered the cold, foul wind billowing up out of the shaft in Stirling, and men laughing and joking one day and then, too soon after, sitting alone in a cookhouse in the middle of nowhere, old hands wrapped around mugs of coffee, sad eyes examining the smoke from cigarettes. Or dead, some small stranger inheriting their skates.

————

Each evening for a week we attended the mission. The visiting Father was young, and he didn't look like a priest or sound like one. He didn't speak like Father Doyle or the nuns or even Miss Annie Christie. He smiled and laughed a lot and told of his experiences in foreign places. I kept waiting for him to tell us how he spread the Gospel messages and the Word of Jesus among the unbelievers, but he never did. I kept waiting for Sin and Penance and the Sermon on the Mount. But when he talked, it was about the world and how all the people in it are unique as individuals and fascinating in their cultural differences. Miraculously, all are one and part of the same mysterious design—the precious creatures of an all-powerful and infinitely good God.

Listening to him was breathtaking, and, as I lay in bed afterwards, his words came back in complete sentences and paragraphs, bringing exotic images with them. One image that stood above them all was of people who owned nothing—not a thing but the rags on their bodies. People who lived in the direst material poverty, but who wanted to know the Truth about the world and about Eternity because they knew that somehow, somewhere in the Truth, they'd find Hope and Happiness. The Word was the truth and it was made of flesh, like me. And everything started to seem logical.

One evening he explained how there's a kind of war on—a war for the hearts and souls of people, a war between the Truth and the False Promise of material progress. Godless Communism was only the most conspicuous of the problems challenging our immortal souls. The world was rotten with problems, largely caused by Greed and Violence. I think it was then that I knew: to be a missionary was to be everything—a teller of the truth; a warrior against the Communists; but, best of all, a traveller in a world of endless mysteries and fascinating conflicts. I remembered Miss Christie's sadness and the mission Father's anger, but only for a moment.

I couldn't wait to tell my mother. She didn't say anything at first—just looked at me with a serious expression on her face.

"That would be wonderful," she said. But her eyes were full of questions.

My father was listening, studying the floor, saying nothing as usual. I tell nobody else, except my dog. We're sitting on a stone near the edge of the cemetery, where it overlooks the strait. The racket of the construction is now inescapable. The gigantic Euclids are clearly visible, rumbling across the face of the jagged cape in patient convoys, dumping massive chunks of granite into the rushing water. According to the *Bulletin*, the causeway is now two-thirds across. The world is that much closer.

I tell the dog: "I think I'm going to be a missionary."

In case he doesn't understand, I point across the water. Over there, I tell him, beyond the cape, there is a troubled, complicated world, and people are waiting for the Word. He seems to understand, and we both watch another Euclid backing carefully to the tip of the approaching causeway.

Then he places his chin on my knee, a sad expression on his face— thinking about a future that doesn't have him in it.

4

HOME FOR GOOD—AGAIN

Some of them have been standing here since four this afternoon, huddling against the dampness and the December chill. They are mostly adults and don't move around much. Jackie Nick and Billy Malone and I, because we are kids, create our warmth in frantic spurts of action. Billy digs Jackie in the ribs or grabs my cap, and a chase ensues, or the dog and I will race back and forth until we are all warm and breathless from the running and laughing. The grown-ups regard our foolishness with a mixture of contempt and envy.

The causeway started under a shroud of fog and a cold drizzle in September two years ago. It now seems destined to finish in the same kind of weather, except perhaps a little colder. The drizzle is more like sleet. It is December 10, 1954. At least fifty people have gathered for the historic moment, the undoing of the strait that nature carved in the landscape incalculable centuries ago.

Among the curious, I suspect, is a newspaper reporter from Sydney. Every few feet of the causeway progress, it seems, has been noted in the papers by story or picture or both. Now it's the moment they've really been building up to. There must be reporters around. I can't imagine what it would be like to be a reporter at a time like this, the eyes and ears of all the people who can't be here—almost everybody on the planet—even for people from just a few miles away who are sick or busy or uninterested or hostile to the idea that Cape Breton will cease to be an island in the pure sense of the word.

Oh sure, there will be the canal, but Jackie Nick points out that there will be a bridge over the canal. Billy, who isn't even from here, argues that there will still be a crack of space at either end of the bridge because it will be a swinging bridge, so we will still, technically, be on an island. And that reminds me that I read in the paper that the big shots at something called the Canadian Board on Geographical Names have decided that Cape Breton will still be an island after the causeway, no matter what anybody says. Jackie scoffs, the way he does at any argument he's losing.

Even though there's a want on him, Jackie tries to sound like a grown-up. You would never mention Santa Claus anywhere near Jackie. He even argued, to the point where you felt like slugging him, that there's no such person as Roy Rogers—until he saw him for himself on his new television set. He and his grandmother got the TV after they were moved off the point and their old house went up in smoke.

There's a man in an overcoat and hat, and he's carrying a large camera and a canvas bag slung over his shoulder. He looks like the pictures of newspapermen I have seen in magazines. He has curly black hair and resembles the Syrian my mother sent away from our door one night. I try to pick out the reporter. I think I know which one he is, if only because there is one large, soft-faced, bareheaded man who shivers a lot and has frequent chats with the photographer. Now and then they wander off towards the canal, where the cars are parked, and return obviously more cheerful.

We can no longer see the trucks as clearly as before, but we can hear them distinctly as they back to the edge of the causeway, now no more than thirty feet away, and unload the crashing, tumbling rock into the racing strait. The water has been moving swiftly for days now, as if in a race to escape the confines of the Gulf of St. Lawrence in a final dash towards the freedom of the infinite Atlantic before this ancient waterway is closed forever.

We've been waiting for this day for months. In late August, Mr. Harry MacKenzie, one of the big shots on the causeway project, was in the newspaper saying that the most difficult part was finished.

"The last couple of hundred feet will be a piece of cake," he said.

As if in response, almost instantly the tides ripping through became more difficult. They snatched a passing freighter and hurled her against a rock, causing significant damage. That story led to another newspaper headline announcing what we all knew already: Tide Through Narrowing Causeway Gap Now Hazardous.

But, clearly, not everybody reads the *Victoria-Inverness Bulletin*. Just ten days ago, a Norwegian freighter on its way to Prince Edward Island for a load of potatoes ran smack into the causeway, even though the strait has been officially closed to shipping for nearly a month.

This morning a little motorboat fought its way through, after three tries, to become the last vessel in history to pass through the strait the natural way. I don't think the people on board were going anywhere in particular; they were just trying to make a name for themselves by being the last to do something—the way people try to become famous by being the first, say, to climb Mount Everest. I'm not sure I understand this hunger to be noticed, even though it seems to be fairly common. I get nervous when I'm noticed because of all the people waiting to pounce on my mistakes and failures.

I'm sure the little boat will be in all the papers tomorrow, struggling through the churning, frothy gap between here and there.

All year, just from watching, I could tell that the strait was becoming moodier, more dangerous. And, as if to assert its awesome power, the shore this spring was littered with thousands and thousands of dead billfish. You knew there was something unusual by the flocks of screeching gulls, wrangling as though there weren't enough dead fish to go around. And all you could see, from the tip of the point to the old pier, was the silvery harvest cast up on the rocks and gravel for no apparent reason.

Now we watch in silence as the last of the monster boulders from the cape are being hauled across in a relentless procession of grim-faced Euclids, to assert the superiority of engineers and drillers and their dynamite over Mother Nature.

Someone points into the gloom and there, writhing and leaping, we can see a school of pollock struggling through the gap. Probably the last living creatures to do so, stealing some of the glory from the little boat that made it through this morning.

I study the crowd to see if the reporter noticed, but he is engaged in a laughing conversation with his photographer.

Earlier there was a rumour that one of the well-dressed men in the tightly packed shivering group of important-looking people is the lieutenant governor of Nova Scotia, the Honourable Alistair Fraser. It's hard to tell because important men all seem to look the same. They wear similar serious hats and coats and faces. They have a way of standing, feet planted solidly, because they know exactly why they're there instead of somewhere else. Their importance travels with them and invests their destinations with a certain majesty.

Mr. Fraser, I have heard, owns Cape Porcupine, where all the rock for the causeway came from—at least ten million tons of it, they say. And now, the last few tons are tumbling into the narrowing gap between here and everywhere else.

I can imagine Mr. Fraser standing there, somewhere in the crowd, adding up the money in his head as the rocks from his ancient mountain tumble into the desperate strait.

Darkness gathers closer. I know it's suppertime. Faint kitchen smells waft towards us from the *Shediac* and the *Shawanaga*, which are moored nearby. The *Shediac* is a dredge, digging the approaches for the new canal. The *Shawanaga* is a tugboat that moves the dredge around.

I know I'm risking trouble standing here, missing supper, but this is a rare historic moment in a place where, until recently, there was nothing but decline and stories of before. It is Friday, and there is no school tomorrow. The only thing tomorrow morning is the usual trip to the camp with Billy for the bottles Old John will have stored away for us. And I find I'm less likely to get in trouble for things like being late for supper since my father moved back home.

––––––––

One of my jobs, before he came back to stay, was to lock the kitchen door before I went to bed and to unlock it in the morning.

Most people around here never lock their doors, but most people around here have men living in the houses more or less all the time. We began locking the door when we started seeing so many strangers showing up around the village in the spring of 1953, when the causeway construction started on this side—just before my father came home and I turned ten.

First I thought it was because of the Syrian. But my mother said, "God, no. There's no harm in the poor Syrian."

"Why couldn't we let him sleep in the house, then?"

"Because you can't take chances when you're alone," she said. "You just don't let strange men sleep in the house when the father is away."

Maybe it had something to do with peddlers. The way people say the word "peddler" makes you think there's something crooked about them—something vaguely dangerous.

My mother was trying to reassure me: there's nothing wrong with peddlers. She told me about growing up in Bay St. Lawrence, when the Jewish peddlers would travel the countryside. People were almost always glad to see them because, back then, country people needed most of the stuff that the peddlers brought. The peddlers brought pills and cloth and pots and pans and tons of gossip. Most of them were fun, my mother said. They'd bring news and stories from the towns and other villages and sit in the kitchen talking the night away. One of them, named Jack Yazer, was young and good-looking, and he'd be full of news from the city and around. And when the news was done he'd recite long poems, changing the verses to make serious poetry sound comical.

She'd recite what she could remember of one of Jack's favourites, "The Charge of the Light Brigade." It was about a massacre, but Jack would make such changes as "Cannons to right of them, cannons to left of them . . . hundreds of thousands of dollars worth of cannons . . ." And everybody would fall over laughing.

They always loved to see Jack Yazer in the lane.

I'd say: "Maybe the Syrian would be like him, full of news and entertainment."

She'd say: "We can't take that chance. The country was different back then. And the men, if they were alive, would be home most of the time. The houses were full of men. The fathers and often a grandfather or uncle. And always, it seems, lots of large strong brothers."

I don't have a brother, either.

The worst part before my father came home were the times when I'd hear the women in the kitchen some nights talking quietly, so I wouldn't know exactly what they were going on about. My mother and my Aunt Veronica and Grandma Donohue at the kitchen table, talking softly about somebody's problems. Or sometimes when I'd come upon one or two of them in the pantry and somebody would be crying.

Part of being the only man in the house, I have learned, is to try to anticipate and avoid what will make the women sad or nervous or angry and prevent those quiet, private conversations in the pantry or, late at night, around the kitchen table.

————

One morning when I unlocked the door, Martin Angus was sleeping on the floor of the porch. He was curled up on an old coat that used to belong to my father but had been turned into a bed for the dog. It was a red and black plaid pattern, but the colour was, by that time, almost invisible under the dog hair.

Martin Angus MacLellan is our cousin on the MacIntyre side, but we don't often talk about it because everybody in the county makes fun of him.

Martin Angus lives in Inverness, but mostly he wanders around the countryside like the peddlers, living off hospitality. Nobody knows quite how to describe Martin Angus. He's tall and thin and very pale. You can tell by his eyes that there's a serious want on him. At the same time, the way he listens to people and the way he understands even what they aren't saying makes people a little bit nervous when he's around. Sometimes I think that Martin Angus can read your mind.

There are a lot of people like him in the asylum in Mulgrave, but they haven't put him there yet because he has an unusual brain and uses it to entertain people. And that's how he takes care of himself.

Here's how he does it: He'll go to a political meeting, say, and listen to the speeches. Then he'll go to visit somebody who will let him in, and he'll repeat the speeches, word for word, for the people who weren't there. Once he came to our place straight from the graduation at St. Francis Xavier University in Antigonish, and he told us about all the priests and monsignors and what the bishop had to say. Then he started reciting the speech that some important person made, and he didn't even stop when my mother left the room to fill the kettle in the pantry. The speech went on and on even when the kettle boiled. He shut up only when she put some tea and sandwiches in front of him.

Some people say, probably because he's related to us, that Martin Angus is witty and has a photographic memory. But when he shows up at our place my mother says, "Oh *Dhia*, look what's coming."

But you don't want to provoke Martin Angus because of the sharpness of his tongue.

Once, when he was watching a step dancer he didn't like much, somebody said, "That fellow has music in his blood." And Martin Angus replied that the step dancer obviously had bad circulation because the music wasn't getting to his feet.

So, this particular morning, there's Martin Angus sleeping on the dog's bed. The dog is curled up in the corner, shivering. And when I opened the door, the dog jumped up and looked at me as if to say: What are you going to do about this? Or, Maybe it's time to put a lock on the outside door as well.

Martin Angus woke up too and asked what he always asks: "Is Dan Rory home?"

"No," I said.

"And when might you be expecting him?" he asked, sitting there on my father's old coat, scratching under his arms and looking cold.

"I don't know," I said.

"And is he still working over in Stirling?"

"Yes."

"That's good," he said. "Working for Mindemar Metals. That's good work—a good place for him."

The way he says things, it's as though he thinks you're lying.

I said nothing, but as Martin was going out the door, he said, "You can tell Dan Rory I was here."

"Yes," I said.

And as he closed the door, he said, "I'll be back."

When I told my mother, she just rolled her eyes.

Martin Angus always says that: "I'll be back."

When I was little, and my father was around for a while one summer, there were also the fiddle players. They'd appear out of nowhere and just move in for days, eating and drinking and playing the fiddles in the evenings. Their whole lives seemed to be like that, going from house to house. In the winter they'd move in for months with someone who had a kid who wanted to become a fiddler himself. There's also a piper named Sandy Boyd who lives like that: wandering around playing and teaching music, getting paid in hospitality.

My father learned to play the fiddle, but stopped after he got married.

"The fiddle is a lovely thing," my mother says. "But it's bad for attracting boozers."

———

Billy Malone is new, though he moved to the village more than a year ago. He comes from the far end of the province, a place called Lower Woods Harbour, which he says is even smaller than Port Hastings. Mr. Malone is a crane operator, and when he came to work here he brought the whole family: Mrs. Malone, whose name is Zella; Billy and his sister, Phyllis.

Billy's real name is Willis, which is also his father's name, and there was snickering in school when he and his sister were introduced. I guess that was when I decided he would be my friend. People giggling at names—Willis and Phyllis, as if that's funny.

He is younger than I am and younger than Jackie Nick, who also became his friend because they live close together. Jackie moved into the old Bellefontaine place, across the road from Mr. Clough's store, after they burned down his old house on Nicholson's Point to begin working on the new canal. Billy's family came here in the fall of '53 and moved into the Captain MacInnis place, where Brian Langley used to live, next door to Mr. Clough's. Brian moved to town when his father got a better job.

Little Ian MacKinnon was saying there wasn't much point in getting to know Billy because he wasn't going to be around for long. Then the Malones built a new place, a bungalow on the other side of the road from the Captain's, practically next door to Jackie's new old home, and moved in there. To me that means they're here for good, anticipating lots of work for crane operators even after the causeway and canal are finished. It's hard for me to imagine that a father who goes places for work would take the whole family and build a new house if he wasn't going to stay.

And that is a good thing, because Billy Malone has become my best friend, and his sister is one of my sister's best friends.

This is what I expect from the new causeway: new friends who bring their different personalities and experiences from other places.

To pass the time while waiting for the gap to close, we've explored what's left of Jackie Nicholson's old lighthouse, which is nothing now but ashes and a few charred pieces of lumber. There is no longer any trace of where the house was or the old outbuildings. There is the beginning of a large trench, which will one day be the canal. The concrete walls are now about a third of the way along to where the first "cell" is to be located. I understand that the cell is where there will be large gates that open and close and control the current so that ships and boats don't swirl around as they try to get through.

Since the spring, my father has been hauling gravel for the concrete they're using for the canal. I read in the paper that they're going to need a hundred thousand yards, which really means a lot more than it sounds.

I try to imagine the ships I used to see moving slowly in the distance as they passed through the unblocked strait. Soon I'll see them up close, halted in the canal, with the land pressed close on either side, waiting to get through the narrow passage so they can continue towards the gulf—or back towards the ocean. I'll actually be able to read the names of the ships and the distant places they come from. I'll see their flags and get to see the people on board.

The flank of the hill leading up to Newtown, where Angus Neil and Theresa MacKinnon used to live, is patchy white from recent snow. But where the canal is being built there is only mud and carved black rock. The air is full of the smell of diesel fumes and the sour aftertaste of blasting smoke.

It is strangely quiet now, the way it always gets at suppertime when day is ending and the night is moving in. But I know it's different from the quiet of before, when there was nobody here but Jackie and his grandmother. The only sound would be, on foggy nights, the sad call of Mrs. Nicholson's foghorn and the nervous response of invisible ships somewhere in the darkness. The quiet now is that of an army of construction men and their machines relaxing briefly on this side, watching the frantic action on the other side in this battle against nature.

I want to ask Jackie Nicholson how he feels, coming here and seeing all the change. How does he feel about the lighthouse that gave his grandmother work for years and years and now lies in a pile of charred timber and powdery ash? But I know he'd just look at me with his puzzled expression. He seems happy in the new house, and especially since they got the new TV.

According to the *Bulletin*, they turned off the big beam at the top of the lighthouse for the last time on November 17. After they burned the lighthouse down, Mr. Jim Spray, who lives in town, was in the paper saying that it was the first time in 150 years that the point was dark. He doesn't seem too happy about it.

According to Mr. Clough, the point won't be dark for long. Where the lighthouse stood for a century and a half will, in fact, soon become a part of the causeway, and there will be more lights than anyone can imagine, starting in the village itself and illuminating the strait from one side to the other along the brave new road. Huge power lines will be draped across the strait from towers so tall they'll need flashing lights on top to keep the airplanes from running into them. And everybody will have TV.

Right now, though, Jackie and his grandmother have one of the only television sets in the village. Murdoch MacFarlane, who has a son in the priesthood and a daughter Mary working for the Power Commission, got the first. Then McGowan. Then Mrs. Nicholson got theirs, which Billy and I are allowed to watch when Jackie Nick is in the mood. Jackie is strange like that. Some days he's your best friend. Then there are days when his face is pale and scowling and his hair damp and hanging over his forehead and you avoid him. One night he and I went to a card game in the school and played as partners after I loaned him twenty-five cents so he could get in.

When I asked him, next day, to pay the quarter back, he said, "Whistle for it."

He's even ignorant to his grandmother when she tries to stop him from eating cookies or shovelling heaping spoons of icing sugar into his glass of milk. He'll speak sharply to her. Mrs. Nicholson just shakes her head and sighs and lets him do whatever he wants. If I spoke like that to Grandma Donohue, I'd be dead—instantly.

———

Everything, it seems, begins with mud. Men and large machines manoeuvre in fields that were, until recently, abandoned, shoving grass and underbrush aside. The growling voices of the chainsaws rise and fall in the woods, the air thick with spicy smoke from brushfires. It is hard to sit at a desk inside a classroom, knowing that everything outside is being transformed.

There are even changes in the small routines of school. On Fridays we have the Junior Red Cross meeting and assign jobs, such as handing out the cod liver oil capsules and checking for dirty fingernails and head lice. One of the best jobs is fetching water, which gets you extra time outside, if only briefly, every morning. There is no running water in the school, so we have to carry water in pails to fill the water coolers. We used to go to Miss Phemie MacKinnon's just below the church, but the old MacKinnon place is empty now, and someone drowned a cat in the well. The house and well will soon be gone to make way for a new road, which will be part of the highway that stretches across the country from one ocean to the other.

Now we go farther away from the school, through the pasture that is beside the school and into the woods, to a little spring where the water is cold and clean.

But now I see them burning brush near that spring, and I'm not sure where we'll go for water next. I wonder what it would be like in a school with running water.

Below Mr. Clough's store they are relocating the railroad, and soon the long, slow turns before and just beyond the railway station will be a straight line, a new passageway hacked through the rocks all the way from Sam Fox's Hill to the end of the new causeway at the point. There will even be a miniature causeway to carry trains over the water at the entrance to the cove. There's talk about moving the railway station. Survey crews appear shouting and measuring and driving enigmatic stakes into the ground in unlikely places. Clusters of men in hard hats and work boots stand in groups around men who wear shoes and overcoats and carry briefcases and long rolls of paper and turn up suddenly in pastures, unintelligible intelligence flowing among them. And across the water, the hulking cape suddenly shudders and shatters. And the causeway inches closer. Mud-spattered cars and trucks line the road between the stores. People say they're even going to tear down the church and the school and all the houses near the road, including ours. Old people are feeling anxious.

My mother laughs. "Don't pay any attention to the wild stories. They'll never touch that church."

It's been more than a hundred years since they started grumbling about the difficulty of getting on and off the island. I often want to ask why anyone would want to live on an island if they were so worried about getting off it.

Back in the eighteen hundreds they were asking the government for help getting people and animals across the strait by boat. Politicians and merchants started talking about a bridge, but most ordinary people couldn't imagine such a thing. The strait is deep and fast and wide. Then, somehow, they suspended a huge cable from a tower on top of the cape to a high pole here for the telegraph service. After that anything seemed possible for a while. But the cable eventually sagged until it was catching in the masts of sailing ships, and the pessimists were all saying: "See? A bridge? Not a chance."

Then they put the cable under the water, and the businessmen and politicians and all the optimists were saying "Progress can't be stopped" and "It's only a matter of time" before somebody with courage and drag and imagination finds a way to build the crossing.

Then there was a long period of time with no talk. People travelled back and forth as best they could, figuring the telegraph cable was the last word in progress. And eventually there was a modern ferry service for cars and even trains. That seemed to keep the people satisfied for a long time.

It was only after World War Two, after Angus L. Macdonald returned from Ottawa where he ran the navy during the war, that the talk started again. There was agitation from people who ran the coal mines on the other side of the island and the steel plant in Sydney—and from Newfoundlanders. Angus L. made it his business to get the government in Ottawa interested in a bridge. They probably figured they owed him, for being a war hero and everything else that he's achieved, and in 1949 they made a decision to build one. A bridge?

People were making jokes about the *bocan* bridge. The word *bocan* means ghost.

Then they changed their minds again. They finally realized that the strait was too deep and the tides too strong. And in the winter the drift ice that made so many problems for the ferries would tear a bridge apart.

"Typical," the Tories said. "More broken Grit promises."

You'd think that Angus L. would have known, without being told by engineers, how, in winter, slabs of ice the size of small ships sail through, sometimes jamming up, grinding and buckling, and piling up on the shore and turning the strait into an icefield, but never still or stable enough to walk across. Even I knew that spanning the strait would take something stronger than the relentless moving ice, something more durable than wood or steel or even concrete.

Something like rock—but not just any rock.

And when they finally announced a permanent crossing to be made from rock from Mr. Fraser's mountain, there was silence even from the Tories. There is something indisputable about words like rock and causeway. There is a sensible simplicity about the notion of carving chunks of granite from the face of old Cape Porcupine to build a road across the rushing water. News of a causeway finally had the credibility that was lacking in all the previous speculation and political promises. It seemed so natural and so obvious, you had to wonder why nobody had thought of it long ago. In time, I suspect, the causeway will be just another part of the natural landscape—a natural offspring of the cape.

———

The cluster of important-looking men parts for a moment, and someone is having a serious conversation with an older gentleman in an important-looking hat. This is obviously the lieutenant governor. He is listening carefully and staring at the ground, deep in thought.

The other day there was a rumour in the paper that they paid Mr. Fraser only $5,500 for the ten million tons of rock they've used, and that they appointed him lieutenant governor to keep him quiet. But he's going to sue them anyway and, from what I hear at home, he can't possibly lose. He's a lawyer. Even ordinary people think he's been screwed.

———

I thought for a while last year, before the mission, that when I grow up I would become a lawyer. I got the idea listening at The Hole and hearing my mother telling my Aunt Veronica that she was going to have to get one to help with her problems.

"That's all there is to it," she said. "You need a good lawyer."

It was another evening when there was quiet talking and sniffling at the table, and I gradually realized that the lawyer was necessary because my aunt has no water on her property and is in a dispute with a well driller she hired to dig a well. His name is Wendelblo, and he isn't from around here. He's one of the new people, which probably explains a lot.

My aunt has always had a water problem. From what I understand, water is a constant source of worry for adults and, when I really think about it, I can understand why. Just from school, I realize how important water is and how hard it is to find sometimes. I hear people complaining that, because of the blasting on the cape, wells are going dry. This doesn't surprise me. At three in the morning at the end of August, they set off two explosions, and I thought the house was falling down. I read later that those two blasts blew 350,000 tons of rock off the mountain.

My Aunt Veronica has no man in the house, just her two little boys, and has to carry her water in buckets from the old town well, which is down at the foot of her street, in behind where Danny MacIntosh lives. The town well is beside what was once another lane before the well-to-do storekeepers blocked it off so the poor people would have to pass their businesses when they were travelling through the village.

So my aunt finally hired the new well driller named Wendelblo to try and find water on her property. And she's been at war with him ever since.

———

Something I've learned since this construction project started is that big changes have a way of sneaking up on you. Even up to the summer of 1953, the changes weren't all that conspicuous. School ended in late June last summer, and I set about my new routine as always— swimming in the cove, wandering in the woods with the dog. Early in July, when Ian's uncle, Big Ian MacKinnon, started making hay, I went there to help.

He uses a horse, named Nellie, hitched to a clattering mowing machine with steel wheels. Nellie plods around the fields in large circles, with Big Ian sitting on the mower hauling on the reins and shouting "Hoo, haw, head up there, Nellie." And the machine rattles and the long spiked blade, slung on one side of the mower at ground level, slashes through the dense hay, leaving it in neat prostrate swaths. My job last summer was to walk along behind the mowing machine with a pitchfork, turning the swath as I went.

Sometimes Little Ian would be allowed to ride on the mower with the reins in his hands while his uncle walked behind with me or just watched. When I asked to try driving the mowing machine, they said it was too dangerous.

On day two we'd turn the hay again. Then they'd hitch Nellie to the raking machine, and she'd drag it along the swaths, gathering the hay in long windrows. Ian often got to drive the raking machine as well because, his uncle and everybody else said, he is as strong as a man. They're always calling him "a great little worker."

Then we'd take our forks and bunch the windrows into haycocks shaped like thimbles. And Nellie would be hitched to a truck wagon, and the hay gathered up to be stored in the haymow of Big Ian's barn. Little Ian could heave a whole haycock with one pitch of the fork, but when I'd try, half of it would fall back in my face.

Then you'd be struggling in the mow just to keep from getting buried, distributing the hay and tramping it down, watching for dampness, because everybody knows that wet hay causes fires, and a barn fire is a disaster. You'd be soaked in sweat, with the hayseeds glued to your neck and back, and even in your underwear. And afterwards, everybody would gather around the big hand pump. Big Ian would pump icy water into a dipper, and we'd all take our turns. A bottle of buttermilk was hanging on a rope in the well, and they'd pass it around. Buttermilk makes me gag, but Little Ian would swallow it down just like the men did, and it would leave a thin white mustache on his upper lip. And they'd be going on about what an able little man he was.

After the haymaking, we'd spend the rest of the summer just wandering around barefooted, wearing nothing but shorts. We'd burn to a crisp at first and go to bed slathered in Noxzema. Then, in a few days, we'd be brown, and the sun wouldn't bother us any more. We'd spend long afternoons swimming in the cove or off the old coal pier, gathering up empty beer and pop bottles along the roadside and taking them to Mrs. Lew, who ran a canteen and paid a few pennies for each. And when we had fifty cents, we'd walk or hitchhike to Rocky Hazel's theatre in town, where a movie cost thirty-five cents, and a couple of bars of toffee or chocolate used up the rest.

Then, in the fall of last year, the Malones moved in, and we got the sense that everything was different. The changes that everyone has been talking about now seemed real.

The Malones speak with a different accent, a little bit like Americans. For *shore* they say *shoah*. Mrs. Malone says *theyah* for *there*. Mr. and Mrs. Malone always seem to be in good cheer. He smokes a pipe and doesn't drink, and speaks to us as if we're grown-ups. Billy says he's from a smaller place than here, but he dresses like the city boys I see in magazines and comic books and movies. He has jeans and a denim jacket, and they fit perfectly. When I'm not wearing shorts, I wear overalls or jeans that never seem to fit properly. I want to ask where his clothes come from, but fear it will only draw attention to my own. I'd love to have a denim jacket.

Most of all, the Malones remind me of the families I read about. They are always nice to one another. Mrs. Malone is generous with the cookies and makes jokes and calls Billy and me "the turd birds." Billy and Phyllis never fight. Mr. Malone puffs his pipe and always seems interested in what we're up to.

Billy has large sad eyes and a serious expression. But in more than a year I've never seen him upset, and now we're together most of the time. I've shown him all the best places I know—Happy Jack's Lake, and the swimming hole in the middle of the cove, and the waterfall out back. Together we hang around the construction work near the railway station, watching the drillers and the large machines moving about, running and hiding when a siren sounds to warn of a blast. Sheltered underneath a building or behind a rock, we imagine we are in a war, with artillery coming in.

When they were in the Captain's house, rocks from the blasting for the new railway line would come almost into their yard.

Once Billy asked how come Jackie Nick and I don't have fathers. I explained that I have one, but he often works away. Billy was impressed when I told him that when he works away, he does what the drillers do and even sets off underground explosions with dynamite. And I could tell Billy was wondering how come he isn't working on the causeway project like everybody else. One of the things I like most about Billy: he knows what not to ask.

Right now he's driving a truck at the canal for T.C. Gorman, because that way he thinks he's his own boss. That is what he says.

We talk about the work we'll do some day. Billy wants to be like his father, running large construction machines like bulldozers and cranes. Or maybe a fisherman like his relatives back home. First I told him that I was going to be like my father, a hard-rock miner, and he thought that was a great idea. Then, when I knew him better, I told him the truth: that I plan to be a priest when I grow up. He just stared at me, as if he didn't understand. Not like Jackie Nicholson, who would have said something ignorant. Other than my mother, Billy is the only one I've told. I find it interesting that my mother stared at me the same way Billy did, with the same dubious expression. The Malones are Protestants, after all.

"That would be wonderful," she declared, but her face indicated doubt.

There is no doubt in my mind. I've even started to make my own rosary out of dynamite wire, of which there is no shortage in the village now. I am making little knots in the thin red wire, ten per decade, with one in-between for the "Glory Be to the Father."

My aunt finally had to go to Antigonish to see a lawyer to deal with the well driller. On the way over, somebody asked me what I planned to do when I grow up, but I didn't want to mention mining or the priesthood, so I said I was thinking of becoming a lawyer. Everybody laughed. The woman driving the car said I'd be making a terrible mistake because lawyers are all crooks.

I felt better knowing that nobody would ever say a thing like that about priests or hard-rock miners.

————

There was no grand announcement when my father moved back home. He just arrived home one weekend driving a three-ton truck. I heard it before I saw it, the big blue truck he bought from Danny Shaw in Stirling, whining up the Victoria Line. Then it turned onto our lane and stopped beside our barn. The door opened, and my father climbed out, looking serious.

First I thought he'd borrowed it, but I could tell by the look on his face, as he parked it near the barn, that it was his. And then he went into the barn carrying the large canvas duffel bag in which he keeps his mining gear, and I realized that he was home for good.

It was shocking, in a way. This was what I had prayed for—not for myself, but for him and the women. I'd been praying for something that would prevent the sadness in the pantry and the quiet conversations late at night, and the tired look on his face when he'd sit on the doorstep with his arm around the dog before he'd go away. I'd been praying for something that would achieve what I, even though they all say I am the man of the house when he's away, could never do—make something complete that is actually missing an important part.

Now the circle was closed, and it felt as though I'd made a deal with God. Ever since the mission, I've been praying that he'll find a way to stay. Not for my sake; just for my mother and himself. And I've decided to become a priest, and my mother seems to think that maybe I haven't really thought it all the way through. But what, really, is there to think about?

The causeway was a third of the way across when he finally moved home. For months, along with the sirens and the blasting for the new roads and railway, you could hear the constant hammering of piledrivers building cofferdams on either end of where the canal is going to be. A cofferdam is like a tongue-and-groove wall, except it's made of iron and the pieces are hammered vertically into the floor of the strait. There are two of these walls at each end of where the canal will be. In-between the walls they dump fill from the hole they're digging for the canal. The cofferdams hold the water of the strait back while they dig.

That was one of the things my father did with the truck at first—hauling the fill for the cofferdams. Working "behind the iron curtain," he'd say, and everyone would smile.

A piledriver going all the time can get on your nerves, but eventually it ended, and they started erecting forms for the concrete that would form the walls of the new canal. And that was when Dan Rory really got busy. The company doing the canal work is T.C. Gorman, and the boss's name is Romeo Larocque. The Larocques live beside the Catholic Church in town. I see them every Sunday, the whole family just walking across the road to Mass. I believe there is some significance to the fact that Mr. Larocque is boss of the canal job and lives practically in the Catholic Church, and my father finally has a truck and a job that lets him live at home for a change.

Sundays we go to church in the truck and, because there isn't room for everyone in the cab, I get to ride on the back, hanging on high up there and seeing everything, and the wind tearing my hair apart.

Lately, listening at The Hole, I hear them talking about the Trans-Canada Highway, a road that will eventually cross the entire country from the Pacific to the Atlantic. It might not ever have got to Cape Breton, because everybody seems to think that Canada ends at Halifax. But with Newfoundland now part of the country, Canada and the new road will have to end up in St. John's. The only way to get to St. John's is through Cape Breton. And when the causeway is completed, the only way to get through Cape Breton will be through our village.

The Trans-Canada Highway, according to what I can figure from listening to them, will cross the causeway and hook up with the Victoria Line behind the church. It is why Phemie MacKinnon's old house is empty, looking shabby and defeated. Soon they'll probably just burn it down, like Nicholsons'. What about Angus Walker's house? I wonder. What about old Sinclair's? What about the school?

"That's what was in the paper," my father said. "It says the new road goes behind the church. It makes sense when you think about it."

And it also makes sense that, if the place grows the way everybody expects it to, we're going to need a new school, anyway, to accommodate all the new people who will move here to live.

You get sad seeing what they're tearing down or burning. But then you think of all the new things coming, and it's like thinking about Christmas.

———

One of the first new people, even before the Malones, was a Hungarian. His name is John Suto, and he is old but very friendly. Now that I know him I can call him Old John, the way the construction workers do. He's in charge of the Gorman construction camp and is always fixing something or sweeping floors. He isn't like older people here who never seem to notice you until you get in their way. He's like Mr. Malone, in the way he looks at you and sees you and hears you when you talk to him.

Gorman's new construction camp is in what used to be an empty field, near the old MacMillan place where the cow continued to find enough peace and quiet and grass to pass her days until just recently. They built the camp in the spring of '53 and, by the summer, it was full of workmen.

It was while passing by, looking for the cow, that I realized the men in the camp drink a lot of beer. They often drop the empties out the bunkhouse windows. I could easily fill a burlap bag, especially after a weekend. One evening, as I gathered bottles, I realized I was being watched. And there was Old John, standing with his arms folded and a serious look on his face.

I just stared back, expecting a blast for stealing bottles he considered to be his. Lots of older people gather bottles. After a dance in the school, I have to get up at dawn to get the bottles that are littering the school grounds before Mrs. Lew gets at them. She also lives close to the school and likes to cut me out of the bottle business every chance she gets. I didn't think there was much danger that she'd get up to the construction camp, but now this old guy was looking at me as if he was about to pounce.

We just stared at each other.

Then he said: "You take the beer bottles."

I wasn't sure if it was a statement or a question, and I immediately noticed the strange accent. The only accents I've ever heard are the French, and Uncle Joe's Irish, and the Malones from the South Shore.

I didn't know how to answer, but the dog trotted over and started sniffing at his pant leg.

He reached down and scratched the dog behind the ears.

"Your dog?"

This was a question.

"Yes," I answered.

He squatted down and took the dog's head in both his hands and seemed to be studying his face. Then, to my astonishment, he opened the dog's mouth and looked in.

"This is a good dog," he said.

"Yes," I said. "His name is Skipper."

"Skipper," he repeated, and then laughed.

"You know he is a good dog," he explained, "by black in dog's mouth. Come here. Look."

He opened the dog's jaws again, and I was amazed by the way the dog just went along with it. I don't think I'd ever looked in there before. The tongue was pink and the teeth yellowing, and he had foul breath. But sure enough, the roof of Skipper's mouth was black, which means that he is quality. And to think that Uncle Francis came that close to shooting him!

"What's your name?" Old John asked.

"Linden," I told him, resisting the urge to make up a new one on the spot.

"Linden," he said. "Good name. Linden tree."

"I know," I said.

"In Berlin," he said. "Is a big street. Unter den Linden."

I didn't know that and, spoken the way he said it, the name suddenly sounded okay.

"Are you a German?" I asked.

"No," he replied, half laughing. "Not a German."

"What are you then?" I asked.

"You ever hear of Hungary?"

Something stirred in the memory. Something from the newspapers. Communists. Cardinal Mindszenty. Prison.

"Yes," I said. "But I don't know where it is."

"Is in Europe," he said.

"Is it near Germany?"

"All Europe is near Germany. This is the problem."

We just stared at each other for a while, and I thought his face was friendly and his eyes were kind.

"You come Saturday," he said. "I tell you about Hungary. And I save bottles for you. Friday night lots of beer drinking."

He laughed.

"My name is John," he said.

Then he walked away.

The main camp is a large building for the workers. There is also a smaller one for their bosses. And a cookhouse where everybody eats. Walking by the cookhouse in the evening, the smells of baking and of meat cooking make your mouth water. Every evening smells like fresh bread and sizzling pork chops, and it occurred to me that, maybe, living away from home and eating in a place like that can't be so bad after all. Pork chops every night, and somebody to pick up after you in a bunkhouse. At home, pork chops are special. Even the dog looks envious.

That evening, after meeting Old John for the first time, I asked my mother about Hungary.

"It's behind the Iron Curtain," she said.

"The Iron Curtain? Like the cofferdam?"

She laughed. "No."

"It's what they call Communism," she said. "An iron curtain that has divided the world in two. It's a metaphor."

"A what?"

Saturday mornings, true to his word, Old John would have boxes of empty beer bottles neatly stored for me. And after we got to know each other better, he'd take me to the cookhouse, where we'd have mugs of tea and he'd ask me questions about school and home and the village and my plans for after I grow up.

I lied and said I wasn't certain. Maybe I'd be a miner like my father.

He seemed impressed that my father was a miner.

"Mining is hard work," he said. Maybe I should stay in school. Get a job where I could wear a shirt and tie. Not end up like him—an old man in a strange place.

But when I'd ask him questions about himself and Hungary, he'd just look away and become quiet.

Once he said: "Hungary is a very sad place. Very sad. Bad people running Hungary."

"Communists," I volunteered.

"Yes," he said. "You know about Communists?"

"From the paper," I said.

"Canadians very lucky people," he said. "No Communists here."

I found a book that told me that Hungary was once part of one of the strongest empires in the world, but that, since the end of World War Two, the Communists have taken over and started persecuting anyone who doesn't agree with them, including priests and bishops and even a cardinal.

I get books from a library in the basement of the church in town. The only books in school are the ones we use for our lessons—history, English, math, etc. There are no books that you'd want to read for fun. But the church library has lots of books for all ages and, ever since Miss Christie, I've been reading books by Pearl S. Buck, who writes about China.

And now that I know a Hungarian, I look for books about Hungary and Communism, and I follow the news about Eastern Europe, and I'm beginning to realize how dangerous and interesting the world really is. And I can hardly wait to be a part of it.

———

My father seems happy to be home, finally working in his own place after years of travelling around the country. I think my father got his job here without any help from politicians. But I know he needed help, and whenever he's talking about his truck he says it belongs to him and the banker. My Aunt Veronica, however, believes in the power of politicians more than ever. It seems a lawyer helped her with her water problem, but I got the impression, overhearing conversations in the kitchen, that important politicians, including Mr. Angus Waye, who is the mayor of Port Hawkesbury, helped her too. They put pressure on the right people, and the well driller eventually left her alone and stopped pestering her or money she doesn't have.

Of course, she still doesn't have water either. Even politicians can't put water where there isn't any.

Everybody was saying Angus L. should be here to see the last load dumped and the causeway connected to the island. Or isn't it a shame that the man who actually dumped the first load of fill into the strait to start the causeway project can't be here to see his dream fulfilled. And how tragic it is that Angus L. is dead.

It would have been shocking even if there had been a warning or if he'd been a hundred years old. But nobody expected it, and he was only sixty-four, which is young for a premier. He worked himself to death, they say. After helping run the country during the war, he went back to being Nova Scotia's premier, and the causeway was one of his priorities. All the work he did to get the causeway started helped to bring him down.

Even our house was full of sorrow at the news.

My aunt, who follows the news more carefully than most people, was saying he caught a cold during a trip to Scotland in November 1953 and never got over it. It was as though she was talking about a member of the family. Then right after Scotland he goes to Edmonton, Alberta, to make a speech. Then he shuffles the Cabinet and gives himself the hardest jobs. Goes to the hospital Sunday night, April 11, and even takes his work with him—estimates for the Department of Highways and Public Works, whatever they are.

Just rest in hospital for a few days, they said. Then the announcement Tuesday morning—he's dead. Worn out, my aunt said. And now he's replaced by that Harold Connolly—which wasn't entirely bad, except that there was no way the Halifax Grits were going to leave him in the job.

It was the biggest thing since the coronation. They even had his funeral on the radio. The Halifax paper said that 85,000 people lined up at the legislature to pay their respects to his dead body. And that there were 100,000 people along the streets watching the funeral procession.

He was as important as the Queen, but the archbishop of Halifax talked about how Angus L. was once "a small boy from a small Cape Breton village, attending the smallest of schools." He became a great man, anyway, and now "we draw a veil over that life so useful, so beloved, so serviceable, so fit to inspire many another boy in the small villages of Canada."

From where I was listening to the funeral, I could look out a window. The trucks were still crawling along the face of the cape, trundling out to the end of the causeway that he dreamed of and made happen. Racing to complete the fulfillment of his dream and not even pausing to lament his death—which is probably what he'd have wanted.

We could hear the funeral from the radio on the top of the fridge. My father was listening, squinting through the smoke of his cigarette. I was wondering what he thought about those words—the small boy in the small Cape Breton village. And what life might have been like if he'd grown up in a village or a town, never mind a city. Or if there had been a doctor or a school.

When it was over he got up and went out, and we could hear the truck starting.

———

From the beginning, Billy Malone wanted to know everything there is to know about the village. I told him as much as I could, about the cove and the old coal piers, and how the place once had more than a dozen stores and places where men could drink liquor until they passed out. There used to be a big dance hall, just across from where Sylvia and Darlene Reynolds live with their parents, William and Anita. But it burned down because some kids were playing with matches.

I told him about all the older people. How Harry and Rannie were harmless, but we're supposed to keep an eye on Danny Black Dan. How Danny MacIntosh had great war stories when he was drinking with the other veterans and, if you were quiet, you could sneak in and listen. How John MacDougall was shot between the eyes in World War Two and still survived. And how Joe Larter had been to Korea and brought a special scarf back for Jean.

He wanted to know about people like Don Riley, who often stays at Jackie Nicholson's place, but I don't know much about Riley, who doesn't seem to have any real connections here. Unlike everybody else, he doesn't seem to have any relatives. He's always been around, and everybody knows him because he's a great step dancer. You step dance indoors to fiddle music, but sometimes you'll even see Don Riley dancing on the road while somebody chants the music for him. De-diddle-di-de-diddle-dum, and Riley pounding the road as if there was a real fiddle player there and hardwood underneath his feet.

Billy doesn't understand why people here like fiddle music and says it all sounds the same to him. Or why people enjoy Riley dancing like the black minstrels we see in the movies.

I think his favourite old person here is Jimmy Cameron, who looks like an elf and always has a crooked pipe in his mouth. Jimmy has a brain a little bit like Martin Angus, because he can remember, word for word, long stories and poems that he learned when he went to school ages ago.

Once Jimmy was working with a gang, clearing rocks off the Victoria Line, and I asked him to recite "Hiawatha" for us. And he did. Billy Malone's big eyes just got bigger and bigger as Jimmy Cameron stood there, leaning on the handle of his shovel, looking off in the distance as if he could actually see the Indians and the woods and the water. And I told Billy afterwards that, next time, we'd get Jimmy to recite his best story, about a skater who is being chased by wolves. But we didn't have time that day because the story goes on and on. And Jimmy was, after all, getting paid sixty cents an hour by the government for working on the road.

And I showed Billy all the best places for gathering beer bottles. Of course, the best place of all is the construction camp where Old John saves the bottles for us.

Billy's father works for T.C. Gorman and seems to know a little bit about Old John. Mr. Malone says Old John has a family back in Hungary and is always trying to get them into Canada and away from the Communists.

I asked Mr. Malone what were his chances, and he said Old John was optimistic. Things seemed to be improving in Hungary since old Joe Stalin croaked.

But Joe Stalin isn't a Hungarian, I pointed out. What does he have to do with Old John's family? Mr. Malone just laughed.

I thought I'd ask Old John but decided to wait until he wants to tell me himself.

The papers seem to think that even though Joe Stalin is gone, the Communists, either in Russia or in China, will start the next world war.

Grandma Donohue doesn't agree. She's convinced that it will be a man named Nasser and that the war will start in the Holy Land. And that is where I plan to be a missionary some day.

———

Easter felt different this year, probably because of Angus L. dying just before Good Friday. A lot of people think that was significant. People were mentioning that he was almost like a saint, and that the causeway should be named after him.

But it seems, when he was still alive, he had vetoed that idea, and nobody wanted to go against his wishes after he was dead.

The Angus L. Macdonald Causeway sounded good enough to me, but his preference was "The Road to the Isles"—the name of one of his favourite bagpipe tunes. And that is probably what they'll name it.

Angus L. was fond of Scottish music. He was always making references to Scottish history in his speeches, and the papers often referred to his Gaelic, as if it made him special in some way. My father doesn't think that Gaelic makes anybody special, but, as is the case with so many things I ask him, he usually answers questions with another question or a joke.

"How come I can't speak Gaelic?"

"Where would Gaelic get you?"

Or, "Where did we come from in Scotland?"

"Uist, I think."

"Where's that?"

"You tell me."

One of the things Angus L. Macdonald did when he was alive was to hire a man from Scotland to act as a special Gaelic adviser to the government. The adviser's name is Major Calum Iain Norman MacLeod. You hear him on the radio some evenings giving Gaelic lessons.

My father will get up close to the radio, listening.

"Caite bheil bean an tighe?" Major MacLeod will say carefully. And some young girl will repeat it after him. Then he'll say what it means: "Where is the lady of the house?"

And my father will smile and say something like "Tha i anns an tigh bheag," which means "She's in the toilet."

Then he goes away, shaking his head, as if "Where's the lady of the house" is the most useless question anybody could ask in any language.

One that I remembered was "Cuir a mach an cu," which means "Put the dog out."

My father said: "Well, that's the first useful thing I've heard out of the Major since he started." You could see Skipper nervously looking out from under the stove, which is where he sleeps when he's in the house.

The Major also plays pipe music, but my father likes only certain tunes on the bagpipes. But when the fiddle music comes on, everybody has to stop talking, and if it's somebody that he knows, like Dan Rory MacDonald, or Little Jack, or Dan Hughie MacEachern, or Angus Chisholm, he'll practically have his ear inside the radio.

I'm not sure what is so special about the fiddle music. I agree with Billy Malone. It all sounds the same to me. At least the bagpipe music makes you feel like doing something, crying or killing. My father says that when I'm a little older, the fiddle will make me feel like dancing. But then I think of Don Riley step dancing to pretend fiddle music on the side of the road—and people laughing at him.

My parents' favourite thing on the radio is a program called *Fun at Five*. The man in charge of *Fun at Five* is called the Old Timer, and he's always making comments about his likes and dislikes. For instance, there's a song he hates: "Good Night, Irene." And every time they start to play it on his program, he stops it after the first few notes and says, "Somebody give me my hammer"—and he proceeds to smash the record right there. You can hear it break and the pieces going into the trash can.

Then, maybe three nights later, "Good Night, Irene" will start again, and the Old Timer will smash it again. You wonder why they keep trying to play it if he's only going to smash it. Records cost money.

Mostly he plays fiddle tunes and cowboy songs by Wilf Carter and Hank Snow, who are famous all over Canada and the United States, but who grew up in small villages in Nova Scotia. My favourites are Eddy Arnold and, of course, Roy Rogers, who, besides being a cowboy and gunfighter, also sings songs on the radio.

The interesting thing to me is that everybody knows that the Old Timer is really a politician named J. Clyde Nunn and that he's a Grit and that, even though he lives over on the mainland, in Antigonish, and works for the Antigonish radio station, he represents Inverness County in the provincial legislature.

This I can't quite understand—being from the mainland and representing a place in Cape Breton.

My father says it wouldn't matter if J. Clyde Nunn was from Mars for all the good that any politician does.

But my mother and my Aunt Veronica and my Grandmother Donohue love the Old Timer on the radio, even though they can't stand Clyde Nunn in politics.

Veronica says she knew him when he was a young seminarian and that the world, and Inverness County in particular, would be a far better place if he'd stuck to his vocation to be a priest.

"After all the great politicians that came out of Inverness County, now we have Nunn!"

During the election of 1953, a half-ton truck drove through the village, and standing in the back was J. Clyde Nunn and a stranger who was playing the bagpipes.

They say Clyde Nunn will be the member for Inverness until Judgment Day. But of course they were also saying that Angus L. would be the premier of the province forever. All things change eventually.

————

Right at six o'clock this huge Euclid pulls up on the other side of the gap, swings wide, then starts to back to the edge. There is a murmur of expectation from the crowd of onlookers, who seem to know exactly what is going on. The photographer moves forward, towards the edge of the point, as if he's going to climb right down to the raging water. This could be the one, everybody seems to be thinking. Jackie, Billy, and I follow the photographer.

The truck stops, but nothing happens. Then I can see the driver of the truck climbing down from his high perch in the cab. He begins to talk to another worker. Then a small crowd gathers around the truck. First I think they're waiting for some signal before they dump the last load. But then the driver climbs under the truck and then somebody comes with a light. Before you know it, there are three people under the truck. And because I know something about trucks, I instantly know the problem.

In the summer on days when there was nothing much to do, I'd walk down to Newtown and wait beside the road until I saw my father's truck, either coming up from the construction site at the canal or heading towards it with a load of gravel from Troy Beach. I'd wave, and he'd stop, and I'd jump in and spend the rest of the day riding with him.

Back and forth over the five miles from the beach to where they were mixing the gravel with sand and cement for the concrete that they're making for the canal walls. We'd just sit there on opposite sides of the seat, elbows out the open window, and the cool breeze blasting in from the motion of the truck.

My father isn't much for talking even when he's with other adults. And adults, generally, don't have much in common with kids and therefore wouldn't have much to talk to kids about. I'd try to get things going by asking questions, but he was always able to answer them briefly. And then we'd resume our silence. Plus it was hard to talk over the noise of the truck and the wind roaring in the open windows.

I'd find different ways to ask about the beach and whether we'd still be able to go swimming there after the causeway was finished.

"That's hard to say," he'd say, which was one of his most frequent answers.

Or I'd ask him about China and Russia and the Communists, and he'd reply that there were some things that were just too complicated for ordinary mortals to understand. As when they executed Mr. and Mrs. Rosenberg in 1953 because they were spying for the Communists.

"Why would they have to be executed for spying?"

"That's what they do to spies," he said.

And then he said: "It's an awful thing."

"What is?" I wanted to know. "Spying or being executed?"

"The whole shootin' match," he said.

Most of the trips were uneventful—you might even say boring. Sitting there in a stuffy truck, driving back and forth over the same five miles. Maybe once in a while, when he had to wait in line at the beach, we'd walk down to the shoreline and see who could skip a flat stone the farthest.

Then there would be the bad luck—the broken axle or the flat tire or the broken drive shaft. And he'd get the tired look and get out of the truck slowly and climb underneath. That's how I knew ahead of anybody else over here what was going on under the Euclid which was stuck at the end of the causeway.

"Broken drive shaft," I said.

"You don't know," said Jackie Nick.

"Yes, I do," I assured him.

Billy wanted to know what a drive shaft was, and I explained it was a long thing like a pole that went from the transmission to the universal joint and turned the wheels of the truck.

This I learned from watching my father underneath the truck, grease to the elbows, sweating and swearing quietly in Gaelic. I have never heard my father swear in English, and he swears in Gaelic only when things are going very badly—when the truck is broken down on the side of the road or in the yard at home.

Swearing doesn't sound as bad in Gaelic as in English.

The holdup at the end of the causeway seems to be serious. Soon there is a lineup of Euclids backed up beyond the disabled truck, and a small crowd standing around watching the men on the ground. On this side, all the important men standing around the lieutenant governor are frowning and muttering. I imagine that the air is blue from the language they're using over there underneath the Euclid.

Occasionally during our drives, and when everything was going well, my father would tell me a story about the mountain when he was young and how being a boy back then wasn't much different from being a man. You started doing a man's work even though you were small because all you had to live on was what you were able to scrape off the land or from the woods.

And I asked him if that was why he never went to school, and he replied that school was a whole other kettle of fish, whatever that means.

And he'd always say the same thing: "I had no shortage of schooling; it was just the book l'arnin' I missed out on."

And he'd laugh the way they do when you're supposed to laugh with them.

Then, out of the blue, he'd tell a real story.

He and his brother John Dan went hunting rabbits one Sunday, which was against the rules because Sunday was supposed to be a day of rest, even though they had to walk about five miles through the woods to Glendale to get to Mass. But hunting rabbits or any other kind of work on the Lord's Day was forbidden. There'd be war if Grandma Peigeag ever found out. Nobody defied Grandma Peigeag.

Anyway, this Sunday they're walking along the mountain road

with the .22, watching for rabbits, when suddenly they hear this loud, unfamiliar sound. They stopped and, sure enough, it was the sound of a car approaching. A car? On the mountain?

It could mean only one thing—a priest. A priest on his way up to visit the old people.

My father was carrying the .22 and, to hide it from whoever was coming, he jammed it down his pant leg. But the trigger caught on something and the rifle went off. He didn't feel a thing at first. And sure enough, a car came around a turn and stopped. And it was the priest. He's sitting there being priestly and asking them questions in Gaelic about who they were and what they were doing. And it was then that my father felt the pain.

The priest moved on, and my father looked down and saw blood oozing around a small black hole in the top of his bare foot. He suddenly felt like throwing up—partly from pain and partly from knowing what was going to happen when his mother found out what he and his brother had been up to.

They both agreed it had to be a secret, but they had to get the bullet out of the foot somehow. When he sat down and lifted the foot for inspection, John Dan declared that he could see a small dark spot under the skin on the sole of the foot and he was sure it was the tip of the bullet. Then he proceeded to dig around the black spot with his jackknife, and, sure enough, it was the bullet. And that was how they got it out.

That was how afraid they were of their mother.

Suddenly there is the loud roar of a diesel engine at the end of the causeway. I can see a huge bulldozer lumbering up to the stalled Euclid. Moments later the bulldozer hauls the truck off to one side, and another loaded truck swings around and backs to the end of the causeway. The massive dump rises slowly, there is a roar, and the boulders tumble into the gap as if in slow motion, splashing and muddying the foam in front of us.

Somebody shouts and points, and we all press as close as we safely can towards the end of the point. And there they are, the giant rocks just sitting there, clearly visible in the swirling torrent that is now like a furious shallow ditch. A couple of workmen move down over the edge, positioning themselves to leap from rock to rock and become the first humans in history to cross the Strait of Canso without a boat or an airplane. But one of them notices something dramatic. The rocks are rapidly disappearing as the rising tide once again asserts the mastery of the water over man and his machines. They scramble back to safety.

And soon, the fragile bridge of stone is out of sight entirely. A churning watery gap of about twenty feet remains between here and there. The strait will not surrender its integrity so easily—not after so many countless centuries of imposing inconveniences on all the creatures on its shores.

One sunny day in the summer, just after we turn off the main highway onto the dirt road leading to the canal construction, my father stops the truck and points at a new sign that's been erected there just that day.

"Look at that," he says, laughing in disbelief.

"What," I want to know.

"Can't you see anything wrong with that sign?"

"No," I reply.

"Read it," he instructs.

I peer at the big words.

"Caution. Intermitting blasting"?

"Read it again."

I did. "Caution. Intermitting blasting."

"What kind of blasting is intermitting blasting?"

"I don't know."

"That's because some smart educated fella got the word wrong. It should be 'intermitt-*ent*' blasting."

"What's the difference?"

He looked at me briefly, then started the truck again.

"You're the fella that goes to school," he said.

Then rapped my knee gently with his knuckle and laughed.

Another time we were just sitting in the cab, waiting in line before he could dump his load of gravel. He had the door open and one leg hanging out and his elbow resting on the steering wheel. We were both watching the same thing: the causeway, now like a fat snake wriggling in our direction.

Then he said, without looking at me: "It'll still be there long after we're both gone."

What?

"That thing is bigger and more important than any of us."

He sounded sad, but I couldn't see his face.

I know that lots of people are unhappy about the causeway. The papers are full of alarm from Mulgrave and Port Hawkesbury, where people will lose their jobs when the ferries stop. Mulgrave is worse off because the trains won't go anywhere near there once the causeway is finished. They say the town will die. And there are people saying that drift ice will back up in St. George's Bay after the causeway and interfere with the spring lobster fishery. And that the water level will rise four inches, which will be enough to change the shoreline significantly.

South of the new causeway, the strait and Chedabucto Bay will become four degrees warmer and drop a bit, and even that small change will interfere with life in the sea.

At Clough's store, however, I hear them saying that these are small prices to pay for progress. Port Hawkesbury is going to be a boom town because of the new industries that will locate here and there. And Mulgrave will just have to accept the fact that communities have their ups and downs, as Port Hastings has learned more than a few times in our long history.

Of course, there are also people who are warning of larger consequences from "mankind tampering with nature." And there has also been some concern that, in the next war, the causeway will be a target because of its strategic importance for the steel and coal industries on the other side of Cape Breton. But some people are saying there can never be another big war like the two world wars in the first half of this century. A war now would mean the end of the world because of the hydrogen bombs they're building.

I'm not so sure. Every day the papers are full of stories about Americans and Russians and Chinese threatening each other over one thing or another. Old John is sure there will be another great war in Europe. And I know from the papers that the Americans killed Mr. and Mrs. Rosenberg for something that would have helped the Russians win it.

My father says people are essentially nutty and, as a result, anything is possible. He says that Mr. and Mrs. Rosenberg thought that, by spying, they could help *prevent* a war.

"So why were they electrocuted?"

He just looked at me for a while. "To make small boys ask questions."

Which is another one of the answers he often gives.

My mother says we have to pray for peace and that this is a good reason for saying the rosary every evening.

My father goes along with the rosary, but when my mother starts adding new stuff, the way she does for peace, you can hear him tapping his foot on the floor, which is his signal that enough is enough.

Grandma Donohue doesn't seem to be half as worried about the Russians and the Chinese as she is about this guy named Nasser. But she agrees: prayer is the only answer.

———

It's good to have your father home, even if you worry about broken axles and drive shafts and the tired look he gets sweating and swearing underneath the truck—which seems to be always looking for new ways to trip him up. And about how, when things really get difficult, he'll come home late with fishy eyes and a goofy grin and a lot of silly talk that makes my mother angry. And then the house will grow cold and, when they're alone, you know things are being said. Afterwards he'll quietly go outside and sit on the doorstep or in the truck, and maybe fall asleep like that.

Friends from the mining days will often drop by when they're on their way home from somewhere or leaving for another job. They'll talk quietly about distant places, and he'll be interested in new shafts that are being sunk and geologists' reports about how rich some base-metal discovery is going to be in some place nobody ever heard of before. And about people they all know flocking off to the new bonanza in Elliot Lake or Blind River or Arizona. Even I get excited and wonder what it would be like to leave your troubles behind and go off to something entirely new in a place that doesn't really matter because you're going to be there only temporarily anyway.

After they leave, you'll see him sitting at the table with an instant coffee and a cigarette, and sometimes he'll have a pencil and he'll be adding things up on the back of an envelope. Then he'll sigh and put it away.

One of his visitors, in the spring, shortly after he came home, was Angus MacDonald from Long Point. They call him Angus Jim Malcolm, and he's a prospector, and he actually grew up on MacIntyre's Mountain too. I was interested in the conversation because I've read a lot about prospectors in Western books and the comics.

Angus Jim Malcolm was talking about a murder, so I couldn't help but listen in.

A friend of his in Quebec had just been charged with murdering some Americans and was going on trial for his life.

I felt a terrible thrill at those words—"on trial for his life." And I was thinking about those same words as they were used before the Rosenbergs were electrocuted in Sing Sing for being spies.

I'll always remember who Angus Jim Malcolm was talking about because he had an interesting name—Bill Coffin.

Angus was saying what a nice guy he was, but that he was a terrible thief.

The reason he was blamed for murdering some hunters was because he was caught with stuff that belonged to them. He kept saying they gave it to him, but nobody believes him.

"He'd steal the eyes out of you, but he wouldn't kill a fly," said Angus Jim Malcolm.

And the men in the kitchen all agreed that Coffin was innocent, but that he was in deep trouble because he was an Englishman in Quebec and because the dead people were Americans.

When the visitor was gone, I asked my father if Angus Jim Malcolm's friend Coffin was going to be electrocuted, and my father said no, we don't do that here.

"What do we do here?"

"We hang them."

For all his troubles, my father is happier at home. You can tell he loves to sit there at his end of the table, eating his *sgadan* (salt herring) and blue potatoes or his corned beef and cabbage like a starved man. Or lying on the kitchen lounge listening to *Fun at Five* or the fiddle music and making a dark worn spot on the wall where he leans his head. And playing cribbage with my mother in the evenings, going to bed for a nap on Sunday afternoons, and, when it rains, going out and sitting in the truck just to listen to the rain rattling on the roof. He says he loves the sound and that it makes him sleepy, because, when he was a boy on the mountain, there was no ceiling in the bedroom where he and John Dan slept and they'd be listening to the rain and the hail and they'd think how lucky they were to be under a roof and not like the poor people who didn't even have places to live.

"Being poor is having neither pot to piss in nor window to throw it out through," they say.

We both love the sound of the wind in the big poplar trees that seem to surround our house—constantly rustling and sighing as you slide off into the magical world of sleep where anything is possible.

All July we were following the Coffin trial in Quebec because we knew somebody who knew him. Every day the paper would have a story, and every day Coffin looked worse. They were even trying to get his common-law wife to testify against him because, according to the lawyers who opposed him, a common-law wife doesn't matter the way a real wife does. Everybody knows real wives aren't supposed to testify against their husbands.

Coffin's lawyers were trying to force the other side to tell them who else they had as witnesses against him. The judge thought that would set "a dangerous precedent." Everything was complicated by the fact that they had to use both English and French because some witnesses couldn't speak one or the other language. Coffin could speak only English and, because of that, my mother said, he's as good as hanged already.

My father said we had to wait to hear his side of the story. That the real truth would come out then and, English or French, in the end they wouldn't hang an innocent man.

Then, in early August, when it was his turn, Coffin's lawyer got up and announced he wasn't calling any witnesses at all. Not one. Not even Coffin.

It was hard to believe, until I remembered what they were saying about lawyers when my aunt had her water problem.

It took only twenty-eight minutes for the jury to announce that Coffin was guilty. The judge sentenced him to hang on November 26, 1954.

It is December 10 and he is still alive. My mother says they're just prolonging the agony.

My father seems sad because of the Coffin trial. I think he knows a lot of men like Coffin. People who, other people say, "are their own worst enemies." People whose lives never quite get started in a direction that might lead them anywhere better than where they started out. Men who are basically good and funny and loyal to their friends, but who never manage to get ahead of where they were yesterday. They start each day a little bit behind where they want to be, then, eventually, out of desperation, they do something really dumb to get a little bit of control over their life.

I think he's had a lot of time to compare himself to guys like Coffin and to figure out what makes him different. Even though he came from the middle of nowhere with nothing, compared to Coffin, he's done okay. He has a family and a home, even though he hasn't been able to spend a lot of time with them. He was brought up strictly: no stealing or crooked work, no matter how tough things get. Faith, too—even though he doesn't show it and taps his foot when the rosary gets too long, and sometimes he gets a strange expression when poor

Father Doyle is rambling on about God's Infinite Mercy and Justice, etc. Even then, you can tell, he has the Faith, and that makes one of the differences between him and Coffin.

And now he has hope. Now there's a chance he will finally get ahead of yesterday. Maybe even get a head start on tomorrow. And it's all because there was a Gaelic-speaking politician from here named Angus L. and a granite mountain five hundred feet high at the narrowest part of the Strait of Canso. And because, within minutes, there will be a causeway.

At eight o'clock there is a roar as another forty tons of rock tumbles from the edge of the causeway and splashes into the water—and sits there. The gap is closed. I see a small group of men race over the edge of the point, into what, a day ago, was a swirling, deadly torrent of angry water. There are five of them. They leap onto a boulder, one behind the other, on their way into the history books. Among them I recognize a neighbour. It is Joe Larter from up the hill, via Korea. Just behind him, Lennie MacDonald, whose father, Mickey Johnnie Sandy, drives the snowplough. And Mr. Wendelblo, the well driller. They scramble through the darkness until I can barely see them now, half crawling up through the rubble on the other side like children, racing to be first.

5

THE *BOCAN* BRIDGE

It glimmers in the pale moonlight.
And you can see it any night—
provided you have second sight—
the *bocan* bridge of Canso.

Two things always tell you that you're in trouble—arms folded across the chest and a certain intensity in the eyes that you know can penetrate skin, bone, brain, and your innermost thoughts when the Irish is up. When the arms are folded and the blue eyes are illuminated by her secret power, you know the war is over before it starts. Defence, denial, resistance, flight—all the normal things commended by your loathsome guilt—are futile. The naked brain, advised I suppose by something ancient in the soul, screams out, "Surrender! Now! It can only get worse."

And so, when, after a long and disabling silence, she announces that she knows I have started smoking, it takes only a split second for me to confess.

Actually, I nod my head. The voice is choked off by a sudden loss of confidence in my knowledge of the language. Then the words trickle out.

"Yes. I was smoking."

"Where?"

"In the woods. Back of the cove."

"You and who else?"

Who else? Here I sense a small margin of room for manoeuvre. How many must I bring down with me? Billy? Ralph and Donnie (new guys, brought in by the causeway)? Jackie Nick? Donald Cameron (who once caused me to piss my pants)?

"Donald Cameron."

"Donald Cameron?"

"Yes."

"Smoking cigarettes with Donald Cameron."

"Yes."

"And you know what the Camerons are like?"

"Yes."

"You remember what Angus L. Cameron did to you?"

"Yes."

"I'm extremely disappointed in you."

I cringe. A beating from Miss Euphemia MacKinnon's braided wire wouldn't sting as much. "I'm disappointed in you." Words of total condemnation when directed at, until recently, the man of the house—the member of the family with the undefined, unspoken, but nevertheless burdensome responsibility to make things easier. At the very least obliged to avoid making things harder in a house where the father is away a lot.

And the reference to Angus L. Cameron is staggering.

Here's what happened. It was after the construction started down below Billy Malone's, where they were moving the railroad. It was early spring, and a spell of snow and rain and heavy machinery had turned the workplace into a sea of soupy mud. The mire was at least eight inches deep.

Angus L.'s father is Finlay Cameron, the railway station agent. Billy and I bumped into Angus L. near the station. He called me Spruce or

Linda or something, and so I said something saucy back. That's how I am. Sometimes I just can't keep my big mouth shut. The chase was on—he after me, through the mud as fast as I could run.

Angus L. is at least five years older than I am, and we have a history. Once when I said something saucy back to him, he caught me, and, while Walter MacKinnon, who is the same age as he is, held me down, he shoved a bun of horse manure into my mouth. Luckily it was old, dried-out horse manure, so it didn't kill me. I kept that incident to myself.

Another time he was pounding me, and my Aunt Veronica came along. He ran, but she chased him. She finally caught him at Mr. Clough's and gave him one on the jaw and asked how he liked it. His father called the Mounties, and they came to see my aunt but didn't do anything when they heard the whole story.

The day he went after me in the mud wasn't something I could easily conceal. He caught me. Then, gripping me by the back of the neck and the back of my pants, he picked me up and sluiced me through the muck face first. Even Billy laughed—at least for a second, until he realized how much trouble I was in.

But then I discovered I wasn't in trouble after all. I was a victim. That makes all the difference in the world. Once when I taunted Binky MacLellan and he slugged me, I went running home for sympathy, my nose pouring blood. My mother checked it out and told me that is what happens when you shoot off at people bigger than you are.

"Damned good enough for you," says she. "Remember this."

But when my mother found out that it was Angus L. and how I really didn't deserve this assault because he started it, she put her coat on and marched down to the railway station and confronted his father, Finlay. This is what happens when their Irish is up. Some people might wait until the father comes home. Not her. She'll go after anybody. Even somebody as important as the station agent, even if it isn't going to do her any good. Her sister is the same way. My Aunt Veronica will go after anybody, no matter how important. And their brothers, even Uncle Joe who isn't much taller than I am—I've heard stories about him and Uncle Francis at the dances down north, and going after people twice their size even if they didn't have a prayer of winning.

My mother barged into the station and gave Finlay Cameron hell. Billy Malone went right to the door and heard it all, and reported back afterwards with his eyes like saucers.

The truth, of course, is that Finlay Cameron did what he always does—denies that any of his kids could ever do anything wrong. After all, they're Camerons, and the Camerons have always been heroes. The *L* in Angus L. stands for "Lochiel," who was one of the most heroic Highlanders in history. And it was scandalous that people went around blaming a good boy like Angus L. for everything. And didn't poor Angus L. almost die once when he and Chum Chiavari were fooling around with a shotgun and it went off and the slug passed through his guts, making a hole the size of your fist?

But according to Billy, my mother stood her ground and got the last word in, which Billy couldn't remember exactly.

And now here I stand: correctly accused of smoking cigarettes in the woods with Donald Cameron, who is Finlay's son and the younger brother of the notorious Angus L. And she's understandably Disappointed in Me, which is the worst thing in the world that could happen. Worse than the Communist takeover of Russia and Hungary and China and half of Korea. Worse than if we'd set the woods on fire the way some kids, smoking and fooling around with matches, burned down the old dance hall and almost took Clough's store and the Reynoldses' house with it.

My moral victory over Angus L. Cameron is erased.

"Where, pray tell, did the cigarettes come from?"

"Donald got them." (The truth.)

"And where did Donald get them?"

"He put them on his father's bill at Clough's."

I imagine a twinkle in the eyes. Everybody has a bill at Mr. Clough's.

"He what?"

"He went to Clough's and bought a pack of Sweet Caporal, a loaf of bread, and a jar of sandwich spread and told Clough to charge them to his father's bill-book. And then we went out in the woods and made a campfire and then made sandwiches and ate them. And smoked most of the cigarettes."

"And Clough didn't ask who the cigarettes were for?"

"He did."

"And?"

"Donald said they were for Eileen."

Eileen is their older sister, and she smokes. And when we were in the woods smoking, we were laughing at how cool Donald was when he told Clough the smokes were for Eileen. Laughing and laughing and smoking, and Donald glowing in all the attention.

"Ask me," he orders. "Pretend you're old Clough and ask me: 'Eileen who?'"

"Eileen who?" I obey, trying to sound like Mr. Clough but laughing and choking on sandwiches and smoke.

Donald puts on his cocky face and says: "*I-lean* over, you kiss my arse."

And, of course, that has everybody on the ground choking and gasping at the courage and the wit of Donald Cameron, who, anybody could tell, was from a long line of Highland heroes and who would have said it right to Mr. Clough's face—if only he'd been asked who Eileen was.

"I don't ever want to hear of you smoking again," she said.

And I swore to it.

"Don't you think we have enough to worry about around here without you going around with the Camerons and behaving like a ruffian?"

In my guilty misery, I make my way to the old cemetery that overlooks the new causeway. Even the dog seems ashamed of me and walks behind me at a distance. He probably just respects my sorrow, but in my contaminated imagination I assume rejection. My mouth is sour from its bitterness.

Below the cemetery there is the new road, from the canal to the village. It is still jagged with blasted rock, still acrid from the chemistry of explosion. Large road-building machines roar below me. The giant Euclids still move about the face of Cape Porcupine, now hauling even larger stones out onto the causeway to be dumped along its flanks to provide armour against the relentless tides. You realize, watching this activity, that, from Nature's point of view, the causeway is just another inconvenience—as with all human installations. Nature will now intensify the effort to remove it—imperceptible erosion, the sudden battery of winter storms, the grinding drift of ice. It might take forever, but Nature has forever to complete her project. Nothing made by man can be forever.

The silent headstones around me briefly note the transience of all human enterprise. Each grave occupied by what was once a person real as me, buffeted outside by Nature, torn inside by something called emotion—forces that are as unmanageable as they are unpredictable because they are responses to the unexpected.

Over there, just beyond the trench that is becoming a canal, is that other cemetery—probably the first cemetery around here, now carefully excluded from the destruction of what was. Only a few weathered tombstones are left. One reads "Douce Elizabeth Balhache, departed this life July 1793." Aged six. Daughter of Douce Hulbert Balhache, native of Jersey. I wonder: what must that be like, losing your only kid? Of course, they say Mrs. Balhache was tough. She got over the loss— even got over it after her husband disappeared at sea. She personally took over their family business, a two-thousand-acre farm, a weaving business. She even ran the quarry at Plaster Cove.

What is it about women? I wonder. Where do they get that . . . whatever they have?

The engineers and drillers, blasters and truckers, all seem to tiptoe around the final resting place of young Douce Elizabeth—and Christina Skinner, and James Skinner. People long forgotten, except for a few words on stones that are slowly being erased by the grimy wind. Even the name Balhache is strange here now, though once it was important. Old maps designate the location of the lighthouse as Balhache Point, but we know it now as Nicholson's Point because of Jackie and his grandmother. And now they are gone too. Soon there will be no name at all, no point. The causeway—that's what it is now, part of a road. A road, the adults say, to bring people home. A road, I know, that will one day carry me away. And on this day of shame, nothing in the future can be soon enough.

My father says that the causeway will last longer than we will. I am reassured.

My father isn't like the women in the family. Maybe it's because he doesn't have any Irish. He doesn't talk much. He is "easy going." They say my father could be a dangerous man if he ever got rattled. Fortunately, he doesn't—at least not very often. And I know my smoking would never rattle him, which is why she didn't bother telling him.

Some mothers around here terrorize their kids by threatening to report them to their fathers. My mother never does that. It wouldn't do her any good.

I have seen him angry only twice and, both times, I was the cause. But the consequences were pretty mild, at least for me. The first time I was teasing the dog by putting my face close to his and growling. Suddenly, the dog bit me. Chomp. One fang punctured just under my eye, another made a little hole at the corner of my mouth. My father heard the racket and went to a tree and cut off a small branch. I tried to tell him it was my fault, but he said it didn't matter. Once a dog starts biting people, that will be the end of him. He has to learn early. And he caught Skipper by the scruff of the neck and whipped him. The dog kept spinning around and yelping and looking at my father with the saddest expression I ever saw, except for the one on my father's face.

Afterwards, the dog crept away and hid behind the barn. My father went in the other direction and sat silently on the doorstep for a long time. Later, the dog crawled up to him, and they were friends again.

The other time was more serious. It was after I got my first bicycle, and I drove in front of a car.

I almost made it all the way across the road before I heard the screech of rubber on pavement. The car clipped my back wheel and sent me and the bike flying into the ditch. I didn't even fall off because the bike somehow landed upright, with me sitting on it looking stupid. I heard someone shout my name, loud and angrily. And when I looked, my father was running down the Green Path, which used to be called Saddler Street. Running! The man who never walked faster than a saunter, who couldn't even ride a bicycle, who almost fell off mine when he tried it once. Running towards me like a sprinter and shouting my name, which I rarely ever heard him say because he always called me "boy" or "bub."

For a moment I thought I was about to be murdered, but then he seemed to notice I was alive and realized it wouldn't make much sense to kill me now. And he seemed to know the driver of the car, who was just sitting there with an amused expression, leaning out his window, looking at me as he slowly lit a cigarette.

My father went to the car, and they were talking about how stunned young fellas are most of the time. And then they were both lecturing me about how we couldn't play on the roads anymore now that there is a causeway, and with the Trans-Canada Highway coming through.

Those were the only two times, though I'm sure he could get as wild as anybody else. And I even heard a story once about how he flattened somebody with one punch when the guy attacked him for no good reason. But, if we were alike, he'd have hated that as much as I do when I get into fights. The way I see it, nobody wins a fight.

Once when I was waiting for the train at the station in town after a movie, I saw two men fighting. They both seemed drunk and weren't doing much harm. But I felt a terrible dread because, I suppose, drunk men fighting out behind the railway station can do a lot of damage if they want to—even kill somebody.

At first this fight was more like kids pushing and grabbing. And then one of the men seemed to be giving up, and he laughed as though it had all been a big game and stuck out his hand for a shake. But when the other fellow stopped and stuck out his hand, the first guy hauled off and smashed him in the face. The sound was like nothing I ever heard before. I imagined something like a baseball bat slammed against the carcass of a pig or a calf hanging upside down in the barn.

The man who was hit just slumped to the ground and stayed there on his knees, as if he was praying.

I could see blood coming out of the corner of his mouth and snot running out of his nose. And then another terrible sound—him whimpering like the dog. And then sobbing and trying to talk. Something about being a returned man, which I know is somebody who was in the war.

It was the sound of him crying, I think. And about him being a returned man. And the blood and the snot. I could feel my knees wobbling and, to keep from falling down, I started running and didn't stop until I had to throw up.

I have never seen my father frightened. And I have never seen him cry.

I'm not as bothered when I see women going after people with their Irish up. Women usually don't try to kill people—just humiliate—and as bad as that might be, you get over it.

———

Suddenly my father was home for good, but we didn't make much of a fuss about it. For one thing, he'd been home for good before. For another, his coming home wasn't always a hundred percent good thing.

I remember other times, and my sisters, who are little girls, going, "Daddy's coming home, Daddy's coming home," hopping around and squealing the way little girls do when they're excited. And I, waiting to see exactly what would happen when and if he did show up. And more often than not, a car with an Ontario licence, or Quebec or Manitoba, stopping in the lane that ran by the house. And men inside talking, just sitting there in the car, with me wondering why he wasn't getting out.

And then, finally, he'd clamber out, and they'd fetch the canvas duffel bag from the trunk and the little suitcase he called his grip. And he'd straighten up and come into the house with short, careful steps and a tight little smile on his face. My mother would be sizing him up while the little girls grabbed at his legs, and he'd look at me and ask how the old place was, and then I'd join the girls and grab him around the waist.

They'd be asking what he brought and he'd say "Nothing," but later you knew he'd have something, and he'd eventually dig it out of the grip and, if he'd passed through Toronto or Montreal, it would be special.

Once he brought me a Toronto Maple Leafs ring, even though I know he wasn't interested in hockey. I wasn't very interested in hockey either, and I lost the ring the day after I got it. But it was exciting to get it and to have it, even for a little while.

It seems he was always coming home for good, especially the time he came home hurt and wearing a cast from his belly to his neck. He'd have plans and projects, but you knew there were no jobs because he didn't have any schooling. And so he'd buy a truck. But, unless there was a big job like paving a road, there was never enough work for the truck because he didn't have any politics. Then you'd see him around the house a lot—just sitting at the kitchen table, drinking instant coffee and smoking cigarettes and staring into space. And, sooner or later, he'd always have to go away again.

So it was, even after we moved home from Newfoundland, where I and my sister Danita, who is the older of the two girls, were born. The war was over, and he was finished in the fluorspar mine and determined to start fresh back where he came from. He'd get some trucks and start up a sawmill on MacIntyre's Mountain. We'd live in the village, happily ever after. This was the plan.

I wasn't very old—two or three. But I still remember things from that time. My Uncle Francis getting out of a taxi on a rainy day wearing a sailor's uniform and dragging a big duffel bag like the one my father has for his mining gear. And bringing gifts for me: a toy penguin and a shot glass. And I remember them all giggling about the shot glass, and hiding it because Father Gallivan arrived suddenly for a visit. And an old brown house with electric lights. And my mother one evening catching a snake just as he started swallowing a toad. And though she's terrified of snakes, she went after that one and beat it to death with a stick. And, afterwards, this snow-white toad came crawling out of the dead snake and hopped away to start life all over again, just like us. And my father being at the mountain a lot, trying to make a go of it. And us moving into the old tailor's place and not having electricity anymore. And noticing for the first time how the grown-ups change and forget you're there when they're talking quietly about money and mortgages and Mr. Walker, who is the banker in town. And the way they were talking, you couldn't be sure whether Mr. Walker was helping us or trying to put us in the poorhouse.

And my father disappearing sometimes, then showing up with fish eyes and his tight little smile and the strange sour smell. And I'd realize that this was probably the look and smell of his anger and his sadness.

This time would be different, I suspected. At the peak of the canal project, there was enough work to keep the truck running day and night, and he hired somebody to drive it when he was too tired to drive it anymore himself.

That seemed to be when a lot of the trouble started. People he hired to drive the truck didn't treat it as carefully as he did. Soon there were problems. Some of the problems were small, like having to clean spit off the door because one of his drivers chewed tobacco and wasn't very good at spitting, and the wind was always blowing the juice back against the truck. Other problems were more serious—broken axles and drive shafts and hoists, and flat tires.

My mother would shake her head. Tobacco spit on the truck door! The handwriting is on the wall, she'd say. But he was optimistic. Once he got his one truck sorted out with a good driver, he'd buy another. And my mother warning that you can't rely on anybody but yourself. And if he bought a second truck, sure, they'd be lining up to ruin that one too.

Once there was a rumour that Mr. Clough was interested in selling his store and retiring, and my father, maybe joking, said he should try to scrounge some money so he could buy it and become a storekeeper.

And my mother saying that would be Just Great—him the storekeeper, and feeding half of out back and never getting paid for it.

To be successful in business, she'd say, you have to be hard-nosed. You have to have a head for business, which means looking people in the eye and demanding that they pay their bills on time. And when they don't, you have to be tough, the way the old-time merchants were—even if it meant taking somebody's property away from them because of their debts, which used to happen all the time around here. It was how a lot of the poor people ended up in Newfoundland, evicted from farms over here by merchants. But that was how certain people became successful and wealthy. And, in the long run, success and wealth weren't worth turning into something like that, squeezing money out of poor farmers and fishermen. At the same time, you wouldn't want to turn into a sheep, being fleeced by everybody who knew you.

She'd say: "Don't think that Mr. Clough or Mr. Walker became successful by being nice to people."

He'd just look at the floor, thinking about what she said, knowing in his heart that she was usually right about people.

What finally convinced me that this time was different was when he went on the wagon.

My father isn't a big drinker. I know some big drinkers around here. You can always tell by the smell off them. There's the sweet smell of wine, and the stale smell of sweaty clothes and the outdoors, where they often sleep. The drinkers wander around a lot on foot because they don't own cars, and their houses are rarely places where they want to be for long. There's a family of Frasers like that, living out back but walking to town several times a week to scrounge money and buy wine.

Angus and his boys. I heard in school that they're distant relatives of the famous explorer, Simon Fraser, and they're the way they are because Angus lost his wife, who was the boys' mother, and they never got over it. You see them walking together out the Victoria Line, then towards town, quiet and shy. Once Billy Malone and I came upon them sitting in the rain, out back of Mr. McGowan's store, eating raw baloney and drinking wine from a bottle.

My father says there's no harm in them at all, except for what they're doing to themselves.

But there are others who wait until they get drunk to go after people they have grudges against, or just to work off their frustrations. I can hear them, and even see them sometimes, when there are dances in the school. I'll stand in my dark room at the open window, listening to the music. Then, suddenly, I'll hear them shouting and see the crowd gathering to watch, some people in the crowd urging them to go at it or go home. And one night I saw a grown man taking his shirt off to fight and looking completely foolish because it was summer and he was wearing long combination woollen underwear, and the crowd started laughing and the fight went out of him because of the mockery. He finally just walked away into the dark without the shirt.

My father never gets angry when he drinks. Sometimes he gets full of big ideas, and my mother just sits in the rocking chair listening and nodding her head. The big ideas usually involve trucks and sawmills. Sometimes he gets silly, and she gets angry. Sometimes he gets sad and stays away from home. Then he comes back, looking sorry for himself, and once, when he brought home pork chops as a peace offering, she threw them at him.

I think he went on the wagon after that.

I don't know much about liquor because I don't see it around very often. And mostly when I do, people are having a good time—as when my uncle Joe Donohue shows up with a bottle and, usually, some priest in tow. Or the Capstick cousins from down north. My mother and her sister Veronica will talk and sing and dance and carry on with them like teenagers. Or when my mother and father decide to have a treat, and they buy some beer and lobsters. And once, when my mother wasn't feeling well and was losing weight, the doctor ordered her to drink stout, which is a kind of beer. And people would make jokes about catching whatever wonderful ailment requires drinking beer for the cure.

Then there are nights when you hear the dogs barking and a ruckus up the hill where people are drinking. There are two bachelor brothers up there living with the family of the third brother, and most of the time they're completely normal and quiet. Then they get drinking and fighting and terrorizing the house.

One night there was a knock at our door, and it was the sober brother coming down to ask my father if he'd be good enough to go up to the house with him and help take a gun away from his brothers, who seemed determined to murder each other. One of them had grabbed a rifle, but the other had the bullets, and they were wrecking the house fighting to get control of both.

My father just put his coat on and, as he went out, he told me to go down and ask Angus Walker, who had the nearest phone, to call the Mounties—and I did. But Angus came back from the phone looking grim and said the Mounties refused to come. They knew the gentlemen in question and weren't interested in their disputes.

This, of course, is a common problem: I've heard it said it's dangerous to get in between fighting brothers, or a husband and wife, because of the strong possibility that they'll forget their dispute and turn on yourself. Mounties obviously know these things, and it was my job to report back to the scene of the action.

My father and the peaceful brother were waiting for the cops, watching the fighting brothers through a window, and seemed surprised when I arrived.

I kept it brief because I was out of breath.

"They won't come."

So my father and the sober brother just looked at each other for a moment, then marched into the house. And through the window I could see each of them go after a drunken brother and, before long, they came out with the rifle and the bullets. And, suddenly, everything inside the house was quiet.

Another night I heard a racket up the hill at a different house, where Mary and Johnny O'Handley live. You'd hear the stories. Mary and Johnny didn't get along very well. Johnny is kind of handicapped by a neck problem, which causes his head to be tilted to one side all the time. There's a man like that down north, and they call him "Ten to Six." They say that when old Johnny gets thirsty he'll go out to the well with the dipper, take his drink, and then pour what's left in the dipper back down the well. If Mary wants a drink, she can go out and get it herself. It's what they say, anyway.

The problem is that Mary also drinks liquor and spends most of what she earns scrubbing floors for people in town on wine and chewing tobacco. You know Mary chews by the small lump in her cheek and the brown stain at the corner of her mouth. They say that, as she scrubs, she spits her tobacco juice into the scrubbing pail, and that is her secret formula for making floors look clean and shiny.

The night of the racket at O'Handleys' you couldn't tell whether it was a fight or a party, but the next morning I knew there was something wrong when I saw the priest's car backing out of their lane.

It was the curate, Father O'Brien, who was filling in for Father Doyle, who had died on New Year's Day.

It had rained during the night and, for a day in February, it was mild. But the rain left the hill a solid sheet of ice. I was at the woodpile and, when Father O'Brien was coming down the hill, I saw his car suddenly begin to slide sideways and slowly drift into the ditch in front of the school.

He climbed out and looked around and, I guess, spotted the truck at our place. So he came up and asked my father if he could pull him out of the ditch. My father agreed and got the truck going and put a chain on the priest's car. Then he got a bucket of ashes from the ash pile beside the barn and spread it on the ice and got the priest's car out without much trouble. When he came back to the house, he said that Father O'Brien had informed him that poor Mary O'Handley had passed away just that morning.

"Died sitting at her table," he said, "with the breakfast in front of her." Isn't that the way life is? they were saying. We never know from one minute to the next.

Poor Mary, sitting at the table, all dressed for the day, with the breakfast in front of her, little knowing as she was preparing it that she'd never live to eat it.

Of course, it wasn't long before the gossip started. And they'd stop talking about Mary when there were kids around. But I could hear it, even if I didn't quite understand or ever get to the bottom of it. About a party and something happening to Mary, and people dressing her up in her good clothes and propping her up at the table and putting the breakfast in front of her to make everything look natural.

Anybody I asked about it would just look at me angrily and wonder where on earth I was hearing foolishness like that. So I stopped asking, but they continued to whisper about poor Mary. And I kept watching to see the Mountie's car going up the hill and turning into O'Handleys' lane. But they never came. And soon Mary was forgotten, like Douce Elizabeth Balhache and all the others who pass through here briefly.

———

From up by the camps now, when we're collecting the bottles Old John saves for us, the causeway looks as though it has always been there. There is something quite natural about it, probably because the rock matches the craggy face of the cape from which it came. Early in January we saw a train creeping out over the causeway, and it was an amazing sight—like someone walking on water. It was moving carefully, puffing and shunting, the wheels squealing on the new rails. Old John said they were using the train to haul out more rails and ties and gravel, so they could finish the job and get the trains moving regularly from the mainland to Cape Breton. Big pressure, he said, because of the steel and coal that had to keep moving.

There's a chain across the entrance to the new causeway to keep the cars off, but somebody cut it so they could drive out and be first to take a car across, even though Mr. Harry MacKenzie had already done that, claiming the fame for being first in the middle of December, just after they dumped the last load of rock. He even got his name in the paper for it.

But by the end of January, you'd see the occasional car creeping over. January 22 there was a little convoy—all twenty-five members of the Inverness County Council. They stopped at one point and got out to take pictures—a strange group of important men on an important mission. They were going over to inspect the asylum in Mulgrave, where, it seems, most of the people are originally from Inverness County. According to the paper, this was "the first official group to cross the now famous structure."

The officials made serious comments. There was nothing in the paper about the reaction of the poor people in the place they were going to inspect.

The paper is saying that the causeway will be officially open for everybody by April, but Old John doesn't think so. Maybe by the end of the summer, he says.

Old John, whose real name is John Suto, is tall and thin and bald and he never seems to sit down. Even when we're there talking, he stands as if he's ready to disappear at any moment. Sometimes I ask him about where he came from, but he doesn't seem to want to talk about it.

Mr. Malone, who also works for the Gorman construction company, says there's a big story hidden in Old John's past, and that just makes him interesting along with being nice. I figure the story has to do with where he comes from, and maybe the war and what happened afterwards.

Hungary, he says, is a sad place because there is no freedom—which, I understand, is because of the Communists, who even put a Catholic cardinal in prison. He seems angry when he talks about Communists. Then some days he seems happier. And one Saturday morning, when we arrived, he was sitting in his tidy little room in the bunkhouse reading a letter. He was so absorbed in the letter that we had to knock on the door, even though it was already open. He looked up, confused. Then you could see how happy he was. He said we should watch the papers because things were happening back home, and soon there would be big surprises.

Hungarians have been fighting outsiders for a long, long time, he said, nodding his head.

So I started watching the papers closely for news from Hungary, but there was nothing but more sad news about people being persecuted.

———

I suppose if we'd lived in a bigger place with a bigger school, there would have been books and people who could have told us everything we want to know about places like Hungary. I understand there are libraries and running water in the bigger schools, and sports teams and organized competitions between schools in different communities.

We have none of that here. There is a bookshelf with some large books called *The Book of Knowledge*. The other shelves are empty. The only evidence that it is a school is the blackboard and the rows of desks and the smell of chalk dust and Dustbane. For the first four months of this school year we didn't even have a teacher.

I'm not sure how it happened, but by late summer last year people were talking about the fact that no teacher was available for the Big Room. The Little Room had Mrs. Martha Hennessey, but from grade six up we were going to have to start the new year with correspondence courses. Our lessons would come in large packages from Halifax, and we would have a supervisor in the classroom to make sure we did them and behaved.

The supervisor, Mrs. Mary Ellen MacNamara, had an awful time. I thought it was great fun, watching the older kids carrying on, coming and going and tormenting the poor woman at the teacher's desk. I was getting my work done at home, under the eye of my mother, who is a schoolteacher herself.

Going to school was crazy, with nobody doing a stroke of work and just wandering around the room as if there was no adult there at all.

By the end of January, just in time to salvage the year, we had a real teacher, Mrs. Dolly MacDonald from Judique, and the foolishness stopped—really quickly.

We call her Dolly when we talk about her, the way we used to call Miss MacKinnon Phemie when she couldn't hear us. Mrs. Katie Gillis was always Mrs. Gillis because she gave you the impression she could read your mind and hear everything you were saying or thinking, even when she was nowhere near you. Once someone had an apple he wanted to share but didn't have anything to cut it. Mrs. Gillis, who is an old lady, took the apple in her hands and, with a quick twist, split it in two pieces as neatly as if she'd used a knife. Even the bigger boys were impressed.

Even out back of the cove, where no adult ever went, you'd refer to her as Mrs. Gillis because, somehow, she always knew what you were up to.

But Dolly was different. She was friendly and always had a kind expression on her face. You couldn't picture Dolly splitting an apple with her bare hands. It took a lot to make her angry, but, when it happened, the whole room would go cold because of her disappointment. So everybody seemed to work hard to avoid upsetting her.

Obviously she noticed that the school had nothing but the bare necessities—not even books on the bookshelves. Shortly after she arrived there was talk about putting on a variety concert to raise money for school supplies. School kids and adults would prepare a program of entertainment. This was something new. In the past we'd have Christmas concerts for the entertainment of our parents, but never before, as far as I know, did we have adults and kids on the same stage entertaining the public.

There were meetings in the evenings, and soon there was a program. I didn't have much to do with it, except for helping get the stage ready, and that suited me just fine.

My part in the Christmas concert the last year I was in the Little Room was a poem called "A Small Boy's Pockets"—about all the junk mothers find in a kid's pants. As I recited each verse, I was supposed to reach into my pocket and pull something out. There was a jackknife, a marble, a rabbit's foot, and a few other things. But to make my pockets look really full, the teacher stuffed them full of balled-up paper. The problem was that she put so much paper in my pocket that I couldn't find the things I was supposed to find to match the verses. It was a terrible struggle, with balls of paper falling out of my pockets and causing me to lose my place, and everybody laughing because they thought my confusion was all part of the performance.

The next day at the mail, Mr. Clough told me it was the best part of the concert and gave me two of the cookies with the spot of jam in the middle. But I knew the truth—my performance had been a disaster, and I was determined not to let it happen again.

Studying the program for the variety concert, I was relieved not to be on it but surprised to see my father's name, Dan R. MacIntyre. He and Angus Walker Sr. were in a "skit." A skit, I understood, is a little performance that's supposed to be funny. My father and Angus Walker Sr.? Funny?

Mr. Walker is a photographer who has a studio near the causeway. He also built a small canteen, attached to the studio, where you can buy hot dogs and ice cream, cigarettes and other treats from his mother-in-law, Mrs. Lew Reynolds. It was one of the first signs of new business when they were building the causeway. Next door, where Johnny Morrison had his blacksmith shop, another Mr. Morrison started turning the old forge into an Esso service station.

My father is funny at home or when he's speaking Gaelic, but not like the performers in the movies or on the radio. And I never heard Angus Walker Sr. being funny at all, which is not to say that he couldn't be comical in private. But being funny in front of everybody is another matter altogether.

There were lots of other performances on the program though, and I soon put my father's out of my mind. There was Angus Walker Jr., who is a talented guitar player and wants to become the next Hank Williams. There was a short play put on by adults, plus the usual fiddle playing and Gaelic singing. And Dolly was going to bring her son Lewis, who, she said, had a nice voice and would render some Scottish selections. That was how she described it—render Scottish selections. Probably "The Road to the Isles" or "Scots Wha Hae."

———

My father is reading the paper at the kitchen table. The story is about Coffin. The paper is using his formal name. Wilbert, not Bill. My father looks serious.

"What's happening?"

"The Quebec courts upheld the death sentence."

"Oh."

"Yep."

"Does that mean they're going to hang him?"

"Nah. There'll be the Supreme Court of Canada. All that Quebec stuff, about English and French and them being Americans from Pennsylvania, won't matter there."

"What about the Boyd Gang guys?" I ask.

I am dubious. Everybody in the country seemed to be cheering for the Boyd Gang and especially Edwin Alonzo Boyd, their boss. Even Grandma Donohue and my mother, who usually think crooks should get what they deserve. But in spite of all their popularity, they still hanged two of Edwin Alonzo Boyd's gangsters.

The Boyd Gang killed a cop, my father says. Coffin didn't kill anybody. He's being railroaded.

Even when you know that things are bothering my father, he doesn't show it. When I say something that older people think is ridiculous, they say, "You're full of shit" or "Your hole is out." Once, when we were talking about the causeway and I said the Communists would certainly destroy it with an atomic bomb in the next world war, Pipe Major Cameron, who was in the last world war, told me: "Your hole is out so far you can cut *washers* off of it."

The worst thing my father ever said was: "You're full of old rope."

After he finishes reading about Coffin, he just shakes his head and folds the paper carefully.

My father seems to keep most things inside his head, even when he's with people he knows well. They sit in the kitchen, men pouring tea into saucers, their caps on their knees. When they smoke cigarettes, they carefully put the ashes in the cuff on the bottom of the trouser leg. When they're leaving, you see them outside, carefully brushing the ashes away.

Sometimes they sit in silence for what seems like an hour. Then there will be a short sentence. Just a few words, and they'll remember a common experience or some common knowledge. And then there will be head shaking and sad glances or maybe a sudden brief explosion of laughter.

This is how it is with friends and relatives, and I realize that the more we have in common, the less we have to say for understanding. And how difficult it must be for my father when he is away, mostly among strangers, having to talk and explain everything he wants them to know. Or maybe being silent all the time.

———

The closer we got to the big concert, the more you could feel the excitement. Dolly had to work hard to keep the classroom under control. At home I would sit by The Hole at night, listening to rehearsals for the short play that the adults were preparing to put on. My mother had a part in it. I couldn't make head or tail out of it.

Once I asked what my father and Angus Walker were going to do, and they just told me to wait and see.

It was going to be a big surprise for everybody.

I'd have guessed a Gaelic song, even though I've never heard my father sing, and I don't think that Angus Walker knows any Gaelic.

Then again, maybe he's been listening to Major Calum Iain Norman MacLeod's Gaelic lessons on the radio.

I haven't heard them advance much beyond "Caite bheil bean an tighe" because my father turns the radio off right after the fiddle music program, which is before the Gaelic lessons by Major MacLeod and a girl named Seonaid.

It doesn't really matter because now that my father is home all the time and has a truck, I hear plenty of Gaelic all around me. People from out back drop in and, when my mother is out of the kitchen, they speak Gaelic. We often visit the mountain, and that seems to be the only language the grown-ups use out there. And it doesn't sound a bit like the careful, slow words that Major MacLeod and Seonaid use on the radio. At the mountain, the words flow like the water in Rough Brook which runs from the big marshlands up behind my grandfather's all the way down, emptying eventually into Inhabitants Bay.

When we go to the mountain, it's usually just my father and me. My mother and my sisters will say they're busy, but I suspect they get nervous when Grandma makes tea for us because they don't think her kitchen is clean enough—especially in the summer when the flies come and go through the open doors and windows as if they own the place. So just my father and I go, and we bring along something like a bag of potatoes or a small bottle of brandy, which Grandma swiftly hides somewhere in the closed part of the house. Even though Peigeag is death on liquor, she likes to have a little bottle of her own for medicine or special treats.

I suggested once that we should bring a bottle of DDT for all the flies. But my father says the stickers hanging in the kitchen do the job and, anyway, there isn't much point in DDT if you don't have screens to spray it on.

Grandma Peigeag always greets us at the door, babbling in a mixture of Gaelic and English. *M'eudail* Lindy, and running bony freckled hands that are surprisingly soft over my forehead and through my hair.

Grandpa Dougald will stand back, hands in his pockets, half giggling and wearing the same old sweater that he always wears, winter and summer.

On the mountain it is like being in a history book. There is no electricity or running water. There are no machines of any kind. They used to have a horse named Tony, but now the barn is empty and leaning over as if it will soon fall down. The walls and floors and ceilings in the house are just plain boards. The kitchen smells of burning wood and, when they stop talking, the only sound is the crackling of the stove and the wind against the windows, or the trees rustling outside or, if it's summertime, the buzz of invisible insects. The kitchen is dimly lit, but the walls and ceiling are dingy from wood smoke.

Once, on a winter day, just before we got there, somebody had been by and left a feed of smelt, which Grandma proposed to boil up with some of the new potatoes we brought.

My father looked at me and smiled. He said that would be great.

The way he looked at me he seemed to think that, like the others, I'm not too keen on Grandma Peggy's cooking either. But I don't mind it, and I like boiled smelt. I also knew that before we'd leave, she'd disappear briefly in the direction of where the brandy went and return with a couple of quarters and some special candy in a box that someone gave her at Christmas, but which hadn't yet been opened.

Nothing ever seems to change on the mountain. Everything is as it must have been a hundred years ago, except that there are fewer people now. I listen to the Gaelic conversations that flutter and flow around me—about the weather and the woods and the people they know. Grandma seems to speak English with her teeth. From what I can see, she has only three or four teeth, and you hear them clicking and sucking as she struggles with the foreign English words. The strain of the unfamiliar language makes her seem older and unsteady and a little simple. But when she speaks the Gaelic, smooth words flow easily from somewhere in the back of her throat, clear and confident, and my father and grandfather mostly sit and listen, nodding in agreement. Her voice deepens and she becomes younger somehow, eyes flashing and face changing every moment, hands flying. In Gaelic she has the authority of a teacher or a priest, and you understand why so many people are afraid of her.

They'll say: Peigeag has a wicked tongue in her head if you ever cross her, and if you're not careful she can invoke the *buidseachd*—even against her own.

But I don't worry about her because I also heard them say that Dan Rory is her favourite, being the youngest and because he almost died like the other two. She keeps a careful eye on him because she believes another old woman on the mountain once put a wish on him for something he did that displeased her. My cousins on the mountain tell me they have heard the talk: old Mary Ann put a wish on Dan Rory, that no matter how hard he worked at trying to succeed, he'd never know anything but bad luck.

They're usually smiling when they say it. But sometimes I feel a chill.

My grandparents live on a bare little hill that was once surrounded by open fields. I think, when I was four, I lived there for a while—but not in their house. I remember a lumber camp that my father built just after the war, just across the road and not far from an old abandoned house they call Big Mary's Place. Big Mary once lived over there with her husband, who was called "Domhnail am biast," which means Donald the Worm, because he was so tall and thin. But they were both long gone by then.

Further up the mountain, you can still see open spaces where there were farms belonging to two MacIntyres known as Big Norman and Little Norman. And the place where Angus Jim Malcolm, who was a friend of Wilbert Coffin, grew up. None of the farms have been there for years. Most of the people, I think, are either dead or in town or in Boston.

Just down below us there is the Dan B. MacIntyre place, and that is near where my grandfather and his brothers and sisters were all born. We are known as the Alasdair Chiorstaidhs, because that was the name of my grandfather's father and it means "Alexander who is the son of Christy." Usually people with names from history are called after the father, but my great-grandfather's father, whose name was Donald and who was born in Scotland, died when they were still kids, so they were raised and identified by their mother, Christy, who was a MacDonald. My grandfather is Dughail Alasdair Chiorstaidh. Dougald the son of Alexander the son of Christy. My father is Dan Rory Dougald.

My strange name doesn't require a *sloinneadh*, but I know that I am still a Chiorstaidh no matter what they call me. And that I'm a mountain MacIntyre.

Old Christy was, they say, like Grandma MacIntyre, a "powerful woman." She raised her kids alone after her husband's death, and then raised the children of her son, Alasdair Chiorstaidh, after his wife died and left him helpless. She raised my grandfather on the mountain, at least until he was big enough to go away.

I sometimes think of that priest in Scotland, telling them at the time of their eviction that their faith would lead them to prosperity. And that he should have seen them in the years beyond the sea. *An cuan siar*, they kept on calling it, even after they got here. It means the "Western Sea," even though it was now east of us. He should have seen them sitting in their dark, smoky kitchens, worrying about the weather and sickness up on MacIntyre's Mountain, or after the August Gale in the 1800s when all their houses and barns blew down. Or today, trying to make a living like a slave, breaking up rock deep in the belly of the earth, the only light available from a little lamp attached to their hard hats. After all those years, still struggling to settle down somewhere with the people they care about—exiled still.

And when we're walking down the mountain, I'll ask again: "How old were you when you went away?"

He'll think for a moment, then say: "Well. Not much older than yourself."

"Tell me again about going away?"

"Well," he'll say. "Going away is special, the first time. I bought a new suit for it. I paid fifteen dollars, and that was a lot of money then. I went to the railway station in Hastings and bought a ticket, but after the suit I only had enough money to get as far as Montreal."

On this day we are walking down the mountain because the snow was too deep to get the truck all the way up. It is a rare day because he seems to be in a mood for talking. The sun is sharp, and there are only a few puffy clouds in the blue sky. I can imagine him being sixteen and coming down the mountain in his new suit, with a few dollars in his pockets and big dreams in his head. Going away for good.

By now in the story it's as if I am not here with him. It's just himself, going away again for the first and last time.

"So I spent all my money on the train ticket to Montreal."

He laughs softly at the skinny boy with the new suit and the big ideas walking down the mountain road.

"The trouble is I was going to Senneterre. Do you know how far Senneterre is from Montreal?"

"No."

"Hundreds and hundreds of miles."

"So how did you get there?"

"In Montreal I found the train that was going north, and I snuck onto a car that was right behind the coal tender."

He shakes his head.

"Imagine what I looked like getting off that train? Black as . . ."

He stops and laughs.

"And after all that, they weren't hiring at the mine. So I had to sleep in the woods for about a week, living off what I could pilfer from gardens."

"Why didn't you ask somebody to let you stay in their house?"

"They aren't very friendly up there," he says. "Nope."

I considered telling him about the Syrian and Martin Angus in the porch at home, but decided not to.

"Not even a glass of water," he said. "They'll put the dog on you when they see you in the lane."

"Really?"

"Don't ever get stranded in Senneterre," he said.

"But you got a job?"

"Yup. Got a job hand muckin' and layin' track."

"What's hand muckin'?"

"Pick and shovel," he said. "But that didn't last long. Before long I was driving drifts and into the real work."

I didn't bother asking about drifts and real work because I didn't want to interrupt this rare moment when he was talking without seeming to notice. And because the sky was an unusually deep blue, and the snow was blinding in its purity. And though it was freezing cold outside, the walking wrapped you in a fine second skin of warmth and your blood sang.

He just talked and talked, and, near John Dan's, I decided to ask: "What happened there, up on the mountain, when you were small? Why did your little brother and sister die?"

"Ah well," he said. "That's a long, long story."

That was what he always said when he was through talking.

At John Dan's, Mae made more tea and asked me questions about school while my father and his brother talked softly in their secret language.

———

The plans for the big variety concert were just about complete, and again I am reminded that a school isn't just for kids—at least a village school. Our school is as much for the grown-ups as it is for those of us required to go there every day to learn math and English and history. I realize that the school has a whole nighttime life and that this is when the school really becomes the village. And that if there were no school here, the place would be like the mountain—a place where nothing happens except in the memory or the imagination.

You realize that the concerts and card games, dances and public meetings are like what happens at the kitchen table at home. People with memory in common get together for a single purpose—eating or praying or doing business or having fun—and it brings out surprising qualities in every individual. The big concert in April was like that in more ways than one.

I understand because I live close to the school and get to see all that happens there. From my room, I can hear the dances and see the people coming and going in the darkness or when they're near the dim light over the doors. The first time I ever saw a movie was in the school. Somebody came with suitcases, hung a sheet, took things out of the suitcases, turned out the lights, and suddenly the bedsheet was alive with pictures. In the movie, somebody murdered a robber by the name of Jesse James.

Sometimes I go to meetings in the school to hear politicians and their promises and to watch the adults get all excited, even though they don't believe a word they hear. I go to the card games when I can afford to, ever since Grandma Donohue taught me to play almost as well as she can. Even the dog comes to the card games, and everybody tries to get him to sit by their table because they think he brings good luck. Recently I won a chicken.

A few days before the concert, Dolly asked the boys to start taking down the partitions between the two rooms. You stood on chairs and removed some strips of wood at the top. Then some strips of wood on the floor. Very carefully, with everybody helping, the walls are lowered to the floor. Suddenly you see all the children in the Little Room sitting wide-eyed, and when the walls are lowered they laugh hysterically at the sight of the Big Room, and Mrs. Hennessey is hopelessly trying to keep them quiet.

Dolly is looking at them, smiling.

All the grade nine and ten desks, near the big windows that overlook the strait, are moved to the centre of the room, and we stack the partitions on sawhorses near the windows and they become a stage, and the excitement in the Little Room suddenly flows into the Big Room like warm water.

The decorating starts. Stuart Kennedy, who works on the railroad and is good at drawing, sketches the Future on large sheets of paper. Then he assembles the parts into one giant scene that covers the windows and forms a backdrop for the stage. Stuart Kennedy's future is all city skyscrapers and highways, wrapped around the new causeway.

His vision of the future, I realize, is shaped by expectations of prosperity and all the activity it brings. And, for a moment, I wonder if it is really possible that the future could happen here, and not, as in the past, everywhere else.

In my imagination, the future is a little bit like Riverdale in the Archie comics—full of interesting and attractive people, where even the silly ones, like Jughead, are popular and funny, and big shots like Reggie learn their lesson, which is that being rich and swanky doesn't count as much as character. And Archie has character. Maybe Port Hastings will be like Riverdale, with its interesting high school and pretty girls and a soda fountain where the teenagers gather to carry on and flirt and eat mountainous banana splits whenever they want to—a place you never have to leave.

The concert was a big success and raised over a hundred dollars for the school. Afterwards they were saying that the highlight was my father and Angus Walker Sr.

Here's what they saw.

The curtain opens and they are sitting on opposite sides of a card table, facing each other. Between them there is a large bowl and two spoons. The bowl is filled with soft ice cream, and they begin to feed it to each other with the spoons. The catch is that they are blindfolded.

I watch in astonishment as they poke heaping spoons of soft ice cream at each other's faces, missing the mouths but plastering it over eyes and hair and clothing.

For a moment I think my father must be drunk. Loaded. But he quit. And how do I explain Angus Walker Sr., who, as far as anybody knows, never drinks?

The crowd goes hysterical, watching serious Dan Rory MacIntyre, the hard-rock miner and truck driver, and serious Angus Walker Sr., the photographer and businessman, behaving like bad boys, attacking each other with spoonfuls of ice cream in front of the entire village.

Worse than the actual embarrassing spectacle, I think, is this wanton waste of ice cream.

The rest of the concert is hazy. The singing and the fiddling. I remember a long delay and restlessness as Angus Walker Jr. took too long setting up an amplifier for an electric guitar and rigging up sticks around an electric light on the end of an extension cord to make it look like a campfire, and finally coming out in a cowboy hat singing "Hey, Hey Good Lookin'." I remember the snickering and people shaking their heads when, for his encore, he sang "Shake, Baby, Shake," which I think a lot of people in the crowd consider a dirty song. The only part of the play I remember is the girl who had to act that she was falling down and doing it so convincingly that everybody thought for a moment she was hurt—and her getting up slowly.

I think the reason everybody remembered that part is because, shortly after the concert, it became obvious that she was pregnant. And people wondered about the baby and why she fell like that. And was she really acting.

That's how it is in a village. Everybody eventually knows everything, for better or for worse.

————

All winter they worked at the canal and the bridge that would cross over it. By mid-April it was almost ready, the last link in the new road that, according to the papers, will be called "The Road to the Isles," after an old Scottish song that Angus L. Macdonald liked. Finally, in April, the bridge was finished. It is the biggest bridge I've ever seen. It sits there by the canal, on the mainland side, waiting to be put to work.

The bridge has its own engine to swing it out of the way whenever a ship comes through, but for the first swing the engine wasn't ready. They attached a cable to one end and a massive bulldozer dragged at it and, miraculously, the bridge started to swing out over the canal until it finally fit perfectly in place. And the new causeway was joined to the new road from the point up to the village.

And Billy Malone was right. There is a space of about two inches at either end of the new swing bridge. And so we are still an island after all—especially when the cofferdams are gone and the canal fills up with water.

There are, according to the papers, big plans for an official opening of the causeway, and they expect to have it in the middle of August. They plan to find a hundred of the best pipers around to lead the way across, followed by fourteen other pipe bands and whoever else wants to make the historic walk.

Among the stories in the paper then, people hardly noticed that 209 railway employees received layoff notices from the CNR. As of the middle of May, they will have no jobs because the railway ferries will no longer be needed. The car ferries will also disappear, and, with them, all the jobs that people once considered permanent.

People are grumbling: if this is what the Future looks like, maybe we should have appreciated the past more.

At Mr. Clough's store, where lots of railway people congregate, there are arguments about change and the price of progress. But there are also jokes. It seems that the Honourable Alistair Fraser, the lieutenant governor of Nova Scotia, is suing the federal government for five million dollars because of all the rock they took for the causeway from his mountain. And everybody finds this terribly funny.

May 20 was a very strange day—the day they started using the causeway for real. I get the impression it was a spur-of-the-moment decision. A few days before, one of the car ferries, the *John Cabot*, mysteriously burned while tied up at the dock in town. Suddenly there were traffic jams on both sides of the strait. Somebody made the decision—open the causeway, right away.

At one in the afternoon on May 20 there was a huge lineup of cars at the new toll booth on the mainland side. They started lining up early. Once again everybody wanted to be the first across the new road to the isles, even though lots of people have been across it already. Nobody seems to mind that it will now cost seventy-five cents. You can buy a book of fifty tickets for $6.25 if you have to cross frequently. And you don't have to pay coming the other way.

Already there are jokes: it costs money to go to Cape Breton; but you can escape for nothing. Old soldiers say the army should have been like that: hard to get into and easy to get out of.

The afternoon of May 20, which was a Saturday on the long weekend, was amazing—cars just driving back and forth across the causeway. According to the paper, seven thousand cars crossed over on that weekend.

I made my first crossing on the Sunday afternoon. I was riding my bike on the road near the canal when what should I discover but a wallet. I was afraid even to open it. What if there was money in it? Or worse, what if there was money missing when the owner got it back? I had to be in a position to truthfully say I hadn't even looked in it.

But what to do with it?

There was only one place to go—to the toll booth on the other side. The toll collectors would know what to do with it. So I pedalled across, dodging the frantic traffic as I went. And when I breathlessly reached the other side, I rapped on the window of the toll booth, and I suppose they thought I was foolish. A kid on a bicycle trying to pay a toll . . . to get off the island?

A stern-looking man in an officer's cap and a blue-grey uniform that indicated significance opened the window and asked me what I wanted.

"I found this wallet," I said, handing it to him.

He flipped it open and looked inside. It seemed to be empty.

"And what am I supposed to do with it?"

He was obviously annoyed at this intrusion on such an important day.

I had no answer. I couldn't understand his attitude. What could be worse than somebody losing a wallet? What could be better than somebody finding it and turning it in and imagining the joy the owner would feel?

But the uniformed man was just standing there looking at me as if I were a fool. And so I wheeled my bicycle around and headed back towards Cape Breton, leaving him with the wallet.

I was almost at the bridge when the thought entered my mind that maybe somebody had really just thrown the wallet away. People do that sometimes. My Aunt Veronica says it's a sure cure for warts. You prick a little bit of blood from the wart with a pin, smear it on a piece of paper, put the paper in an old wallet or purse, drop it on the road, and whoever picks it up will get your warts.

It's guaranteed to work, she says, because nobody can resist picking up anything they think might have money in it.

And I suddenly prayed that she was right. And that the important man in the toll booth would wake up on Monday morning covered in someone else's warts.

It was clear, after the weekend, that the causeway work was almost finished, and I listened carefully for indications of what might happen next. I was particularly listening for the anxiety that is always a sure sign that he'll be going. Now that there were hundreds of ferry workers with no jobs, it would be that much more difficult for him to stay around. I didn't want to be caught by surprise. But there was nothing but quiet discussions about ordinary things.

Then I got a job, and I realized that the more I could do to support myself, the better off we'd all be.

The job came as a surprise. William Fox, who is a little older than I am, had a paper route for the *Post Record*, the newspaper in Sydney. One day, out of the blue, he asked me if I could take over his paper business for a few days. He had a large parcel carrier, big enough for a stack of newspapers, on the front of his bike, and he transferred it to mine. He took me around and showed me who took the paper every day, and through the camp and down to the tug, the *Shawanaga*, and the dredge, the *Shediac*, where some people were interested in the news. And if there were papers left over, you rode across the causeway and stood at the toll booth, and tried to sell them to people who stopped to pay the toll.

After the incident with the wallet, I was a bit shy approaching the toll booth, but soon realized nobody there had a clue who I was. There was no evidence of unusual warts on any of the toll collectors, and I was relieved about that now I had to deal with them on a regular basis.

As it turned out, William Fox had pretty well decided to get out of the newspaper business and was secretly hoping I'd like it enough to take over from him—which I did.

I enjoyed going to the camp and meeting up with Old John, who walked with me from room to room as I offered the paper to people, some of whom would actually dig out the six cents to pay for it. Some would even give me a dime and tell me to keep it. Old John seemed to treat me more as an equal, now that I had business at the camp. And after I'd finish my trip through the bunkhouse and the staff quarters and the construction offices, he'd often take me over to the cookhouse and feed me.

I think I actually started to get fat, selling the papers. After eating at the camp cookhouse, I'd head for the tug and the dredge and, as it happened, the cooks on both vessels wanted the newspaper and were always trying to feed me, because they'd be cooking supper when I arrived. It was almost impossible to refuse, and I'd watch in amazement as they dragged big trays of steak or pork chops out of their fridges and threw them into the huge frying pans that sizzled in smoking pools of melted butter. At home, steak and pork chops were for special occasions, and my mother never wasted butter the way these cooks did. There was always a massive cake with icing between the layers, and deep sweet pies.

Of course, I had to eat again when I got home, because my mother or Grandma Donohue always had my supper ready, and it would be sin to waste any of it.

Besides my talks with Old John, there were always long conversations with the cooks on the tugboat and the dredge. The captain of the dredge was particularly friendly and always interested in gossip from the village. Often they got me to explain the news for them so they'd have a head start when they got around to reading the paper for themselves.

The rooms in the camps were tidy, thanks to Old John, but the boats were a little messier. The captain on the dredge, however, who had the biggest room, always kept his room immaculate. It smelled of shaving lotion and hair tonic. Best of all, he had stacks of glossy magazines with stories about crime and strange behaviour by famous people.

I'd just sit there leafing through them. And in one I found a shocking story: "What the Kiddies Don't Know about Dale Evans!"

The headline just screamed at me. There were lots of photographs of Roy Rogers's wife when she was younger and not wearing her usual cowgirl clothes. In these pictures, she'd be more often wearing things like a bathing suit with large feathers and her hands on her hips and her legs kicking out. My mother calls it cavorting.

There was a long story about her, plus a picture of Roy himself, with his cowboy hat, smiling. Roy is always smiling, I find. I didn't read much of it before I started feeling sad and maybe a little bit angry, the way I do when Jackie Nicholson is sneering that Roy Rogers is just an actor and a singer and a phony who couldn't put a bullet in the broad side of a barn door if he was standing in front of it.

I stopped reading the captain's magazines after that.

The good thing about selling the paper was that I got interested in real news. And every day I'd be watching for surprises from Hungary.

Best of all, I was earning my own money and receiving inspirational mail from the newspaper about how many famous people, such as Walt Disney, got their start peddling papers when they were boys like me.

Then it was summer and, on a Saturday afternoon, Billy Malone and

I were walking to town for a movie in Rocky Hazel's theatre. It was a sunny day, and we weren't having much luck hitching rides. There was a good chance that we were going to miss the beginning of the show. The cars and trucks, when they appeared, just rumbled by. The road, past the end of the pavement, was particularly dusty because construction machinery had already started preparations for paving. One of the first benefits from the causeway was paving the roads into and out of Port Hawkesbury and some of the town's back streets.

Then, out of the dust, I saw, coming in our direction, a white car, and it seemed to be slowing down, as if to talk to us. As it got closer, I could see it was brand new. And when it stopped, I saw my father at the wheel.

"Where are you two heading?"

"Heading for the show," I said.

I could see Billy admiring the car.

It was a brand new '55 Chev.

"Jump in," says he, even though he was heading in the opposite direction.

We climbed in, and he turned around in the middle of the road and headed back towards town.

"What do you think?" he asked, smiling.

"Is this ours?"

He nodded, looking somewhat pleased with himself.

I was astonished.

Clearly something good was happening somewhere in the universe.

————

Having a regular commitment changes the summer routines. No more lying in bed in the morning trying to figure out what to do with the sunshine and the freedom—to prowl the cool forest or flounder in the deep cove water until your skin shrivelled and your teeth chattered;

or build a raft on the shore or a shack in the woods; or ride imaginary broncos through the rolling fields out back. Now I have responsibility, and the days find their shape around the schedules of the *Post Record*.

Late morning the bundle of papers would arrive at Angus Walker's canteen, and much of the afternoon would be consumed by the business of getting rid of them. The best days were when they'd be gone without the necessity of crossing the causeway, even though I found it interesting to stand at the toll booth, watching all the travellers—cars from all over Canada and the United States. Just standing there watching, trying to imagine what their distant lives were like, would somehow absorb the dreariness of the wait. And somehow, in spite of all the dreaming, the papers would be gone and my pocket heavy with coin. I could easily clear a dollar a day, and sometimes more—which was more money than I'd ever had at my disposal in my life.

I wasn't at it for long when I had thirty-five dollars saved up, which was the price of a new bicycle.

The new car also opened up new summer adventures. One Saturday my mother asked if we'd be interested in an expedition to Louisbourg, where, long, long ago, there was an important French fortress. My mother loves history, and I am fascinated by all the adventure stories you can find hidden among the dry bones of the past. Teachers don't seem to find the adventure stories important, but it's through the stories about places like Louisbourg and the Highlanders and the Irish people and the Acadians that I've learned that Nova Scotia is one of the oldest parts of North America—and that the most important day in the history of North America happened on Cape Breton Island in 1758.

We left early on the Sunday, because it's a long drive to Louisbourg. The sun was shining. We stopped for Mass along the way. Passing the city of Sydney, we could see the red clouds of dusty smoke over the big steel mill. The air, filled with steam and smoke from the Sydney coke ovens, was prickly in the nose.

Between Sydney and Louisbourg, we encountered a serious accident with smashed cars and steam and ugly puddles on the pavement. And people lying under blankets, even though, by then, the day was hot. Seeing them left me queasy, and, by the time we were in Louisbourg, I felt a heavy sadness that only increased as the sun disappeared and a dense fog drifted in from the sea.

In 1955, there isn't much to see at Louisbourg, even in the sunshine. After the second time the British captured it, they destroyed almost everything, just in case the politicians in England would be tempted to give it back to France in some treaty, the way they did once before. So the soldiers, after their victory, did their best to knock everything down and even haul away as much of the stone as they could carry. But the fragments of old walls and fortifications and batteries are still there, and there's enough to build on in your imagination—especially with the fog blotting out everything but yourself.

A distant horn sounds like someone groaning. The moving mist reveals what could be the ghosts of soldiers marching silently and in slow motion over the boggy ground. You feel a chill. History is cold and damp and full of mysteries.

There is actually an old history book that is just about Cape Breton. It was written a long time ago by an Englishman named Richard Brown, and it has an amazing story about how important the battle of Louisbourg was and how the British won it almost by accident. It is why I think the most important day in North America happened here—June 8, 1758.

Here's the story as I remember it.

The British couldn't defeat the French by attacking the fortress directly, so they sent some boats, under the command of the famous General Wolfe, to attack from behind. They went along the shore to a place called Fresh Water Cove, now called Kennington Cove, and launched an assault from there. But the French were waiting for them there, too, and were firing cannon balls and grapeshot from the surrounding hills. In addition, the water was almost too rough for the little landing boats.

When it looked as though the British weren't going to be able to get ashore that way, either, General Wolfe, who was in a small boat leading the invasion, took off his big officer's hat and waved it in the air as a signal for everyone to retreat. But some of his soldiers, in another little boat, misunderstood the signal. They thought he was urging them on. So they just kept on going—right through the grapeshot and the cannonballs and the bullets. And, by some miracle, they got ashore. And that was the beginning of the end of Louisbourg, and Quebec, and all the glory of France in North America.

Just think about it—British North America is British because a few soldiers, braver than bright, misunderstood the wave of an officer's hat!

And it all started here. On this little island that some people are trying to say isn't an island any more.

———

The way I see it, Mother Nature never approved of this marriage between Nova Scotia and Cape Breton Island. It was clear in the way the tidal currents seemed to become increasingly furious the closer the causeway got to the island. And how, in the winter of '54–55, the angry drift ice piled up in the bay behind the causeway; and how, south of the causeway, just out in front of the village, the water became unnaturally still and stayed clear all winter. It seemed almost melancholy, cut off from its own history—which is the way it will remain forevermore, I guess.

The face of Cape Porcupine also wears a miserable expression now, like some old wounded veteran who came home bitter and who, we

214

all know, will stay that way until he dies. Angry and resentful, always reminded of his trauma by an ugly scar.

And then there was what happened to Philip Ryan, who was twenty-one years old and working for a pal who needed a day off, when a crane tipped over and killed him up near the canal construction site; and George White, fifty-four, who was killed in a rock slide on the cape. And, of course, Angus L. Macdonald himself, whom nobody ever expected to die before his causeway job was finished.

If there was any doubt about how Nature feels, it disappeared on August 10—three days before the official opening of the new cause-way—when the paper reported that Hurricane Connie was 430 miles east of Jacksonville, Florida, and heading for the Carolinas. We all know what that means. Everybody remembers last September, when Hurricane Edna ripped through here after her holidays in the south. Now it's as though Nature has scheduled an early storm, just to ruin the big celebration and all the fun and games and the kilts and spor-rans of the eighteen pipe bands they've booked. And to spoil the fancy suits and hats and dresses of all the big shots coming in from every-where that you can think of to claim a bit of credit for this remarkable achievement.

The radio had a program called the "Reluctant Piper," about some-body here refusing to play at the official opening because he thought the causeway was a bad idea and "praaaaw-gress" would be the ruina-tion of the village.

I listened carefully, then asked Mr. Clough what he thought, and he reminded me that the ruination of the village happened long before the causeway and that a little bit of Progress is exactly what the doc-tor ordered for all our ailments. And not to worry about Hurricane Connie. Moreover, the "Reluctant Piper" was all made up by some-body who didn't know what he was talking about.

And it's true that hardly a day passes without a story in a newspaper about what a grand place Cape Breton Island will become, now that it has been connected to everywhere else.

It will become "a famous vacationland." You get the impression from over on the other side of the island, in Cape Breton County, that they figure the causeway will do great things for the rusty old steel plant and the ancient coal mines. The melancholy strait, thanks to the causeway, will become a harbour—the deepest harbour on the Atlantic seaboard and a magnet for business and factories of all descriptions. Progress and prosperity are just around the corner, everybody seems to think.

A big-city reporter named Charles Bruce—who, I found out, grew up just over on the Guysborough shore—is writing about some local history that nobody ever heard of. We've all heard of the Highlanders coming after the Clearances in Scotland, and the starving Irish, but he is writing about refugees from *Florida*, if you can believe it. They were people who had to come here after England sold the place to Spain, mostly Americans who had moved to Florida to escape the revolution. Then they had to come here, to the Strait of Canso, and they would have starved if it wasn't for the kindness of the Acadians in Isle Madame—which is a part of Cape Breton.

The *Post Record* reminds people that Cape Breton was once politically separate from Nova Scotia, and that there are people who think it might be time to become a province of our own again. We should, perhaps, revive the Snell Plan, a scheme by a Sydney businessman named Larry Snell years ago to break away from Nova Scotia.

I can't exactly explain Mr. Snell's logic. But it seems he was upset because Ontario stopped buying Cape Breton coal, and he started organizing a campaign to make people stop buying Ontario cars. Then he was talking about independence—provincial status. When he started getting a lot of attention, one of the car companies in Ontario got nervous and sent somebody down to buy four train cars full of coal in Glace Bay. Then they shipped it all to Ontario with a huge sign on the train, saying "This is Cape Breton Coal!"

Mr. Snell's scheme pretty well fizzled after that—but here they are again, talking about how Cape Bretoners are always being hard done by mainlanders. But all that is about to change.

Then I notice that everything settles down just before the big day—August 13. No more complaining or boasting. Even Hurricane Connie backed off and seemed to change her mind when she was still about 200 miles off a place called Myrtle Beach.

For me, the excitement started with the arrival of a seaplane on August 2. You heard it first somewhere in the sky, but, since the causeway started, it wasn't unusual to see low-flying airplanes as photographers took pictures and strangers flew by to inspect the progress of the construction project.

But this one landed on the water near the causeway. Then people were climbing out onto the rocks.

According to Old John, who was watching from up by the camps, these were the people who were arranging final details of the official opening ceremony.

It's going to be big, he said—the new premier of the province and big wheels from Ottawa, priests and bishops, tens of thousands of people. And all those bagpipe players. Poor Old John was trying to imagine the racket they would make, hundreds of them all blowing at the same time.

On the Thursday before the Saturday opening, they broke a cofferdam and started flooding the canal. On the mainland side of the causeway, you could see the outline of a grandstand, just about where they'd cut a ribbon to mark the official and final opening of the new road over the water.

They have decided, according to the paper, to call it the Canso Causeway *and* the Road to the Isles. There will be a green sign, with both names in white. A lot of people still thought it should be named the Angus L. Macdonald Causeway, but, when he was still alive, he said that would be wrong.

I find this reaction unusual for somebody important. But that's why everybody admired Angus L. He was modest, which is how I think real heroes are supposed to be.

Friday, you knew for sure that this celebration was a big deal. Up by Murdoch MacLean's abandoned house in Newtown, where Beulah the cow once seemed to be the only living creature, they filled the field with great military tents for food and entertainment—a gigantic *ceilidh* for after the official ceremonies and the parade across.

And not far away a carnival, with a Ferris wheel and other rides and wonderful games.

We all stood in amazement, watching how they slapped everything together in what seemed like minutes. The big wheel was assembled in sections, the way you'd put together a simple toy on Christmas morning. Even Jackie Nick was impressed and just stood there watching with his mouth open, stuck for words for once.

And that evening we drove up in the new white Chev, just to take a look. Even then the traffic was all backed up, but nobody seemed to mind.

I was in the front seat, with my mother and father. I was actually sitting by the window, with my mother in the middle. As we were creeping past the carnival ground, which was just across the road from where Angus Neil and Theresa used to live, a pretty girl with dark hair and a beautiful smile stuck her head in the car window and said "Hi, Lin," practically touching my face with hers.

I almost died.

My father looked over with a smirk and said, "Who was that?"

My mother gave us both a look, and I couldn't help feeling about two feet taller.

I couldn't really say who it was. I think I spoke to her once at Mrs. Lew's. Somebody named Joyce, I think, from Prince Edward Island, staying up at Larters'. But I'm not certain.

Later, I was thinking about my plan to be a priest and how there would be no Joyces after that.

Oh, well.

There was nothing but the sound of cars and people talking when I awoke on August 13. When I looked out the window, they were everywhere. I suspect the conversations were all about where to park. The roads were lined with cars. They packed the yard in front of the school and the church, and they lined the back roads up as far as you could see. People were wandering around looking for the best places from which to see the big event. The strait seemed to be filling up with boats. Down near Mulgrave, the navy cruiser HMCS *Quebec* crouched in the misty morning, a dark grey ghost.

When they weren't talking about where to park, the other conversation was about the weather. The skies were gloomy. People studied the clouds, looking for the hopeful glow of sun behind the murky billows.

Then they'd shrug. Rain or no rain, it'll be a great day, anyway—a day to talk about for the rest of your life. The day that Canada joined Cape Breton. Ha, ha.

By mid-morning you could see the big buses manoeuvring past all the cars and pedestrians that packed the roads—yellow school buses and brownish army buses and big blue and white Acadian Lines buses. People in Highland dress pouring out of them. And then you'd hear the skirl of pipes. Men and boys and girls walking slowly by themselves, facing away from everybody, tuning up. The air suddenly filled with the brave doomed cries of history.

I suddenly remembered business—the *Post Record*. I'd been told there would be a special edition of the paper, and it would cost more. And, this being a Saturday, my share of the price was larger than on weekdays. I'd make a killing—more than enough for the rides and games at the carnival down in Newtown. And best of all, with all these people and because it was a special day, the papers would be gone in a flash.

I had time to spare and so, when I bumped into Mr. McGowan and he invited me to go out on his boat to see all the vessels in the strait, I said Thanks and Sure.

Mrs. Lew's husband, Lew Reynolds, built Mr. McGowan's boat, and we watched him as it all came together over the course of nearly a year. It was like watching the unfolding of a mystery, Mr. Lew quietly going about the task, shaving and bending boards, tapping and chiselling as if he had all the time in the world—never uttering a word. Lew is hard of hearing, so, quite possibly, he wasn't aware that we were there watching. Or maybe it's because boat builders are like artists and, when they're at work, they're conscious only of the job they're doing.

He built a beautiful boat. It looks like the smack that comes around to buy lobsters, a little cabin on front and a long, open area behind. And though Mr. McGowan is a storekeeper, he was unusually generous in letting kids aboard the new boat and taking us for rides around the strait. Sometimes he even let us fish over the side or from the stern as the boat was moving. And sometimes we'd catch mackerel or pollock.

That day the strait was full of boats. I read afterwards that there were a hundred. And, in the middle of them, this big grey giant, HMCS *Quebec*, now moving closer to the causeway. With her massive guns pointed at the sky and sailors in their white hats and bell-bottoms lined up along the rails watching and waving as we slowly sailed around them, nobody said a word, we were so amazed.

Mr. McGowan was going to watch everything from the boat, but I had work to do, so he brought me ashore.

And sure enough, when I arrived at the canteen, the papers were there ahead of me. A massive stack of them—each one weighed a ton. I'd be able to carry only a few at a time—a minor problem on a day like this.

Then I started noticing a lot of people wandering around with the newspaper under their arms already. And they hadn't bought any from me.

It didn't take me long to figure things out. Not far from the canteen, a group of grown men who should have had better things to do that day were milling around a whole *truckload* of newspapers shouting, "POOOOOST RECK-ERD . . . COME AND GET YER POOOOST RECK-ERD . . . SPECIAL EDITION, ON SALE HERE . . ."

I felt sick, and I wanted to ask them what they thought they were doing, taking over my turf without so much as telling me in advance.

Frustrated, I went back to the canteen and just stood there, looking at the stack of giant papers and, in the background, listening to the city guys hollering as if they were back on a street corner in stinking Sydney, where everybody is too loud and pushy anyway.

And I said: "To hell with them."

I walked away and left the papers where they were, and joined the crowd and the historic day.

It's all a blur when I try to remember details. They say there were more than 40,000 people, and I believe it. One reporter writing in a Toronto paper afterwards said 50,000, and I can believe that too. The reason I know about the Toronto story is that everybody was saying the reporter is actually from here—William MacEachern from Judique. And how exciting it is that one of Johnnie and Phemie MacEachern's crowd is a famous newspaper reporter in Toronto, where people from here usually get work only in factories or digging ditches.

The sun never broke through, but nobody noticed. Neither did it rain. The roads and hilltops were packed everywhere you turned. The air was filled with a dull rumbling, and I eventually realized it was the sound of excitement. All those people talking at once—and cars and buses coming and going.

The speeches and the formal ceremony were on the mainland side. I couldn't get near it for all the people packed on the causeway. C.D. Howe, a big Cabinet minister from Ottawa, cut a ribbon with an old claymore—a sword—and Angus L.'s widow later cut a cake with it. They said the claymore was used in the Battle of Culloden, more than two centuries ago. I don't know a thing about the battle, but they say we're all here because of it. I was wondering about all the blood and rust, and how they got it sharp enough for the ribbon or clean enough for the cake.

There were loads of big shots making speeches. Mr. Donald Gordon from the CNR seemed to go on all afternoon. But the only speech the people here were talking about afterwards was the one by Angus L.'s brother, Father Stanley Macdonald.

They asked Father Stanley to say a few words in Gaelic, but they gave him only a minute. After he complained, they backed down and gave him two minutes. And from what I hear, he used the whole two minutes to talk about how ignorant the people from Ottawa were, trying to limit the one speech of the day in the language of Adam and Eve to a minute or even two minutes. But how he forgave them because you had to remember that Ottawa was still a young and unsophisticated place compared to here.

Half the crowd was laughing and applauding because they understood, and when the dignitaries on the grandstand saw this enthusi-asm, they all started applauding too, because, I guess, they figured he was flattering them the way they were all flattering each other in their speeches. And that made the people in the crowd laugh even harder.

They were saying afterwards that surely Angus L. and all the other Gaelic speakers, including Adam and Eve, were up there in heaven laughing their heads off too. And that, if Mother Nature had her way, it would have rained on everything, but that Angus L. put a stop to that, even if he couldn't arrange sunshine.

And when it was over, HMCS *Quebec* shattered the sky with a salute from her massive guns. And, suddenly, air force jets were screaming out of the clouds and roaring down the strait, causing the birds hiding on the naked flank of Cape Porcupine to scatter in a panic.

Then a pipe band struck up a lament for Angus L. Macdonald. And, when they were finished, all four hundred pipers there stepped out in their kilts and sporrans and spats and their cocky little hats, cheeks bulging and faces red. And, with chanters and drones a-howl, they walked across the Road to the Isles as if marching into battle with the whole world walking behind them.

Although I'm only twelve, I think I can say there has never been a day like this in all of Nova Scotia. Nor will there ever be again. The crowd crossed the causeway and, where it joins the road to the north, they turned left and marched all the way to Murdoch MacLean's field in Newtown, where thousands more were waiting to begin the party.

And then it was Sunday morning, as though it had never happened. Everything was gone, except for the causeway and the expectations.

6

BROWN BRAINS

Afterwards I found out that Old John had a lot on his mind, though you'd never have noticed. Coming and going around the time of the official opening, he was like everybody else—kind of high on all the attention the place was getting from outsiders. Of course, he was part of the big project that created all the buzz, and he seemed to take an even greater pride in his camp the closer they got to the end of the job. It was only much later that I found out some of the details about the family in Hungary and how he dreamed of bringing them to Canada. And about the legacy he thought he could recover from the Communists after old Joe Stalin died and things loosened up in what the papers called the satellite countries.

Whatever his problems, Old John was unfailingly friendly, but you sensed that on some days he had to work harder to project good cheer. And it was only much later that I was able to put things together and realize that the little hints of despair behind the smiles and chatter were tied to the ups and downs in his personal life. And the significance of the fact that, though he was living here, his personal life was somewhere else and he had no control over it. That can't be easy for anybody. When you're a kid, it's as if you've got brown stuff for brains sometimes.

It took me a long time to realize how much he had in common with my father. Living in a bunkhouse; eating in a cookhouse; family far away and somehow cut off by politics and economics. Both foreigners, in a way. My father was born here, as were his father and grandfather. But English was also his second language, and his education wasn't good enough for here either. He and Old John had a common dream: to live among the people who mattered most to them. And they always seemed to be frustrated in reaching that simple goal, so accessible, it seemed, to everybody else around me—Ian and Billy Malone and the Camerons, the Cloughs and McGowans and the Walkers. And yet, somehow, Old John and my father were able to keep the frustrations and the disappointments to themselves, so you never really understood what made them tick until after it was too late. As far as I know, they never met.

Looking back, I suppose the place was full of men like that—in the construction camps and on the dredge and tugboat. I'd be running into them every day as I went around delivering the paper, and they always made me feel special—talking to me as if I mattered, paying me extra for the papers, and stuffing me with food, which I found strange at the time. It was only later that I figured it wasn't really me they were talking to or feeding. I was just a substitute for other people.

———

It's peculiar how quickly we adjust to new circumstances. New people come, and it's as though they were always here. Or they die, and soon fade from the mind. Even before the official opening, it was as if the causeway had always been there. The traffic was heavier, and you had to be more careful on the road. Angus Walker's canteen was busier, which greatly improved Mrs. Lew's cheer. Robert Morrison opened a new Esso station where Johnny Morrison had his forge. Mr. Clough no longer had the only gas pumps in the village, and his big round Texaco sign suddenly looked old-fashioned. But that didn't seem to bother him. He still had his political drag and his customers, and his store was still the centre of attention at mail time. But the new gas station suddenly became the place to hang around, at least for young guys who were keen on cars and talking dirty. Morrison's service station became the place to go if you were looking for excitement. There was always a card game in progress. The older boys with girlfriends would be exchanging French safes, which they stored in their wallets, probably just for show so you'd think they were really doing things that only married grown-ups do. They'd never think of playing cards or dare to pass around French safes at Mr. Clough's at the mail or any other time.

Before long, Charlie Beaton and his wife, Catherine, opened a new canteen on the north side of the gas station. Later they hired Jean Laidlaw to work there with them. Small stuff, but nobody doubted that there were big things coming in the near future.

People were optimistic, but I kept expecting the bottom to fall out of the paper business. The camps would inevitably close. The dredge and tugboat would finish up the canal work sooner or later. But it seemed that there was plenty left to do and, as the summer dissolved into autumn, I relaxed. Old John was still running the camp and saving the empty beer bottles for me, and the cook on the dredge was still throwing perfectly good pork chops at the seagulls, just to watch them fight among themselves—or to see the shock on my face.

If there was one remaining question mark, it had to do with my father's plans. That one wasn't so easy to defer. You knew that the trucking was just about finished, at least until they got serious about the new Trans-Canada Highway. That still seemed to be a distant prospect, with at least a long winter to endure before anything would happen here. According to the papers, the politicians in Halifax and Ottawa were still haggling over who was going to pay for it.

I'd find myself eyeballing the canvas duffel bag in the barn when I'd be out there to feed Beulah or to fetch a hod of coal or an armload of firewood. Just wondering. Or watching him for evidence of restlessness, or the slack-faced vacant look that was the usual sign of trouble. Or listening for the quiet conversations with people like Angus Jim Malcolm, or his old buddies Neil MacAskill and Harry Taylor, or John Duncan Beaton about new mining prospects in strange places, or a new shaft somewhere with Paddy Harrison. Young fellows from around the county were coming home smelling of cologne in fancy cars with fender skirts from some place called Elliot Lake, where the money was just pouring into their pockets. But the duffel bag showed no sign of disturbance as it gathered dust and cobwebs in the corner of the threshing floor where he put it after Stirling.

Then, through The Hole in the floor, I noticed that small snatches of conversation were starting to take on a particular shape. Gradually I realized it was the shape of a plan, and that the plan was a project, and the project was another sawmill. The old man was going into business—again.

I started praying again, and I reminded God that, while I hadn't actively discussed it for a while and was once briefly distracted by the eyes and smile of a girl named Joyce, I was still committed to my end of our bargain.

———

It was early September and raining as I sloshed through the mud down by the canal, heading towards the machine shop where I was usually able to unload a paper or two. Even if I didn't, I loved going there just to watch the welders. Next to the drillers, I loved watching the welders, with their ferocious torches and face-guards that made them look like spacemen. They were like heavyweight wrestlers flinging around the heavy tanks of oxygen and acetylene gas, and fearless as they manipulated daggers of blue fire to cut through solid steel. Plus, it was always warm in the machine shop.

This day it was cool and wet outside, and I hadn't even looked at the paper I was selling. One of the welders spied me in the doorway and said he wanted one. I handed it to him, and he told me to keep the change from the dime as he unfolded it for a quick glance.

I was putting the dime away when he exclaimed: "Well, I'll be gad-damned."

"What?" I asked.

And he started to laugh, and slapped his thigh with a heavy glove.

"Sonofabitch," he said.

"What are you reading?"

"You don't read your own paper?" he said in amazement. "Look at this."

There it was in the middle of the front page: "Facing Gallows: Coffin Escapes . . ."

"Let me see," I said.

"Good for him," he said cheerfully, pointing at the paper.

The headline continued: " . . . but Recaptured."

Then he frowned as he continued reading.

"Shit," he said.

"What?"

"He was in the clear . . . then he went back."

He read some more, shaking his head.

"He's fu . . . *finished* now."

The paper was vague on the details, but the whole place was buzzing with the news. Even my mother, who believes that people usually get what they deserve, was disappointed. She'd been saying all along that Coffin was innocent, and this was all the proof anybody needed. He was being railroaded by the *Fraingaich* in Quebec to appease the Americans. And good for him for taking matters into his own hands.

And surely anybody with common sense would realize that a guilty man wouldn't just march back into the lion's den the way Bill Coffin did.

My father smiled but didn't say anything. And I had this feeling that he could see the future, and that it wasn't good.

The paper the next day had more details. Coffin made a fake gun out of soap, then fooled five jail guards in Quebec City; escaped, flagged down a taxi, rode around for a while . . . then told the taxi driver who he was and that he was on the run!

What was he thinking?

The taxi driver says, Hey . . . just take the car, head for the Trans-Canada . . . keep on going. If he'd taken that advice, I bet they'd never have heard of him again. Certainly not if he'd headed this way.

Instead, he gets the taxi driver to take him to his lawyer's place, and the lawyer persuades him that his best chance for survival is to put himself back in jail.

It was September 7, and he was scheduled to be hanged September 23. But he took the lawyer's advice and went back to jail anyway.

Lawyers.

———

I had my doubts about this mill plan, but I guess when you look out the window and see a new car in the lane and a reasonably new truck parked in front of it, and the old fellow in pretty good cheer and sober all the time, you tend to get optimistic.

I had some vague memories of the last mill, but they were still kind of warm and rosy. I guess I was only about four years old then, but I remember some of it clearly. I remember the men pouring steamy mugs of tea from big pitchers and the sweet smells indoors and out. I remember how the trees whispered when the new day was starting up and the fringe of pink on the clouds between the deep green of the tree line and the empty blue of the early morning sky. And long sunny days exploring as far as I dared on soft rutted roads that vanished into an endless forest full of bears and *bocans*. And voices in the night, men talking and laughing quietly. And sometimes louder, if there was a jug of moonshine on the go, which was when there would also be singing. Some guy chanting a few lines through his nose, and everybody else joining in at the chorus, and the feet banging out the steady rhythm, as if they were marching slowly. And the daytime roar of engines, and my father's uncle, Dan L. MacIntyre, face grim, hand on the lever that sent the log flying back and forth past the screaming saw that was visible only when it stopped, and fresh lumber tumbling and releasing a sweet sticky perfume.

All warm memories, but surrounded by shadows and confusing feelings of something lost.

I suppose I could have remembered the whole scene back then if I'd really worked at it. But I didn't, and I guess that's the way bad memories are. You don't really notice them until you absolutely have to, which you might never have to do if you're lucky. You don't remember the urgent conversations when an engine suddenly stopped or somebody discovered something wrong with the sweet white lumber. Or a truck, at some crucial moment, stalled on a lonely roadside with the hood up. Or your mother walking into the middle of the Gaelic moonshine singsong and everything going quiet suddenly, until you could hear only the creaking insects in the dark outdoors and the hollow sound of your own blood inside your head.

Being busy makes it easy to avoid the shadows, and I was very busy. Grade eight was tough, and every day I'd go straight from school to Mrs. Lew's to pick up the papers. I'd make my rounds, racing against the evening. Then home and chores and supper and homework. In addition, selling papers got me interested in the news, and I discovered that the world is full of stories far more interesting than anything that ever happened here, or even in the story books I borrow. Stories in the news never seem to end. They're like the serials they show before the movies in Rocky Hazel's theatre in town. Always new developments, and you're always left hanging from one day to the next.

Some stories were special and jumped out from the page because of things I already knew. Miss Annie Christie had told me about China and the Communists who changed everything there. And so I noticed that hardly a day went by without something on the Americans and the Chinese and the United Nations and the danger of another war. I'd be thinking how unhappy poor Miss Christie must be now, with all this animosity. And, of course, I kept watching for something to happen in Hungary. Old John wouldn't say much, but it seemed he had inside information that whatever happened would be good for everybody. Sometimes I wondered if he was really some kind of a secret agent and his job at the camp was just a false front. A lot of the older people here still think that anybody with a foreign accent is a spy. This, of course, is changing, now that there's a steady stream of strangers through the place.

And there was the Coffin story. It was particularly interesting because I knew somebody who knew him. And there was something familiar about him. He was from Quebec, but the way they talked about him he could have been from here. A poor fellow always out on the edge of things, struggling to get ahead, but never getting the breakthrough. A fellow from the middle of nowhere with a case of perpetual bad luck.

A couple of days after he went back to jail, Coffin's lawyer asked the court to postpone the hanging which, after all, was only days away. It seems that only one of the nine judges in the Supreme Court made the decision not to listen to his argument that he'd been railroaded by the police and lawyers and judges and politicians in Quebec. Some of the other eight were indicating they might have made a different decision. Coffin's lawyer wanted a chance to talk to all of them.

Then I read that the hanging was postponed until October 21. Maybe the lawyer wasn't such an idiot after all.

Reading the paper every day made me realize, probably for the first time, that everything that happens, no matter where, seems to affect everybody on the planet. I suppose I should have known that just from the war veterans Danny MacIntosh, John MacDougall, and Joe Larter, who got sent off to places they probably never heard of for reasons I'm sure they never really understood. I always thought they went to the wars because they needed the work or, perhaps, because they wanted a real adventure in some exotic place. Now I was coming to see things a bit differently. Wars are about people trying to crush weaker people for selfish reasons. And once they start, nobody knows where they might finish up—which is why people, even from the middle of nowhere, have to stand up and get involved. The way things were looking in about ten different places on the planet, it was a ninety-nine percent certainty that my turn was coming in the not too distant future. Of course I'd be a chaplain—a chaplain who shoots people if necessary.

And so, every day, I'd be trying to catch up on developments in China or Argentina or Gaza or Cyprus among the latest revelations about Eddie Fisher and Debbie Reynolds and Princess Margaret and Group Captain Peter Townsend, who was a war hero and a divorcee and wanted to marry Margaret. I gather that being a war hero was a good thing, but that being a divorcee was a problem for everybody in England. One story would comment on how happy the princess looked. The next one would report that she was looking sad.

Eventually Eddie and Debbie got married. Margaret and Peter didn't.

Figuring out China and Argentina and Gaza and Cyprus was easier than figuring out why there was so much commotion about the movie stars and Princess Margaret, who is very pretty and seems nice, even when she's sad. I eventually gave up on Hollywood and royalty.

I suppose, looking back, stories about adult romance had left a sour taste in my mouth ever since the scandalous magazine article about Dale Evans.

It's a good thing that priests don't have to worry about any of that foolishness.

Two things happened in the middle of October. First, Coffin's execution was postponed again because the government in Ottawa decided to take a second look at the case. That was good news, and I couldn't help thinking he was as good as in the clear. Second, the government in Halifax announced that an American company was planning to build a $35 million pulp mill somewhere in "the Canso Strait area."

The new mill would create five hundred new jobs.

Surely, I thought, even a fellow from out back who had absolutely no schooling would get one of them—that we'd all be spared another experience with a sawmill.

It was about this time that I noticed a pile of what looked like pulpwood in the field alongside the Green Path.

He's started cutting pulpwood, I thought, in anticipation of the new mill they were talking about in the newspapers. But, on closer examination, I noticed that the sticks of wood were longer than pulpwood and sharpened on one end like fence posts. This was mysterious. The field already had a perfectly good fence around it; Beulah could no longer go wandering the way she did before all the construction.

The causeway was completed, but the village was still a mess of broken rock and mud. They were still working on new roads and the rerouted railway line. They seemed to be building large piers at either end of the new canal, which was why the dredge and tugboat were still around and why there were still men living in the camps.

The fence posts were a mystery until I discovered my father with his shirt off one chilly autumn afternoon driving them into the ground with a heavy sledgehammer.

I had just come back from delivering the papers, and my mother told me to find him and tell him that supper was almost ready. It was already almost dark. He didn't see me at first, as he stood there on a wooden box swinging the heavy maul. I heard him grunt every time it whacked the top of the post. When he stopped to catch his breath, I asked him what the posts were for.

He seemed almost pleased to answer—the way you are when you have a hard problem on your mind and suddenly get a chance to think out loud. He was talking to me, but I might as well have been the man in the moon.

He had his serious face on and, with his hand outstretched, explained that the posts were the first step in building his new sawmill.

He had it all in his head. He'd set the posts in the ground in two parallel lines and brace them so they'd be absolutely solid, like a miniature railway trestle. In fact, he'd then build a track on beams that ran along the top of the posts. A carriage, a little bit like a railway flat car, would travel back and forth on the track. The carriage would transport the log, secured by hooked clamps, back and forth past a large circular saw. When the log was adjusted precisely on the carriage, the saw would slice off whatever size lumber you wanted. Everything would be hooked together by cables and belts and pulleys, so all the power you needed was coming from one big engine.

He explained how you'd make four initial passes by the saw, each one taking off a slab of bark and wood, until the log had four smooth flat sides. Then you'd carve it into boards or planks. Everything had to be perfectly level, he said, because people need all those boards and planks to be cut exactly according to "specifications." In other words, he said, you can't have a two-by-four that's two-and-a-sixteenth-by-four-and-an-eighth, or a bunch of boards that are all different shapes and sizes.

I pointed out that the boards in the walls of our house and the old places on the mountain seemed to be all different sizes. And that the planks and beams in the barn seemed to have been carved with an axe.

He laughed. Things have changed, he assured me.

Then he walked down to where he had a stake driven in the ground and said the trimmer would be down there. The trimmer was a little saw that would square off the ends of the lumber and, when it wasn't doing that, cut up all those slabs into stove lengths for firewood.

"Who would run the trimmer?" I wanted to know.

"We'll think of somebody," he replied.

I was prepared to help, but I had school and my papers to deliver. In any case, I got the impression that this project was so particular there wouldn't have been much I could contribute to it even if I had the time. So, when I had nothing else to do, I'd just sit there on the cold ground watching, occasionally making a quick run down to McGowan's store for nails or screws. Or home for a pail of water when he was thirsty.

Watching him work there with his shirt off and his white skin glistening in the wintry air, it was like he was alone in the world. It seemed odd. Men rarely work alone, I'd discovered, from all the activity connected with the causeway. They were always in groups of two or three, and often more, helping each other, gabbing endlessly, making jokes, and always—you knew in the back of your head—struggling to impress one another. He was different that way.

When I'd ask why he didn't have people helping him, he'd reply that good help costs money and that everybody who wanted work already had a job at the construction or away in Ontario.

And, anyway, there are certain jobs you have to do yourself, he said.

Sometimes it's easier just to do it than explain it.

I don't think I could ever forget the sight of this solitary, ghostly man racing against the gloom, pounding long posts into the ground deep enough to avoid distortion by frost or instability from the rolling carriage and the heavy logs. Now and then he'd pause and take a drink from the pail or quietly roll a cigarette and light it and stare through the smoke at the sawmill that only he could see.

During those pauses, we'd both notice the cars on the now busy road through the village. Before the causeway, you'd automatically look and, nine times out of ten, recognize whoever was driving by. It was different now. Almost all the cars carried strangers.

Things are changing, he'd say. And maybe then he'd give me a wink and ask what I was thinking.

And somewhere in the back of my mind I'd be remembering another mill and another time. And I'd try to think of something encouraging. But all I could think of were questions, and I already knew there are no answers for questions about what hasn't happened yet.

———

Having a car changed little things. It made surprises possible. They'd say, out of the blue: "Let's splurge on a show." And we'd go to town to see a movie—sometimes even on a school night. Going to Mass was much easier. Before, when he'd be away, it would be on the church bus. When he'd be home, it would be on the back of a large truck, which was great when the weather was fine but miserable when it was cold or wet. Now we had a new car, and we'd drive up to the church feeling just as fine as all the town people.

Sundays would be for visits. Out to the mountain or people in Troy or Long Point or Glencoe. Usually somebody with a connection to the past or to mining or when my mother was a young teacher around here.

Teachers, when she started out, hardly got paid at all. Maybe three hundred dollars for the year—and then only if the people in the school district could scrape together the money to pay her. The government paid nothing. The teacher would survive by getting free room and board, but it would usually mean moving around a lot from house to house. People didn't have much to offer.

My mother seemed to have made a lot of good friends like that, and we'd visit some of them on Sundays. MacMasters down in Long Point or Jack and Annie Catherine MacDonald in Troy, who were brother and sister. MacMasters' place was fun because John D. had a store and kept foxes for a while, and because there were kids there who were older but friendly. And, in Troy, Jack, who was always called Troy Jack, would have beer bottles. And their mother reminded me of Peigeag on the mountain, even though she was twice the size of my grandmother. She'd be dressed in black and carrying on in Gaelic with my father.

My mother told me that they tried teaching her to speak Gaelic when she lived with them, but that she learned only things that she couldn't repeat.

But she told me about one particular night when they saw an old neighbour coming to visit. Jack said to my mother, "Here's a chance to try out your Gaelic." I suppose she should have realized what was coming.

He handed her a rolled-up newspaper and said: "When he comes in the door, you give him the newspaper and say 'Bheil do thon salach a'nochd?'"

She assumed that it meant something like "Have you read today's newspaper?"

She found out only later, when the old visitor almost died and the others practically strangled laughing, that it meant, "Is your arse dirty tonight?"

She never seemed to mind them talking Gaelic there, and I noticed there was none of the tension you'd feel when people from out back came to the house and spoke quietly in Gaelic while studying the floor.

My mother was actually living with Annie and Jack and their mother when she met my father. She was the teacher in the little Troy school, and one of the things they'd do to raise money for the school was put on dances. I think they met at one of those dances.

It's hard to imagine your parents meeting for the first time at a dance or how they might have acted with each other then. Getting married seems to be like two people passing through a door into another personality. Sometimes I think I understand when I hear them laugh at some private joke or when they're playing cards. The house is never so comfortable as when they're sitting quietly at the kitchen table playing cribbage, their cups of tea and cigarettes alongside, teasing about bad plays or bragging about good ones. But mostly they're talking quietly about important things and, sometimes, not talking at all. That, to me, is marriage. I can't imagine their first encounter in the little school in Troy, when they had nothing in common to talk about. I've never seen them dance.

I know it's wrong, but you always think of them as they are now, older and serious and often worried. But I've seen photographs of when they were young and laughing all the time. There's one of my father in Montreal, and you'd swear he was a city man, walking down a busy street with his friend Archie Dan MacMaster and a young woman I don't know—all of them looking like they're in a movie. My father is wearing a fancy overcoat and a big hat with a floppy brim. Archie Dan, who is now the barber in town, is wearing an overcoat and little glasses that make him look like a professor. And they're just hard-rock miners, out of the north country for a little holiday.

Then there's a photograph of my father and Annie Catherine standing together on the running board of a big old car, and I know that it was his, something he brought home from Quebec where he was working at the time and earning good money.

I look at that picture and think of how successful and complete everything seems to be. He's all dressed up with a fancy car, and Annie Catherine in her apron, her hair hauled back in a bun, looking like the country girl who is embarrassed by all the attention from this good-looking successful man from away. If you could read his mind, I'm sure it would be saying: I'm Somebody; I've got it made now; I took a chance . . . I left the mountain and went away; I got a job and worked hard; prosperity is close at hand . . . just a matter of working longer and harder; I've arrived.

It's like he's thinking: all things are possible, no matter who you are or where you're from. It's like he still believes all those things they tell you when you're a kid. Get up early. Wash your face and comb your hair. Work hard. Respect others. Say your prayers and obey the laws of heaven and earth. Sooner or later you'll have it made.

He hasn't yet learned about the one thing you can't control.

Luck.

———

There's a monastery on the mainland. I've heard about it many times. Older people would go there for retreats, which are weekends of prayer and silence. Before the causeway it was a difficult trip: to town, on the ferry, and then a long drive over the cape and along the twisty road to Antigonish. Now, with the causeway, it's simple—especially if you have your own car. One Sunday afternoon that fall they announced we were going over to see the monastery.

It's run by Augustinians, mostly men from Europe, and it's been there for years. Long before the Augustinians, back in the early 1800s, the Trappists started the monastery to serve Acadian settlers and Indians and try to convert a few dozen Protestant Negro families living in the area. It was closed for a while but has been operating again since the thirties.

I can't think of a quieter, more peaceful place on the planet. Tree-lined lanes and ivy-covered brick buildings and barns. Cultivated fields and indifferent animals munching and resting. A cool, sunny fall day with trees that seemed to be on fire, light shadows from curdled clouds that hung low, trees so dry that when the wind puffed on them you could hear the scratching as they rubbed against each other. People were singing somewhere, a sad holy song sung slowly in a large room. Though it was Sunday, there was a monk on a tractor hauling manure, and it had the rich rank musk of life itself. He smiled a kind of shy smile as he drove by, and I was suddenly bursting with what I guess is happiness. The day we were there, looking back through the peephole of memory, seems like the last relaxing day in my life—at least this part of it. And that's kind of sad because it was probably one of the most hopeful days I can remember.

We got out of the car and started wandering around, and almost instantly everybody seemed adrift. The girls headed for the barn. I could see my father wandering in the direction of a pile of logs. I think the monks also had a sawmill. My mother was walking with her arms folded in the direction of the chapel.

I saw a sign that said Way of the Cross, and soon found myself following a small group of strangers. They seemed to be making the Stations, which is a series of prayers in front of small shrines representing the various stages of Christ's journey from the Agony in the Garden to the Crucifixion.

I'd never seen the Stations outdoors before. They're usually along the walls inside a church. There was something real about these, outdoors. After all, the real events—the Agony and the Scourging, the Carrying of the Cross and the Falling and the Crucifixion—were all outdoors, even if not in a place as holy and peaceful as this.

And I found myself quietly praying that everything would work out and that, out of all the changes and turmoil around us, there would emerge, somehow, the kind of quiet stability that I was feeling right then and there.

After the Stations, I found a little fountain that was, basically, a pipe connected to a spring. Standing there, it was so quiet that I could hear somebody telling someone else that the spring produced natural Holy Water. And that, if you drink it and say the right kind of prayer, there's a pretty good chance you'll get what you wish for. People, she was saying, were cured right here, the same as at St. Joseph's Oratory, Ste.-Anne-de-Beaupré, and Lourdes.

I waited until they were gone. Then I took one of the little paper cups they provided in a dispenser and filled it. A fellow from the mountain can use all the help he can get. The water was clean and cold, and I just knew, somehow, that everything was going to be okay in the long run.

When I found my father later, he was talking to a monk who was dressed in working clothes like the ones the old fellow wears most week-days—baggy work pants, plaid shirt, knee-high rubber boots. A stranger wouldn't have known who was the monk and who was the miner. When I got close enough, I could hear that they were talking about sawmills.

This is another sign, I thought.

And, later, my mother told me that the boys I noticed wandering around in small groups actually lived there and went to a school that the monks ran in one of the buildings.

"A school?"

"Yes," she said, "a high school."

Then you could see the wheels turning. We studied each other long and hard. But nobody said anything. Port Hastings school goes only to grade ten. Going on after grade ten is always a big question of where. Most from here don't bother.

Finally she said: "It's something we can think about."

As if she was reading my mind!

241

Winter set in early, around Remembrance Day. There were big snowstorms and freezing cold. The new sawmill was pretty well assembled and, by late November, my father was spending most of his time on the mountain cutting logs for his new mill. Sitting in school, I'd be waiting to hear the sound of the saw howling as it sliced slabs and plank and boards from trees older than he was. But that would have to wait. The early winter wasn't helping. It was hard to get logs out of the woods and off the mountain with deep snow everywhere. He'd come home on Saturday complaining about the cold in the old place, and how his mother would keep the fire in the kitchen going until he was in bed. But then, because she had some premonition about house fires, she'd sit there by the stove almost all night watching the fire die down to where it became harmless.

Even then the house was like a deep-freeze.

The weather got worse in December. Just before Christmas, the married couple who looked after the lighthouse on Margaree Island disappeared after setting out from Broad Cove in their little boat. Days went by without a trace of them, though the boat was found smashed on the shore. It was as if the sea just swallowed them up and kept them. People soon stopped talking about it. Another lighthouse keeper, on St. Paul's Island, off Cape North, was killed trying to get supplies ashore from a boat.

Hard times for lighthouse keepers, I thought, wondering what was going through the mind of Mrs. Nicholson, who'd been a lighthouse keeper for years and hardly ever spoke about it. I'd be at Nicholsons' a lot, now that the weather was so bad, watching television with Jackie and Billy Malone—mostly wrestling and hockey games. Jackie still had one of the only television sets in the place, probably a small reward for moving off the point.

There was even a snowstorm on Christmas Day.

You always knew he was home from cutting logs on the mountain by the reaction of the dog. Skipper would be sleeping under the stove, and then he'd suddenly start scrambling out and run to the door whining. You'd be letting him out when you'd hear the sound of the truck coming down the back road, which was officially called the Victoria Line.

One night in January he caught us all by surprise, even the dog. He just walked through the door, kind of breathless and pale. All he said was that the truck had broken down out back.

Later I heard what happened. A couple of miles out, by the crossroads at the Long Stretch, the truck just quit. There was no warning. He was driving along and, just as he approached the crossroads, the engine died and wouldn't start again.

He got out of the truck. It was snowing lightly. As he walked away, he looked back to make sure he'd turned off the headlights. That was when he saw the woman standing beside the truck staring at him. He started to walk back, but she seemed to drift away. This made him nervous, so he turned and started walking home.

He tried to forget about her, but every time he'd look back over his shoulder she'd be there, as if she was following him. And once, just as he was passing Archie the Piper's, which is at the crest of the hill where the village begins, he looked back again and she was almost close enough to touch. He still couldn't see her face because she had a kind of shawl over her head and was clutching it at her throat, so it covered most of her features. But he could see that she was dressed the old-fashioned way, in black wool from head to foot, the way Grandma Peigeag dresses.

He panicked then and ran the rest of the way home.

The next morning he went out to where he had left the truck, and it started right away.

Afterwards I heard a legend about a woman who once lived out back of here and who lost her children during an epidemic. They say she still wanders around on stormy nights looking for them. And some day I want to ask my grandmother on the mountain about the children she lost to an epidemic. If that's why she sits by the stove trying to keep her house warm for the one who managed to escape the clutches of disease. And whether she wanders around sometimes on stormy nights looking for them. And whether she really can see the future and, in particular, shadows where my father is concerned.

————

One morning in February I heard on the radio that Wilbert Coffin was dead. Just before the news, I'd been looking out the window and it was a brilliant sunny day. There was fresh snow, and the reflection of the sunshine almost hurt my eyes. The strait, without the drift ice, had the same sharp electric blue as the sky. It was Friday and I was feeling happy. I like Fridays so much that I usually start feeling good on Thursdays. Friday night I could stay up. Saturday started with fresh doughnuts. I felt free on Saturday, even though I still had the papers to deal with. Saturday morning the dog and I would call for Billy Malone, and we'd wander up to the camps to see Old John. If the papers came early enough, we'd still have time to go to a movie in town.

Listening to that announcement on the radio, all the joy went out of Friday. I couldn't believe it. They killed Coffin.

I was shocked when they sentenced him to hang. But that was a long time ago—more than eighteen months. They'd postponed the execution half a dozen times. A lot of people doubted that he did it, including Angus Jim Malcolm, who is from here and who knew him as well as anybody.

"He'd steal the eyes out of you," I heard Angus say. "But he wouldn't kill a fly. I seen him brush them away when he could have swatted them. No. He didn't kill anybody."

Angus had been in the bush with Coffin the week before the Americans disappeared.

244

People actually seemed to get to know Coffin during the eighteen months he was in the news, and what I still can't figure out is how anybody can get up the nerve to kill somebody after all that time to think about it. Especially when there were so many people doubting that he really did it. I can understand killing in a war when everybody is frightened and confused, or when somebody is drunk and angry. But important people with education and religion sitting down and deciding to kill somebody in cold blood sounds like something only criminals would do—whether it was killing the American hunters or killing the poor fellow they decided among themselves was guilty of the terrible deed.

I didn't want to read about the details, but I did anyway. How he protested his innocence to the end but died like a man, climbing the steps to the rope on his own and even shaking the hands of the guards who went up with him. And how the premier of Quebec, Maurice Duplessis, who everybody says is a dictator, refused Coffin's one last wish to marry the woman he loved for the sake of their little boy. I never realized before that they had a kid. His name is Jimmy, and he's only eight years old. And suddenly it just seemed worse.

My father was on the mountain that day, cutting logs, and I was glad. I was also glad that nobody in the house seemed to want to talk about it. I didn't need to hear the words. I knew what they were thinking: that if he'd been rich or if he'd had important friends, he'd still be alive. But he was an English-speaking Protestant Quebecer from a place that didn't matter. The dead people were well-to-do Americans, and somebody had to die to even the score—even if they were hanging the wrong man.

All I could do was say a prayer for the poor fellow, which I did, and one for his boy, Jimmy Coffin, who was going to have to go through his life with this on his mind. Always wondering: what really happened? Always asking why.

I prayed hard, but I had the strangest feeling that nobody was listening. And it occurred to me that God could have put a stop to this but didn't. And, for the first time, I was asking myself: whose side is God on anyway?

———

The thing about news around our house is that, whenever there's a story that gets us down, we know we won't have to wait long for one to cheer us up again. Between Princess Margaret and poor Bill Coffin, 1956 was getting off to a bad start. But, suddenly, there was Grace Kelly and Prince Rainier to take your mind off all the discouragement from the Middle East and South America and the Mediterranean and Europe, not to mention Quebec.

Grandma Donohue just couldn't get enough news about Monaco and Grace Kelly, and I suspect it wasn't just because Grace was an Irish Catholic. It was because she was an American, and my grandmother, who had lived and worked in the United States earning two dollars a week, believes that Americans are superior to everybody else in the world. I suspect that she often regrets that she ever came back to be poor and proud in Cape Breton, so I don't begrudge her the excitement she gets when good things happen to Americans, even though I, like my father, think it's a lot of foolishness.

"Sounds like bullshit to me" is one of his favourite lines, and he kind of sings it, laughing at the same time.

He can actually be funny sometimes—as when my mother adds too many extras on the rosary and he'll start banging his foot on the floor to make her stop.

And there was school to make you forget about the troubles of the world. School was tough. The year before, in grade seven, we had half a year with no teacher at all, and half with Dolly MacDonald filling in. Now we had Mrs. Annie McGee, who is a very nice lady from up the hill, near the Piper's place, but who either didn't like teaching very much or who hadn't been in a classroom for a long time.

She seemed shy, and that was a big handicap in a room where discipline had pretty well been breaking down for over a year, ever since the iron hand of Mrs. Katie Gillis disappeared.

There are several new people in school, and one in particular is a teacher's worst nightmare. His name is Neil MacIver, and he's one of those people who can create chaos out of nothing. The teacher can never get angry because he's so clever about being funny. For example: you'll be working on your math problems and suddenly hear giggling and snorting; you look up and everybody is stealing sideways glances at Neil MacIver, who is brushing long tresses of imaginary hair with an invisible hair brush. Eyes half shut, acting like he's all alone before the mirror in his boudoir.

Watching him, you actually start to see long, golden locks billowing out from his hand. He's like a hypnotist. He tosses his head, fluffing the luxurious invisible hair with a serious look on his face. The more you try not to laugh, the harder it gets—until somebody loses control and blows a wad out of his nose or something that's even funnier than what Neil is up to. And then the whole place is gone. And it's only then that poor Mrs. McGee notices, and it's too late to do anything but laugh along with everybody else and try to persuade Neil, who hasn't made a sound, to behave himself.

Another time he'll be imitating old Herb Moore, who is a carpenter and rolls his own cigarettes. Herb can spend half a working day rolling a cigarette, squinting and twisting his mouth, sticking his tongue out, and Neil has him down perfectly. People go crazy laughing.

This happens a lot.

Then one afternoon I saw Mrs. McGee sitting at her desk with her head down and, when she lifted it, I could see that her face was red and puffy and there were big tears running down her cheeks. And for a terrible moment I thought I was going to cry too. A woman crying is one of the worst things, but the older kids didn't even notice her distress. Or if they did notice, it didn't matter.

I'm thinking: whoever comes to teach here after she's gone is going to have her hands full. Little did I know at the time what the future had in store.

In the Big Room, the higher grades get to sit closest to the windows. Grade ten actually sits right next to them. Then there's grade nine. I'm in grade eight, still close enough to see out. I spend a lot of time just staring at the blue, ice-free strait and the cape, which has gone completely quiet now, half listening to the drone of instruction that will become relevant to me only in the years to come, when I'm in nine and ten.

The opposite side of the strait is quiet. The big Euclids and bulldozers and draglines are gone now. The blasting is finished. The cape has a battered look where they removed the stone. But it's dramatic, more interesting than before. It's like a scar on someone's face. You know there's a good story behind it.

Soon the work on the canal will be finished. The camps will close. The workers will go away. Old John will find another job, somewhere else, continuing to dream and worry about his absent family. Port Hastings will change into something new. The seeds of prosperity have been planted.

In grade nine they're talking about the invention of the machine gun. My ears prick up. Mrs. McGee, with a history book in hand, is explaining how the machine gun made it possible for Europeans to colonize Africa. I suddenly see the little black people, brandishing their spears and blow-pipes, running after all these big white men. And the sudden violence of the bullet-spitting machine. And their little bodies in a brown and bloody tangle on the ground.

Even Neil MacIver has a serious look on his face.

Half listening from grade eight, where the details don't matter yet, I get this dark picture of human progress. History is really about machinery. New machines that add power to the human being. Power to travel longer distances. Power to change what is useless into something of value. Power to dominate.

Sitting nearby, the prettiest girl I've ever seen takes my mind away from the stammering machine gun and the writhing African bodies. She is prettier even than the girls you see in movies, including Debbie Reynolds. She is Neil's sister Mabel.

There are other interesting girls in the room: Sylvia Reynolds, Ann Fraser, Isabel Fox. But lately I've become invisible to them as they carry on with the older guys, including Neil. Mabel seems different. And even though she's older than I am, she sometimes walks with me as I deliver the papers and talks about herself and how she wants her life to be. Once she even revealed her fondest dream: that one day she will become a professional figure skater. That will be difficult because we don't have a rink. The only decent places to skate are Happy Jack's Lake, which is deep in the woods behind the cove, and Long Pond, which is down north, by the Ghost Beach. But this doesn't seem to be a problem for Mabel. And there, beside the road, she suddenly demonstrated the form of a professional figure skater. Standing on one foot with a long leg stretched behind, leaning forward, arms and hands extended, graceful as a gull's wings, her face suddenly transformed by the imaginary place she's gone to.

And when she returned, she seemed a little bit embarrassed, so she asked me what I plan to do. I said I wasn't sure.

And suddenly it was true. Walking along with this friendly, pretty girl telling me about her fondest dreams, I was suddenly filled with a sorrowful confusion about people and their tragic expectations. And how great it would be if dreams came true.

One day in the early spring, Mrs. McGee is interrupted by a roaring sound. It is a sound unlike any of the machinery we became accustomed to during the building of the causeway. A loud racing engine, and then the high-pitched howl of the large saw racing through a log. A momentary drop in the sound, and then the howl of the saw repeated. Over and over again.

People are squirming, confused. Mrs. McGee is trying to get their attention.

"Class . . . please . . . pay attention . . ."

But nobody is listening.

I know exactly what it is, and I want to say aloud: That's the sound of a dream.

But of course I don't. And it's a good thing, too, because by the next day the mill was silent again.

The newspapers forgot about the causeway for a while, turning their attention to the problems of the wider world. With Grace Kelly married, Grandma Donohue was devoting most of her attention to Nasser and making dire predictions about world war three. Then we'd be back in the news. There would be a small story about the planning for the new highway that was going to slash through Cape Breton on its way to Newfoundland. Then hardly a week would pass without another worried story about the future of Mulgrave and Point Tupper and Port Hawkesbury now that the ferries were gone. Speculation about a new pulp mill had a new tone of desperation. All the talk about the causeway in the beginning had been about the wealth it would bring. It was only late in the day when somebody said, "Hang on. We have three or four hundred people who worked at getting cars and trains over to the island. A few of them will get jobs as toll collectors. What about the rest?"

Then a politician would stand up and describe the boom that will follow the causeway because the strait will magically become an ice-free harbour. Deepest Ice Free Harbour on the Atlantic Seaboard, they say. Potentially bigger and better than Halifax. Hell, they're saying New York and Boston will be nothing compared to our new harbour.

I look at it every day now. And every day, after the deliveries to the houses and what's left of the camps, after I've visited the dredge and the tugboat, I ride my bicycle across this monument to one man's stubborn determination. One man from a place even smaller than the village I live in, from a school even smaller than the one I go to, made this happen after fifty years of talk by lesser men. What was his secret?

But in the long run, what does all this mean?

You could tell at first that the men at the toll booth were thinking I'd be interfering with the traffic as I tried to sell my papers. It turns out that my customers hardly have to slow down to complete the transaction. They nod towards the bag, I hand a paper in, they pass back a dime and usually tell me to keep the change. But even if I have to give them the four cents back, there's hardly any delay. I'm faster at selling my papers to the drivers than the toll collectors are at taking money from them. During the slow periods, I'd let the toll collectors read the paper for free. Then they started buying it. Now they're friendly. They come out and talk about the news, testing me with hard questions about people like Nasser.

With the arrival of summer, the sawmill was running almost every day. The logs he cut on the mountain during the winter were now piled on skids, ready to be rolled onto the carriage and reduced to boards and planks and firewood. I'd sit on the log pile and watch my father as he stood, flecked with sawdust, lips compressed and eyes squinting, as the terrible saw howled and tore the logs apart. Back and forth the carriage went, relentless, pausing only as he made careful adjustments to ensure the precision of the cut. A small conveyor belt carried sawdust away, and the growing pile became a measure of his success.

He pulled it off, I thought. With his bare hands he put a mill in this field where there had been nothing. With his bare hands he wrestled ancient trees from the icy grip of the mountain and is now converting them to lumber which, in time, he will convert to cash. And he will have arrived then at the fulfillment of his simple dream—to live at home, the master of his own small economy.

One evening at supper he had an amusing story: while picking up the mail at Clough's, Mrs. Billy MacLean, who is of old quality in the village—a musician and an artist and a pillar of the church—accused him of creating an eyesore in the middle of the village.

"You think," he said. And he laughed.

"An eyesore? In the middle of this place? Think about it."

And I did for a moment and quickly saw the humour. The place is full of abandoned buildings. Just below the mill there is an old store once run by another MacLean, and it is falling down. Mrs. Billy herself lives in a homely house that was once a store. One of the few new buildings in the place, Murdoch MacLean's house in Newtown, is boarded up because he died before he finished it. And the old Quigley place next to us—falling down. The old abandoned coal piers, down by the railway station, are slowly collapsing into the strait. The wharf is rotten.

There are only two things here that aren't crumbling—the new causeway, and my father's sawmill.

The village has been falling apart for fifty years, and she thinks a new sawmill is an eyesore?

"She better get used to it," he says. "The sawmill is just the start. There'll be a lot of eyesores around before too long. And just in the nick of time, before everybody has to move out. Yes, sirree."

I felt a lot better about everything. And then he announced that they were going on a vacation. *They.* Mother and father. Just the two of them. Going to Ontario. *Ontario!*

A place you only dreamed about—like Boston and Florida and Europe, huge and mysterious. Going to visit Aunt Kay, who is my mother's sister, and her husband, Angus Brown, who runs a hobby farm for a rich Toronto businessman named Brawley.

"Why can't we all go?"

"Nope. Not this time."

Actually, it was a vacation for us too. We stayed at our Aunt Veronica's and went swimming every day. Her older boy, Barry, was big enough to hang around with by then, and we amused ourselves pretending we were brothers. And it felt oddly exciting. It had never occurred to me that having a brother might be a welcome relief from all the females in our lives. My father being around all the time was unusual. And even when he's home, he's struggling against the forces that keep trying to drag him away again. Barry's father, Mickey, hardly ever comes home—something you don't talk about. But, I suspect, it was an interesting experience for both of us, having each other.

Barry is more adventurous than I am, and I found myself constantly hauling him back from the brink of small disasters. Always too close to the edge of the cliff, or heading into water that was too deep, climbing into places that were forbidden, making plans for trips to places I knew we'd have a hard time getting back from before dark. But I, in contrast, tend to be too cautious. They say I take everything too seriously, so being with Barry loosened me up.

I draw the line at smoking cigarettes.

The time passed quickly, and they returned from Ontario looking younger and happier than I remembered them. They had photographs of all the places they had been. My only moment of jealousy was when I saw them in raincoats on a boat beneath Niagara Falls. But that's okay, I thought. Some day I'll see Niagara Falls myself. And that will only be the beginning. For them, the way they talk about it, the visit to Niagara Falls is like the end of something—an experience they don't expect to have again.

———

Then things became strange. I look back now, and it's like the sky started to grow dark with gathering clouds.

I remember the date only because I've gone back to double check. August 11. It was a Saturday. In the morning I noticed Old John walking along the road in the direction of Mr. Clough's store, which was also the post office. He was moving quickly, head down, lost in thought it seemed. Whatever, he didn't notice me.

I hadn't seen much of him in the months previously. The camps were almost empty. A few engineers and bosses remained in the staff house, which was a separate building from the main camp. One of them was taking the paper on a daily basis, so my trips to the camp were brief. Also, because it was the summer, I'd be anxious to finish with the newspapers as quickly as possible so I could go swimming at the cove or just wander through the woods with Barry or Billy Malone or Jackie Nick.

Maybe, I thought, watching him disappear into the post office, he's forgotten me. Maybe he's already moved on to another place and another job—at least in his mind.

I'm sure it's like that for people who work on construction projects or in lumber camps or hard-rock mines, which are, more or less, just projects. Temporary. You get to know people but realize that, sooner or later, you'll be saying goodbye and the usual words that express the hope you'll hook up again some day, even though you know it's unlikely. Or if it does happen, you'll have become different people because of the experiences that occur when you're apart and you'll have to start from scratch, becoming friends again.

I know lots of people like that, from the camps and the dredge and the tugboat. People much older than I am who liked my company briefly because of what I am rather than who I am. Somebody who reminds them of somebody else. Plus, I'm friendly and love to talk to adults, which is probably from being the man of the house for so much of my life.

Old John was like that—one of the most interesting people I've met. He never told me much about himself, but that made him even more interesting. He was from an unimaginable place, infinitely mysterious and moderately tragic because of the vast distance between where he was and where he wanted to be. I suspect most of the best men in the world are like that—keeping their tender places under wraps.

That Saturday afternoon was overcast and cool for August. In fact, the whole summer had been unusual for the amount of cool, wet weather we had. It wasn't a swimming day, so I was taking my time with the newspapers.

On Saturdays the papers were heavier. In July they'd changed the name of the newspaper from the *Post Record* ("Today's News Today!") to the *Cape Breton Post*, and they were getting rid of the weekend supplement, the *Standard*, and replacing it with a fat load of fill of their own called the *Cape Bretoner*. Saturday was a day of heavy lifting.

The paper that day, like most days that summer and fall, had another huge headline about Nasser and the fight over who will control the Suez Canal. Most people think the way Grandma Donohue feels: sure as hell there's going to be another world war over this.

If that wasn't enough to get you upset, there was an uproar in Cyprus because the British hanged three young "terrorists" in a jail in Nicosia, and I'm left asking myself, What has that achieved? You'd think with a world war shaping up over the Suez Canal, the British would be too busy to be hanging young guys who just want them to go away.

Canadian politicians were making a racket because the Bank of Canada has increased its interest rate by one-quarter of a percentage point, and now it's at an all-time record three-and-a-quarter percent, which is supposed to be almost as dangerous, in economic terms, as the row over the Suez Canal.

It's all beyond me, and I'm just thankful that I have only to drag the paper around to the readers rather than figuring out what's in it. I feel sorry for the men and women who have to write all that stuff down.

I actually had a lot of ground to cover on my paper route. At least a couple of miles along the main road, almost all the way to Troy. Then I'd double back and turn down towards the camp, drop the papers there, then carry on to the dredge. If I still had papers left, I'd pedal across the causeway to the toll booth.

At a certain point, remembering that afternoon, things get kind of fuzzy—like a dream, after you've woken up.

I'm riding down the road to the camp. The first stop is the staff house, which is where the big shots live. Off to the right of the staff house is the cookhouse, where Old John often takes me for sweets and tea and chit-chat. I wheel my bicycle towards the smaller building, which is closest to the road, and lean it against a tree.

I see Old John right away and call out. He doesn't answer. He's busy, as usual. In my experience there is always a cleaning job or a repair job demanding his immediate attention. You rarely ever see Old John sitting down. He's always moving quickly. Seeing him, I often think of Grandma Donohue's expression: "He's moving so fast you could play checkers on his coat-tails."

But now he isn't moving at all. He seems to be repairing the door-step at the front of the staff house.

He's actually seated on the step, and he is leaning forward with his head between his knees. It's as if he's looking for something on the ground or underneath the steps.

"Hey, John," I say. "What's going on?"

No answer.

I step around him, and it is when I look down to see what he is doing that I see a rifle poking out from under him. It actually seems to be across his lap, the barrel sort of pointing up over his right forearm in my direction.

Rats, I think. He's been shooting rats, and one got away on him and has taken refuge underneath the step. I consider stopping to watch, but I don't like killing—not even rats.

I pause briefly inside. The bedroom doors are open, revealing narrow cots with their grey blankets tucked neatly underneath the mattresses. I inhale the soft odours of hair tonic and shaving lotion and tooth paste. No trace of the feminine. No evidence of family or other lives.

I drop a newspaper on a tidy bed, then turn and leave.

Old John hasn't altered his position, hasn't made a move. The sky is dark and the air heavy. A soft breeze sighs through the trees that shelter the staff house. My eye settles on the motionless rifle.

I now imagine that I stood there for a long, long time, waiting for his greeting, listening to the breeze that, experience tells me, will grow cooler and, sometime during the coming night, wring the moisture from the dark, heavy air. And I imagine the beginning of a headache that will be real tomorrow. In the memory the moment goes on and on, subtracted from all that has gone before and all that will come afterwards.

And then it is a different moment, a normal moment linked, like all the others before the moment at the staff house, to the rest of time. I am on my bicycle and I am riding down the steep hill towards the canal, and there is a vehicle making its way up the hill, but I'm not certain if it is a car or a truck. I am aware of the low, dark sky, clouds almost touching the leaden waters of the strait. I feel the bump of the stony, unreliable road and, when the vehicle has passed, I can taste the dust it leaves behind. Up near the old cemetery that overlooks the new causeway, I hear a crow. "One crow, sorrow," Grandma Donohue always says.

And then I am approaching the canal, now wheeling the bicycle because the ground is so rutted by trucks and heavy machinery. The heavy bag of newspapers thuds against my hip, threatening to trip me. I suddenly feel tired. I imagine that the dredge is deserted. It is, after all, a Saturday. The men have gone ashore or home. The tugboat is nowhere to be seen. There is a peculiar silence all around and, I suddenly realize, inside my head.

And then I am home, carrier bag still half full of unsold papers.

It is Saturday. On Saturday we get the *Star Weekly*, which is a glossy newspaper from Toronto and full of wonderful comics—*Dick Tracy*, *L'il Abner*, *Terry and the Pirates*. My father's favourites are *Pogo* and *Juniper Junction*. I retire to my room with the comics, and I fall asleep.

Later, I think, an adult came by, and there was quiet conversation in the kitchen accompanied by sidelong glances in my direction. And then the adult left.

My mother was very quiet.

"I'm sorry," she said.

"About what?" I asked.

She looked at me oddly.

Then she said: "About Old John."

And that was all she said.

After Mass the next morning, you could see the little groups of people and imagine what they were all talking about. Old John. The Hungarian from the Gorman's camp. Shot himself.

But what I was thinking about was Father MacLaughlin's little sermon, just minutes before.

As usual, right after the Gospel, he went to the lectern and, instead of the usual explanation of what he'd read, he just stood there for a moment looking at us.

Father MacLaughlin hadn't been here for long, and people mostly remarked about his housekeeper, who was unusually good-looking and, unlike most priest's housekeepers, young. And about how you can often hardly breathe in the confessional during the Christmas and Easter seasons because of the smell of booze coming off the priest.

All of which, they always say, is understandable. "Poor Father Spotty," which is what a lot of people call him because of his freckles, "went through hell" in the war. I guess he was an army chaplain and saw things that nobody ever likes to think about. He drinks to forget and, if he gets a little comfort from a good-looking housekeeper, more power to him.

That's what I hear them say about Father MacLaughlin. And nobody ever criticizes him, even for the booze and the pretty housekeeper—especially not the war veterans.

On that morning, after the longest pause I can remember by a priest on the altar, he spoke quietly about a tragic incident in Port Hastings on the day before. Something at the Gorman's camp.

I could feel my stomach tightening and pressure building behind my eyes, just as you do before you start to cry. But I couldn't stop listening.

He talked about an unfortunate man who worked at the camps, a man from a distant country who was alone here, isolated from everything he knew and cared about. Probably lonely and, eventually, in a state of despair. And how, in this terrible state, and with nowhere left to go, he took his own life. He paused, just staring out at us, and you'd think he was somewhere else, somewhere cruel and far away.

All I could hear in the church during the pause was my own heart beating. My throat and my entire head ached. I prayed that he was finished speaking. But he wasn't.

Father MacLaughlin then talked about church doctrine on suicide. How suicide is supposed to be a mortal sin, a deed so terrible that it cuts us off from God's grace and any hope of salvation.

That's the teaching of the church, he said.

You could hear people clearing their throats then and squirming a little. We all know that two kinds of people are excluded from God's grace and salvation when they die: unbaptized babies and people who kill themselves. Once there were other categories, like poor Paddy Murphy in Bay St. Lawrence, whom the priest put outside the cemetery because he missed his Easter Duties.

Because they are excluded from God's grace, they are excluded from the consecrated part of the cemetery and must be buried somewhere else—anywhere outside the fence; sometimes in the ditch.

But Father MacLaughlin was saying he had a problem with this teaching by the church. You could hear the place go quiet again.

Basically, he said, to be in a state of mortal sin, you have to be aware of what you're doing and know that it is a mortal sin and still not care.

The way he figured it, the last thing in the mind of a man so lonely and miserable that he'd rather die than live is mortal sin. A man that desperate is incapable of reasonable thought. And if you are incapable of reasonable thought, you can't be in a state of mortal sin.

That's how he sees it anyway.

Our infinite God, he says, is distinguished by an infinite capacity for mercy. And for that reason, this humble priest is going to give Old John Suto from the Gorman construction camp the benefit of the doubt. Old John Suto is going to get a church funeral and a Christian burial here. Tomorrow. Ten o'clock. Period.

He turned on his heel, then, with a swish of vestments, and resumed the Liturgy.

And, after a short funeral Mass on the Monday, attended by a few people from the camp, they buried Old John in a shady corner of the St. Joseph's Parish cemetery. There he'll remain until the day of the Final Judgment, when he and Father Spotty can both face the music side by side.

Afterwards, George Fox, one of the older boys who sometimes helps Mr. Clough at the store and post office, was saying that Old John arrived that Saturday morning to pick up a registered letter. It was obviously important, and he must have read it right away. You could tell by the look on his face that it was bad news. He just put that important-looking letter away without saying anything and headed back to the camp.

They found it later. It was from a big-city lawyer somewhere. The lawyer regretted having to tell John that the authorities in Budapest had relayed a firm and final refusal to reimburse the money they had confiscated and that it would be pointless to continue pursuing his efforts to reunite his family.

A few weeks later, Nasser and the Suez Canal were gone from the front page of the newspaper. Now the stories were from Europe. They were calling it a revolution. The headline on October 25 was huge: Hundreds Killed in Hungary.

The next day there was another even bigger headline: Fighting Rages in Budapest.

I sat for a long time on the platform in front of Angus Walker's canteen reading. Soviet troops were in pitched battles with Hungarian students and other civilians who were being supported by parts of the Hungarian army.

It went on and on, day after day, until, inevitably, the Soviet army crushed the uprising. But not before hundreds of thousands of refugees fled the country to find new homes. Thousands came to Canada.

All I could do was shake my head and ask the pointless question: why couldn't you have waited? And I felt something like anger mixed in with the sorrow. Surely you knew that even a disaster would leave some room for hope.

But Father MacLaughlin, of course, had already given me the answer. Despair leaves no room for reason in the human heart. And in the absence of reason, there is no place for hope.

7

BUIDSEACHD

There are three old women on the mountain, and they all have special powers. That's what my cousins tell me. People come to them when they have problems doctors and priests can't solve. They also have the power to make bad things happen. One of them is our grandmother, Peigeag.

Once my grandmother was helping a young woman to have a baby. The woman wasn't married. Plus, there was something seriously wrong with the baby, and it made a mess coming out. It almost killed the mother. My grandmother was so angry she put a curse on the unknown father, even though it could have been someone she knew and cared about. That's what my cousins told me, and there is no doubt in their minds that the man who was the father of that poor baby would suffer as much as the woman did—unless someone with equal powers took the curse off him.

The curse is called the *buidseachd*. And it always seems to be women with the power to put it on or take it off. You rarely ever hear of a man putting the *buidseachd* on somebody, or having the special power to do things.

My Aunt Veronica, for example, reads tea leaves and predicts the future—and she usually gets it right. She can get rid of warts, or cause them, and make your hair grow back if you're losing it. If you break a dish, she knows how to put it back together again as good as new. She can also make good things, including medicine and wine, from weeds and wild berries. But I've never heard of her putting a curse on anyone, though I suspect she could remove one—if you asked her to.

My cousins told me there is a *buidseachd* on my father. Here's how it happened. Years ago, before he was married, he came home from the mines in northern Quebec for a visit. He was prosperous. He had a car and was quite pleased with himself. But he insulted one of the old ladies on the mountain because he neglected to offer her a ride in his new car to Mass one Sunday. So she put a curse on him.

She could probably have made him sick or caused him to have a car accident, but it was a more serious kind of curse. It was that, for as long as he lived, he'd never have the benefit of good luck. And as everybody around here knows, you don't get anywhere in life without a few lucky breaks.

Knowing my father, he'd just laugh at the idea and would never go to the bother of having somebody remove the curse—even though his own mother had the power to do so. When I mention things like the *buidseachd* and *bocans*, which are spirits, he just laughs as though he doesn't believe in any of that.

I'm not sure whether I believe in it, but it would make me nervous to know that some old lady had cast a spell on me. And if I knew another old lady who could remove it, I would go to see her and get it removed. And the bad things that have happened to my father are enough to convince me that my cousins are right. On the mountain they're always saying: Poor Dan Rory never had any luck that wasn't bad.

He went to work in a mine in St. Lawrence, Newfoundland, where I was born, and now almost everybody he worked with there, including my godfather, Alonzo Walsh, and his brothers, are sick or dead of some mysterious disease. My father has trouble breathing sometimes and coughs a lot, and he must worry about whatever is killing his friends in St. Lawrence. After he left St. Lawrence, he tried to start his own business, a sawmill on the mountain, and everything that could possibly go wrong went wrong. And the mill disappeared. After that he was working in another mine in Newfoundland and broke his back. He buys trucks that keep breaking down and costing him more money than they earn, and eventually he's forced to go away to the hard-rock mines again. I know he has tried to get work in the big mines of Elliot Lake and Kirkland Lake and Sudbury, where there are unions, so that men work safely and get fair wages, but they say he can't pass the physical for those places. He has bad lungs, they say. Probably because of the sickness he had when he was a boy, or from working in St. Lawrence, or both. So he mostly goes to work in mines where there are no unions and where they don't check as closely on your lungs as in places like Elliot Lake.

I confess that, for a while in the summer of 1956, I thought his luck was changing for the better. It occurred to me that, maybe, during the winter when he'd been living on the mountain and cutting logs, he broke down and got his mother to lift the *buidseachd*. Or maybe that would be one of the things they were doing when they'd be talking Gaelic as if I wasn't present in the room—and she'd be doing most of the talking while he and Grandpa Dougald would just sit and stare at the floor, leaning forward a little bit with their hands folded on their knees. But I don't think so. And it became obvious by the end of the year that the curse was still in full effect.

He sawed a lot of lumber in the spring and early summer of '56. Then he started running out of logs. It's hard to imagine a shortage of trees on the mountain, but they have to be a certain size and quality for lumber, and it gradually became harder to find them. Finally he made an arrangement to lease some more woodland in Troy.

There are two old bachelors there, MacDonalds, named John and Neil. Their father's name was Rory, and he had red hair. So the bachelors are known as Neil Red Rory and John Red Rory. That summer, he even built a small camp there and hired George the Wheeler, who is a MacQuarrie, to live in the woods and cut logs. He bought a small bulldozer, which he said he'd need to haul the logs to the road. Horses, he said, are pretty well on the way out. Plus, they require too much looking after.

Meanwhile, he was sawing the last of the mountain logs and trying to get a decent price for his lumber from the big dealers in Sydney. His problem, as I eventually understood, was that he was never in a position to make advance arrangements for delivery or price because he was never sure of his log supply, and he could never anticipate breakdowns in machinery.

Still, from time to time, there would be a special day when he'd work long after dark, optimistically loading his lumber on the back of his truck to take it down to Sydney, hoping that he'd hit a day when they were desperate for it and prepared to give him a fair price.

I'd help him, and then watch in fascination when the truck was loaded as he'd walk around with his pencil and little notebook, very intense, eyes squinted, calculating the board feet on the back of the truck and how much money he'd have to get per board foot to at least break even.

On the eve of one of those trips, I asked if I could go with him to the city when he sold his lumber. He thought about it for a moment, and then he said I could.

He even told my mother that he thought it would be a good idea for me to see how the world works, whatever that meant. I figured it meant that it would be the same as school, getting to see what a city was like. And Sydney was a particularly interesting place because it had a very large steel plant and coke ovens right in the middle of it.

We were up before dawn on the morning we were to go to Sydney with the load of lumber. I remember dressing in the dark, hoping I got things on right. My mother made a big breakfast for us. I could feel the rising excitement, knowing that we were on the move long before anybody else in the village. And that we were going to the city.

Months before I'd had a letter from my friend Angus Neil MacKinnon, who moved to Sydney with his family because of the causeway and changes on the railway. He was inviting me to go and visit for a while. Stay with them in Whitney Pier, where I'd be amazed at what I saw. There were Black people there, and families with names you couldn't pronounce. People who came from Europe years before to work at mining coal and making steel. There were homes in Whitney Pier where they spoke only in Ukrainian and Polish. The kids in Whitney Pier were tough, he said, but he had no doubt we could handle ourselves. Plus, we'd go to the Sydney Forum to see the wrestling.

We were all huge wrestling fans, and Billy Malone and Jackie Nick and I would watch faithfully on Jackie's new TV set, practising the holds and the flips until Mrs. Nicholson lost patience and chased us all outside. I could easily handle them, because Billy was smaller and Jackie so thin.

"Jackie Nick," you'd hear the older boys pronounce, "is so skinny you can smell the shit through him."

We'd just look at them, thinking about what we'll do when we're as big and nasty as they are.

To see professional wrestlers at the Sydney Forum would be like getting to the World Series, I thought. I loved Whipper Billy Watson. I loved hating Gene Kiniski and Killer Kowalski.

I had no fear of the city, but my mother did. She decided I shouldn't go to the Pier to visit Angus Neil. It was too rough there. Also, the thought of us at the Sydney Forum with all the rowdy wrestling fans was a bit too much.

But going to the city with my father to sell a load of lumber would be educational, she thought.

You actually smell the city before you see it. The air is full of the tang of burning coal, a gassy, dusty smell that hangs everywhere. It gives the place a seriousness you never feel in the country, where the air is bland. And I was amazed by all the traffic. You suddenly find yourself surrounded by cars and trucks in parallel lines driving straight ahead or around turns, but never getting close to bumping. Other lines of cars stream along to meet us, but they never cross the line on the middle of the road. And then there would be a traffic light, which everyone would notice simultaneously. And everyone would stop at once, as if up against some invisible barrier.

Stopping was more difficult for us, and my father would have to gear down because, he said, the brakes couldn't be trusted with the heavy load behind.

Just before the main part of the city, we turned down a steep hill and, on the way, there was a large sign telling us that we were entering a cooperative lumberyard.

"We'll try here," was all my father said.

Try?

I sat in the truck alone for a long time before my father returned. He was with a man who was wearing dress pants and a shirt with the sleeves rolled up. They walked out of view, but I knew they were examining the lumber on the back. Then the man in the dress pants was walking past my side of the truck, and he disappeared inside the building.

The door on the driver's side opened, and my father climbed back inside. He didn't speak, but his face was serious. He started the engine, and the truck groaned away, up the steep hill, back towards the street that I remembered was called King's Road. And on into the city.

LINDEN MacINTYRE

I'd never seen so many houses packed together—houses everywhere I looked. There were streets running off King's Road, up a steep hill, and I could see nothing but big wooden houses painted in all the colours you can imagine. Across the harbour, new houses in a place called Westmount. And, off to the north, the shadowy outlines of other towns—North Sydney, Sydney Mines. Nothing but wooden houses.

You'd think the easiest thing in the world to sell to city people would be lumber. It should be like selling water in the desert.

The traffic became more intense and there were people everywhere, crossing in front of us and on the sidewalks. I saw a building with a large new sign: The Cape Breton Post. I saw small boys with new red carrier bags like mine trudging along the sidewalks, loaded down with newspapers, shouting out the name of the paper—*CAPE . . . BRITTEN . . . POST.* I thought that everybody at home would know I'd gone completely foolish if they heard me walking up the road yelling *CAPE BRITTEN POST!*

I forgot about my father's serious expression.

And then we were at another lumberyard, and there was another long wait. And another man who was wearing better clothes than my father's came out. He walked around the truck, writing on a clipboard as they went. This time my father went inside with him. After he returned we drove around to the back of the woodyard, and my father climbed up on top of the load, undid the chains and rope that held the load in place, and started throwing pieces of lumber down.

I asked if I could help.

"No," he said.

Afterwards we stopped at a liquor store, and he came out with a small paper bag in his hand. He uncapped a little bottle without removing it from the bag, took a long swallow, sighed, and put the bag away, under the seat.

Afterwards we stopped at a liquor store, and he came out with a small paper bag in his hand. He uncapped a little bottle without removing it from the bag, took a long swallow, sighed, and put the bag away, under the seat.

269

Finally, he smiled.

"Let's go to a restaurant," he said.

A restaurant?

So we went to Joe's Steak House on the Esplanade. Once, on the way to the restaurant, his frown returned.

"Highway robbery," he said.

And that was all. I didn't ask him what it meant because, for that brief dark moment, it was as if I wasn't there.

———

There was another significant development that fall, and it was a mixed blessing. My mother started teaching school again—in the Big Room.

The year before, her friend Peggy MacIsaac, who was a teacher at the Convent School in town, became sick and had to go to the hospital, and my mother filled in for her for a month. Now she was full time—in Port Hastings, in the Big Room, where I was a captive.

It meant a bit more financial security in the house. But it also meant your mother standing over you from the time you got up in the morning until you were back in bed at night. There's also the stigma of having your mother for the teacher—though the fact that I was the only kid in grade nine reduced that problem somewhat. And it didn't take my mother long to establish for the whole room that there was a whole new regime in place and that things were going to be different from here on in—especially for me. If anything, I would feel what the Bible calls "the rod of correction" more than anybody. We were back to the Katie Gillis days of discipline, and "make no mistake about it."

But I wasn't worrying about that. I was far more concerned about the fact that, over on the far side of our hayfield, just beyond the crest of a hill and alongside the Green Path which the older people still call Saddler Street, there was only silence. The mill just sat there, seemingly abandoned. The sawdust pile, no longer fresh and sweet, was settling down into a dense mass, changing colour as the time went by. An eyesore, as Mrs. Billy predicted.

For a while, my father used his truck to haul topsoil for landscapers who were trying to cover up the scars of the construction at the end of the causeway, especially around the new tourist information bureau. The little bulldozer he bought for the lumber camp in Troy was getting rusty, over beside the barn.

Whatever hope there was for him, and the hundreds of former ferry workers thrown out of jobs by the causeway, had been dashed earlier in the year by a story in the Halifax newspaper. The American company that had been considering building a pulp mill in the area had decided against it.

The politicians were still optimistic. The new mayor of Port Hawkesbury, Mr. Gillis, was saying that prosperity was inevitable. New industry would come, he said, if for no other reason than that the hydrogen bomb was forcing big industrialists to decentralize their operations, moving factories away from vulnerable places in the midwestern United States and central Canada to remoter places like the Strait of Canso.

People just rolled their eyes.

We had to be patient, he said. But Mayor O'Neill from Mulgrave, where, the older boys were saying, "things are flatter than piss on a platter," was beginning to lose patience with politicians in Halifax and Ottawa. His comments were becoming more critical, perhaps because he's Irish. My father isn't Irish, but he seemed to be more on the wavelength of Mayor O'Neill than Mayor Gillis.

But then he'd sing his little ditty, "Sounds like *bullshit* . . . to me"— which was to say, "I don't really have any faith in any of them."

And even when my mother would be tacking on extra prayers at the end of the rosary just to nudge along the prospects for some of what the politicians are calling "industrial development," you'd still hear him tapping his foot on the floor.

"Just move along" is what the tapping foot would be saying.

Then one morning when I was in the barn to feed the cow, I noticed that the canvas duffel bag in which he kept the mining gear was no longer where I'd been seeing it since the summer of 1953.

———

All fall there was great excitement in our house—at least among the women. There were unmistakable signs that there would be a provincial election at any time. And this time there was little doubt: the Tories were going to win.

The Grits had, for reasons best known to themselves, picked Dr. Henry Hicks, who was a university professor, to lead their party. Dr. Hicks, everybody said, was extremely intelligent. He had been a Rhodes Scholar at the famous university in Oxford, England. But he didn't look like a politician. He looked more like a banker. He wasn't very tall, and he lacked the military elegance of Angus L. He had squinty eyes and bad hair and an unpleasant little mustache. He used fancy words, and his voice had a pompous edge on it.

The women at our place were delighted. They'd been worried that the Grits would pick the man Angus L. wanted to take his place— a man named Harold Connolly. Mr. Connolly had a lot of political experience and a pleasing public style. He had a friendly appearance and a sense of humour. More frightening to the women at our place was that he was of Irish descent and Roman Catholic. All that made him extremely attractive and difficult to dislike. He could probably defeat the new Tory leader, a man named Robert Stanfield, whose family had made a fortune manufacturing and selling underwear—an impressive man, but kind of dry.

Now they say that Mr. Stanfield can't lose because the Tories did what the Grits were too confused to do. They picked the resurrection of the great Angus L. Macdonald to lead their party. Mr. Stanfield is

272

everything that Angus L. was—except a Catholic and a Cape Bretoner. The fact that he's a Protestant is fine because it wouldn't really be fair to have two Catholic premiers in a row anyway. Mr. Stanfield is a mainlander—but that doesn't matter so much anymore, now that there's the causeway—and he's wealthy, but, in spite of that, he's as honest as the day is long. Just like Angus L.

Grandma Donohue and my Aunt Veronica were quite convinced that the Tories would be in power before Christmas, and if that should happen, someone with my father's Tory background shouldn't have any problem getting work.

What Tory background? my father would ask.

Sure your mother and father and all your relatives are Tories. And isn't Ronnie (what we call my Aunt Veronica) working day and night for the Tory candidates, Al Davis and Archie Neil Chisholm?

And, in any case, once the Tories are in power, we'll see the good times roll.

My father never argued with the women. I never heard him discuss politics. But if I were he, here's what I'd be saying.

Good times? Haven't we just had four years of good times? Haven't they just spent about thirty million dollars on a new causeway and canal and practically demolished the village for new roads and railways? Haven't we been hearing them talk about new industry here for the whole time? And what's the latest? The American company that was the best bet for creating new jobs here has changed its mind.

Good times are for other people, other places. And, when all is said and done, how much can we really expect from "good times" in the long run? As the old politician in PEI used to say, good times won't put another tit on the cow.

What they weren't saying was what everybody knows and doesn't have to say. Liberals were going to be booted out of jobs all over the place after a change in government, and that they would rapidly be replaced by good strong Conservatives. Liquor store people and highway workers, including the snowplough drivers and road foremen, would be fired—even the forest rangers. Tories are lining up to take their jobs. A Tory with a truck would be sitting pretty with all the roadwork planned, and especially the new Trans-Canada Highway.

And that was something else. Who could say when that job would start or where the road would go?

My father was never interested in any of the political talk. He disapproves of people losing their jobs just because of how they vote. He says he'd rather starve than take a political job.

But it isn't just how people voted, the women say. People can vote however they want, but they should keep their mouths shut about it. Also, the Liberals didn't hesitate when they were shoving the poor Tories out of their jobs, when the shoe was on the other foot.

You live by the sword, you die by the sword, they say.

The old man would just sit there, smiling, the way his father smiles when there's no choice but to agree or keep quiet.

It's the same on the mountain. My understanding of Gaelic is flimsy, but I could understand practically everything Grandma Peigeag was talking about when the conversation turned to politics. You'd think the Lord Himself had come back to run the province the way she crowed about Mr. Stanfield.

What is it about women? I wonder. What is it that makes them more pragmatic than the men? Or is it only here, where the women become tougher than the men because the men so often have to go away?

And then, one day, the duffel bag was gone from the barn altogether.

————

Delivering the newspapers was becoming less interesting by the day—mostly a matter of dropping them on doorsteps or, if there was someone home, placing them wordlessly in a hand extended past a storm door. Of course, there were exceptions. The old Fox brothers, who were bachelors and lived alone, always insisted I come in to chat, and sometimes they'd make tea. Lennie MacDonald, who is from town, was the timekeeper at the Gorman project and one of a handful of people still working in the offices there. He always liked to sit back and shoot the breeze when I showed up with his paper. But a lot of my old friends were gone. On the dredge and the tugboat, they were pushing hard to finish the project—there was another big one waiting somewhere on the St. Lawrence River. They didn't have as much time for talking or reading newspapers.

The Gorman construction camps themselves were practically deserted, adding to the strange feeling that grew stronger inside me every time I went there after what happened to Old John. I wanted them to be gone forever. I wanted the place to grow up in trees, and for time to erase everything that had been there and had happened there.

For days afterward, there was a dark place in the gravel just in front of the doorstep where I last saw him.

The first time I saw that stain, on the day of his funeral, which was two days after the Saturday I saw him sitting there, it startled me. Then I realized that I didn't want to think he'd been dead and that it had been important for me to believe he had been alive when I spoke to him. It sounds stupid now admitting that I convinced myself he was alive. But there had been no doubt in my mind at the time. He couldn't have been dead. Surely I'd have known he was dead. Surely I'm not such an idiot that I could step over a dead body and talk to it *twice* and carry on as if everything was normal. You'd have to be a complete moron not to recognize a corpse.

That Saturday night and Sunday at Mass and at the funeral, I kept telling myself that I had been the last person to see him alive.

It surely happened after I was gone. But looking at that stain on the ground in front of the staff house, I realized that this deception wasn't any comfort at all. Pretending he was alive and not a corpse when I went by only raised the disturbing possibility that I should have done something to distract him or maybe even help him. That maybe, if I had reacted to the rifle, for example, I'd have interrupted his plan. Maybe if I had asked what I always asked, how things were in Hungary, that would have got him talking—and everybody knows that talking is one of the sure cures for despair. Now I'm questioning myself. And I'm quickly realizing how easy it is to get into the muck of asking questions that have no answers, the worst of which always begin with the words "What if . . . ?" And I'd say, "What if nothing" in reply.

Then I'd see that brownish patch on the gravel again.

On the Monday it looked as if maybe somebody had spilled motor oil. But you never see flies crawling over a spot of motor oil. And it was right about where his face would have been when I walked by.

And I'd find myself just standing there staring at it, my brain flooding with strange thoughts and questions. And realizing how little separates the living from the dead—a bit of fluid passing through tissue.

And then the real questions. When did he do it? Just as I was pedalling down the road? I know that a .22 doesn't make a very loud noise. And why did he do it? How can somebody become that desperate?

He had a job. He had a place to live. He had friends. He had all the food he could eat. You could tell by the quick way he moved and how easily he'd bend to pick something up and by the colour of his skin that he was healthy for an old man of sixty-two.

Could it be that living far away from your family, and losing any hope of ever seeing them again, can cause such desperation?

That Monday, after staring at the dark spot on the gravel for a while, I kicked at it, but when the gravel scattered I could see the stain was still there, imprinted on the hard earth below the gravel. And there it stayed for as long as I continued delivering newspapers to the camp.

Or did I just imagine it?

But then the camps were finally empty, and there was no longer any need for me to go there. And the stain became a part of that hard place beneath the gravel of memory.

———

The first clue that things were bad came one day when my father called me over to the truck. He'd just arrived home for supper and had obviously stopped for the mail on the way. He had some envelopes in his hand. He held one up.

"Look at this," he said.

"Who is it from?"

"It doesn't matter," he said.

But obviously it did. He instructed me that anytime I pick up the mail, any letter that looks like the one in his hand was not to go in the house.

"Right?"

"Right."

"You put it here instead," he said, opening the truck door and indicating the space behind the driver's seat.

"Okay," I said.

"Look at the envelope again," he said.

I complied.

"What do you see?"

"A letter with a window in it."

"Very good. A letter with a window. What do you do with it?"

"I put it in the truck."

"That's the boy."

In the weeks ahead, there would be a lot of letters with little windows.

———

School can become a welcome distraction from reality. There was no more daydreaming with my mother at the front of the classroom. Even Neil MacIver settled down. Occasionally he'd put on a brief show when he sensed that her mood was appropriate. And, usually, she'd laugh along with everybody else—for about a minute. Then the tone of voice would change and we'd be back to business.

Being alone in grade nine, I often found the line between home and school significantly blurred. On days when there was a lot to do with the other grades, she'd leave my schoolwork for when we were home. That was particularly true for Latin and algebra, two subjects she seems to consider the keys to all success in life. I'm not sure what they're good for. We all know Latin is a dead language, outside the church. I can see the value of arithmetic. But algebra is just a series of puzzles. They can be fun if you're in the mood, and there is a definite feeling of accomplishment when I've translated a Latin story and finally figured it out, or after I've successfully finished a page of algebra problems. But the long-term value of these exercises remains a mystery to me. I understand why we should know subjects like English and history. I realize you never have the feeling of having arrived at a conclusion. The process is endless, and I can see how people spend their entire lives studying history and literature, and growing more uncertain as they go along, and finally ending up completely in the dark.

The stories in history and literature are all about human behaviour, which is impossible to understand no matter how much we know. That much I know from reading the newspapers that I drag around the village every day. But even though you never fully understand them, the stories in the newspapers and the history and the literature all have a particular shape, and the more you read and study and observe, the more similarities you recognize in what has happened before and is happening now, in what is real and what is imaginary.

In September, just after the start of school, he went to a place called Tilt Cove in Newfoundland. Half of Inverness County was over there by the sound of it. Inverness County is famous for its hard-rock miners. And, for my father, the best thing about Tilt Cove was that there was no union there, so he knew the physical would be a piece of cake.

My mother explained that it was a temporary arrangement. They needed good miners. He was a *great* miner. Once the place was in full production, he'd probably be made mine captain. He'd make good money quickly. Then, when we were out of the hole financially, he could pick up where he left off—whatever that meant.

I had my doubts. And then one day there was no longer any doubt. I don't believe in the *buidseachd* and I don't believe in omens. But sometimes there are moments that just smack you between the eyes and, for an instant, you can see where things are going.

That moment came for me at noon hour one day in the fall of '56. We always went home for lunch because we lived so near the school. I remember that this was a rainy day and it was cold. There was a small truck with high sides parked near the barn.

"Whose truck is that?" I asked.

"Ernie MacKay," my mother said.

"Ernie MacKay," I repeated, with a hollow feeling where my stomach is.

"Yes," she said.

She was slicing bread and had her face turned away. I leaned a little bit and saw that her cheeks were flushed.

"Ernie MacKay is . . ."

"It was Ernie MacKay who sold us the cow," she said, trying to sound cheerful.

"That was a long time ago," I said.

"So now he's come and he's been good enough to buy her back," she said.

"But we still need the milk," I said.

The voice was sharp this time.

"We need the money more."

There was no more to be said. I went to my room, no longer hungry. But she called me back. The food was made. It had to be eaten. It is a sin to waste food.

I could see through the kitchen window as Ernie MacKay led Beulah towards the truck on a short rope. I imagined she was staring back at me in confusion. She stumbled on a little ramp leading up to the back of the truck.

Where are we going? I could almost hear her ask.

And, of course, I knew the answer. But she was hidden then behind the high boards around the back of the truck, and I wouldn't have told her anyway.

When Ernie MacKay wasn't selling young cows for their milk, he was butchering old ones for their meat.

———

It is almost winter. At Mr. Clough's store, the talk is about anticipated improvement in snow removal. How much better the Tory snowplough drivers will be. How, after the election, the ploughs will be going up lanes that were never ploughed before. Nobody has to mention that the lanes are where the Tory houses are. And, to rub it in, they mention that the Liberal lanes will also still be ploughed, which is to say that the Tories are more civilized.

Mr. Clough has a sour expression, but you have to imagine it because he turns his back towards the people who are making the comments, pretending to ignore them. He stares out the back window at the strait, probably imagining all the industry that will soon line the shores of this deep new harbour, no matter who wins the election. That would cheer him up—new industry, new people, new money for his store.

He says nothing to contradict the people who are talking about the likelihood of a new government because he, like everybody else, knows that his power will soon be diminished. He hears all the talk: that the fall of the Liberal government in Nova Scotia will just be the beginning of a big political change that will sweep across the country. The papers are full of a new Tory leader in the national party—a man named John Diefenbaker. And speculation that he will defeat the Liberal government within a year.

Diefenbaker?

"Poof," says Mr. Clough. "Nobody named Diefenbaker will ever lead the country."

"Wait and see," the Tories say.

And you can almost hear everybody asking the same question—the one they dare not speak aloud: how long can old Mr. Clough expect to hang onto his post office after the federal Tories take power?

Nobody says it aloud because, secretly, they fear that Mr. Clough just might be right. That Mr. Stanfield, by some stroke of bad luck, will lose. Or that no prairie lawyer with a name like Diefenbaker will ever get to be the prime minister of Canada, a country always run by men with Anglo-Saxon, Scottish, or French names. And that being so, Mr. Clough's political clout isn't likely to disappear anytime soon.

Plus: no matter what happens, the Masons will always run things no matter who is in power in politics, and Mr. Clough is one of the biggest Masons around.

When the talk isn't about the Tories and the Grits, it's about the new Trans-Canada Highway and what route it will follow passing through the village.

The old MacKinnon house, where Phemie and Mary lived, is now empty and will soon be torn down or moved. It is right beside the church. Will that be next? And then the school? And our house?

There are rumours that all the houses below the road will have to go. The brown house we lived in briefly after Newfoundland, the old MacFadyen place. MacQuarries' and Bernie Ryan's, which used to belong to Miss Christine MacKinnon. And even Mrs. George MacLean's, one of the biggest and grandest old houses in the village.

I've heard that the politicians are having trouble making up their minds about where to put the road, at least on this end. And that there are sections, further inland, where they've already started digging.

Not that it would make much difference for us. My father is back underground.

———

Then you notice the good things more easily. Angus Walker Jr. put together a country music group called the Radio Rangers, and his career as a cowboy singer seemed to be taking off. The Radio Rangers were getting a lot of airtime on *Fun at Five*, the big radio program around here. The host is called the Old Timer, but everybody knows that his real name is J. Clyde Nunn and that he represents Inverness County in the provincial legislature. People find it strange that someone who lives on the mainland would be a political representative for Inverness, but, because of the radio show, everybody considers Nunn to be from his place, no matter where he lives. Inverness is a two-member constituency, and the second member of the legislature from here is another Grit named Rod MacLean.

Tories criticize J. Clyde Nunn because he lives in Antigonish, and

Rod MacLean because, they say, he's homely. But they keep getting elected.

And October 30, 1956, was no exception. Even though Mr. Stanfield's Tories ended twenty-three years of Liberal government in Nova Scotia, they couldn't crack Inverness County.

A very bad sign of things to come, my Tory women said, shaking their heads.

Then, shortly after Mr. Stanfield was sworn in as premier of the province, a big company in Sweden, called Stora Kopparberg, confirmed that it was interested in building a pulp mill in the Strait of Canso area.

And the Liberals were saying, "Ah, well. The politicians don't have much to do with it in the long run. And better the Swedes anyway. The Americans already own too much of Nova Scotia."

One afternoon in December I was on my way to pick up my papers at Mrs. Lew's and strike out to the north on my bicycle. It was raining slightly and cold. As I passed Robert Morrison's Esso station, I saw a familiar car at the gas pumps. It was the Malones.

I hadn't been seeing much of Billy. For much of the summer he was away, back visiting relatives in Lower Woods Harbour, and when he returned he had his cousin Roger Nickerson with him, and they seemed to be busy doing things together a lot of the time. I had the paper route, which was an interruption every summer day, though I took a break for a couple of weeks—in Dingwall at my Uncle Joe's place, hanging around with my cousin Lester Donohue. It was fun, but I kind of lost touch with my friend Billy Malone. Then, when school started, I was busy with grade nine.

And there, suddenly, was the Malones' car at the gas pumps. Mr. Malone was standing beside it, and he was dressed up. When I approached the car, I could see that it was so full of bags and boxes that I almost missed Billy and his sister, Phyllis, jammed into the back seat, looking very small.

Billy saw me and rolled down the window and just stared at me, without saying anything. He had a sad expression on his face.

His father was smiling and came over with his hand out. I shook it.

"Bill," he called out. "Come here and say goodbye."

Goodbye?

"The job is finished here now," Mr. Malone said. "We're heading back home."

"Home? I thought this was home."

Mr. Malone laughed. "It feels like home," he said. "And we'll always come back for visits and whatnot. But home is down the south shore."

South Shoah.

And I realized I'd forgotten that they weren't from here, and, now that the causeway was completed, there was no reason for them to stay. I suddenly felt very small too.

Then Billy was standing there beside his tall, gaunt father, who always reminded me of those fathers in the comic books or in the movies, with his warm smile and his pipe.

"I guess I'll be seeing you," Billy said.

"I guess," I said.

"Maybe I'll write."

"Okay," I said. "You write first because you know the address here."

"Okay," he said.

But he never did.

The last I saw of him, he was looking back from the car as they headed down the new road, past the new tourist information bureau, towards the new bridge over the new canal that our fathers helped to build. And it was a strange feeling, watching them disappear over the new causeway that everybody thought would be mostly for bringing new people here—not for sending them away.

———

I really didn't expect him home for Christmas because the finances were obviously in bad shape when he left. But he came home and the cheer was strong. You'd hear them talking about how we were finally getting back on our feet, with the teaching job and the fact that he'd been making some good bonus pay at Tilt Cove.

I had a small pile of letters with windows stashed away, but when he took them his face didn't get the heavy expression that I expected. He winked.

I got a .22 for Christmas, and at some point over the holiday we visited the mountain to check on the old folks. We took the new rifle, to try it out on some rabbits. I'd never hunted rabbits before. It was time to learn to do it properly, now that I had my own rifle.

It was the usual visit. Wall-to-wall Gaelic, with Grandma doing ninety percent of the talking.

As usual, I sat there watching and listening. Grandma looked, I realized, like photographs I've seen in *National Geographic*—pictures taken of people who live on remote islands in the North Atlantic; old women with long dresses and shawls, their white hair blowing in the wind.

She had clear blue eyes and a bony face, and when she spoke in her own language the opinions flew like sparks. You could easily believe she had special powers. I wondered how you'd go about persuading her to put them to work for you. I guess that, at the very least, you'd have to speak to her in Gaelic.

And then I had the strangest feeling. It is a feeling I often get on the mountain when I hear the wind struggling and sighing in the trees. And the fact that it is Christmas now makes me realize that this feeling has something to do with a Christmas long ago.

I've always loved going to the mountain. How my cousins there are always laughing and carrying on, and their mother never seems to notice, no matter how rowdy we get, inside or outside. And how, in summertime, you can run forever through the cool woods, your feet springing back from the rubbery moss, and the tree limbs dense as a roof above. Crashing over Rough Brook, shoes soaked and pants wet to the knees, but not concerned because they'll dry before anybody notices. And anyway, it's only water. John Dan's Mae chuckling and saying, "You only have to worry about getting wet if you're made of sugar."

What I couldn't explain was the dark feeling that would come over me without warning from time to time when I was there, as at this very moment. Sitting listening to them talking seriously in Gaelic, while the stove snaps and cracks and hisses.

And then it's as if I've fallen asleep and am dreaming. And there's an abandoned truck, nose buried in the bushes. A deep rut in a wood road, with a small spruce growing in the tread tracks. A sawdust pile, flattened by time and weather, slabs and trimmings interlaced with weeds, almost out of sight.

And there is a sound, as if the forest sobs. And there is no other sound. And then a chill.

I am on the mountain, but it is still the early autumn. The hills rising gently around us are blinding reds and yellows and flaming orange. The air is moist and cool and smells of earth. There is a truck, and now I can recall that my father named it Leapin' Lena, and every time he mentions it I want to laugh. But now he's handing the keys to Leapin' Lena to another, older man. He had a horse for working in the woods. The horse's name is Tony. My grandfather is standing near the gate at the end of the hill below his house, and he is holding Tony by the bridle.

Behind them the mill is silent. There is a tangled pile of long, thin spears of wood that they call edgings. There is a small mountain of slabs, which can be used for firewood. A sawdust pile, in which my cousins and I would leap and roll and become hopelessly covered in the itching, scratching particles of wood, looms over the silent circular saw.

I see my father climb into a car with other men. The car drives away. The older man walks to the front of Leapin' Lena and starts the engine with a crank. My grandfather speaks to Tony, who tosses his head, then turns, and they walk off up the hill towards the house.

This is what they call the past. I struggle back, into the present. Into the dingy kitchen, with the winter sulking in the hills outside. And now I strain to understand the droning Gaelic conversation. Maybe something in it will help me to see the future. The name Stanfield comes up a lot. My father is smoking a cigarette, carefully placing the ashes in the cuff of his trousers. He has one leg balanced across a knee. Grandpa Dougald is at the corner of the table picking at his fingers. He has a floppy woollen cap on his bald head.

I stand. Nobody notices. I walk out to the porch, where I can still smell the faint sour smells of milk from the time when they kept a cream separator there. Old coats and caps are hanging on nails driven into the wooden walls. I pick up my new .22, which is leaning in a corner, and walk outside, admiring the smooth shining wooden stock and dull black barrel.

Near the barn I pause. A crow squawks, lifting off from a corner of the barn roof. "One crow, sorrow," my mother always says. Just like her mother.

The past returns. It is another Christmas. There is snow. It is my mother's birthday, but she is unhappy. She has been unhappy for some time now. I first noticed the sadness on a morning before the snow when I found her in the yard in a housecoat watching the sunrise, holding a fist with a clenched handkerchief to her face.

When I asked her what was wrong, she said, "Nothing."

But though I was only, maybe, four, I remembered. Leapin' Lena driving off, and Grandpa Dougald leading Tony to the barn. And me, lost and invisible in the sadness of the adults. And my father saying nothing, just getting into a car with the other men. And then they drove away.

"You go back inside," my mother says. "I'll only be another minute. We'll make some porridge."

And we did.

That night her friends came by—William and Anita, Elsie, Roberta, Laidlaw—and they had a small flask. There was music on the radio, and they turned it up. A person had to celebrate a birthday, no matter what.

It was also Christmas. A week before, I'd seen the notice from the post office. There was a large Christmas parcel at the railway station—a large catalogue order. There is always a large catalogue order just before Christmas—COD—which means cash on delivery. And sometime, shortly after the cash is delivered to the station master, the order comes home. The door to the living room is locked, but you can see through the keyhole that there is an unopened package inside. And you know that although all the good things of Christmas come from God and Santa Claus, sometimes They use the post office and the CNR and Eaton's or Simpsons to make the good things happen.

But that year when I peeked through the keyhole a week after the notice came, the parcel wasn't there.

Now it is her birthday, which falls ten days before Christmas. The happy music plays. The voices become louder and merrier. I hear the rare sound of laughter. Then there is a crash, the sound of breaking glass, then silence, followed by the murmur of regretful voices. No sounds of anger.

I peer down from The Hole near the chimney, which passes through my room. Someone is apologizing for breaking something. My mother, happy now, is saying, "It really doesn't matter . . . honestly."

But you can tell the party is over. They are in their coats, gathered at the door. But one hangs back. The man named Laidlaw hovers near the table.

Then he leaves too, and when he is gone I see the twenty-dollar bill he left behind.

The next day I got the mail at Mr. Clough's. There must have been a hundred Christmas cards. My mother was flipping through them anxiously, and then there was an envelope that was not a Christmas card.

"Thank God," she said, laughing.

"What is it?" I asked.

"The baby bonus," she said.

Now there was the baby bonus and the twenty-dollar bill. And when I checked the keyhole two days later, there was the parcel in the corner of the locked parlour.

We had our Christmas. We had a tree and got to Mass. There were gifts and there was turkey. But there was something missing. Somehow I knew I wasn't supposed to ask when or if my father would be home.

And then it was the New Year, and there was still no mention of the missing man.

New Year's Eve we coasted on new sleighs until dark over by MacKinnons'. And when she came to take us home, she was trying to be cheerful. But the falling darkness seemed to be soaking into her expression.

I asked what was wrong, and she said New Year's always made her sad. Another measure of time gone. No way of knowing what the next chunk of time will be like. Getting older and no further ahead. Nothing you have to be concerned about when you're a child, she said, and yanked my arm, trying to start a game.

"Where's Daddy," my sister asked.

"We don't know," she said.

———

I examine the .22. It tells me that I am growing up, soon to be a man with choices. I think briefly of Old John and the choice he made. The choice to die. I feel a brief shudder. Nothing can be that bad. Nothing can be worse than the Christmas when he wasn't with us. And he hasn't missed one since.

I was by the edge of the trees, then, crouched to see beneath the bushes where the white of the rabbit's winter coat would show up against the dusty brown of the underbrush. I didn't hear my father come up behind me.

"What about over there," he said quietly.

I looked. He was pointing off to my left and, just at the edge of the woods, where the snow tapered to a shard of ice, I saw the rabbit crouching.

I turned, cocked, and took aim. Fired. The rabbit turned his head and looked at me indifferently. Then he hopped a few yards into the bushes and stopped again. I flipped the bolt and thumbed another bullet into the firing chamber, cocked, took aim, and fired again. This time the rabbit didn't move.

"Let me see those bullets," my father said.

He examined one, then reached for the rifle, loaded it, cocked, and fired. The bullet snipped a small twig from a bush beside the rabbit's head. This time he vanished in a blurry bound.

My father was examining the rifle barrel.

"Ah. There's our problem," he said.

What?

"The sights," he said. "They aren't lined up."

Later, when I told my mother, she just smiled.

I asked about the smile—insisted there was something wrong with the new rifle. I, inexperienced, might miss a rabbit. My father never would.

"Unless he wanted to," she said.

It was different after he went back. Somehow you knew you'd see him again before too long. But you also knew that, from now on, he would be a visitor. That would be okay. Not perfect, but better than nothing.

8

TED

His appearances always seemed to catch you by surprise. I suppose my mother knew when to expect him, but she'd usually keep the information to herself. The places he invariably found work weren't exactly easy to get away from, so, at best, she'd be guessing if she said when he'd be coming home. But you always had a rough idea where he was and that, whenever the opportunity presented itself, he'd be home for as long as he could possibly extend the visit. The only time we had any real doubt about where he was or when he'd surface was after the first sawmill on the mountain.

Christmas and New Year got by that year with no word from him. Now that I'm older, I can see his point. He'd have left a lot of unsolved financial problems behind and probably figured it was best if the folks back home could truthfully tell people we had no idea where he was.

That time we got by on the goodwill of our neighbours and the line of credit at Mr. Clough's. And, sure enough, he reappeared eventually. He'd been working like a dog in some remote part of Ontario, a hard-rock mine in a place with a name like Pickled Crow—something like that. Somewhere altogether off the map. But he'd been making good money there and was almost ready to start paying off some debts. And how is everybody anyway?

I don't even want to try to guess what the answer might have been.

This time, after what I call the causeway mill, there was no dramatic disappearing act. This time he just went away in the normal fashion. Packed his gear, hugs all around (including the dog), a bit of jokey advice about looking after things since I'm the man. Et cetera.

Then they loaded the duffel bag and a suitcase into the back of the car and headed for the railway station in town. I watched them drive away, wondering how long it would be this time.

It was all for the best, my mother said when she returned alone. We were in dire straits again financially. But it wouldn't take him long to clean the slate now that he'd have a steady income and with her teaching school full time.

With the cow gone, the chores were reduced. And now that the work on the canal was coming to an end, the paper business was hardly worth the effort I was putting into it.

I was in grade nine and finding the schoolwork pretty easy, having been eavesdropping on the course content since I was in grade six. My mother was impressed by my ready knowledge of the role of the machine gun in the conquest of Africa. But I was no longer paying as much attention to the subjects in the grade ahead of me. Too much emphasis on algebra and geometry, and an awful English grammar course that involved a book called *Using Our Language*. I'd sit there daydreaming about the possibility of skipping grade ten altogether. Or maybe actually going to boarding school at the monastery.

That, I presumed, would be determined by the availability of money—assuming you had to pay to go to school over there—and there was no guarantee that we'd be out of the hole by then.

There was another factor distracting me from academic matters. I was noticing subtle changes in people I'd known forever but never took very seriously—girls such as Sylvia and Ann and Isabel and Mabel. Suddenly they were not so much girls as some new species, taking on the appearance and shape and mannerisms of women, without actually turning into adults like your mother or grandmother. Not entirely a desirable development, I realized, because of the cruelty that seems to come so naturally to adolescent females when dealing with men and boys they see as being insignificant.

I knew and accepted that I, just by virtue of my age and lack of a car or driver's licence, was about as insignificant as you could get.

But still, it was a visually interesting process, watching the flat places and sharp angles filling out and turning round. Noting the care they took to conceal parts of themselves that nobody ever used to notice. Chests and legs and rear-ends, mostly, but in their new awareness of these parts, also choosing at unexpected times to reveal them to the unsuspecting. Accidentally, of course.

For all their newfound powers and casual arrogance, the girls in the grade ahead of me were becoming more pleasant to stare at with every passing week. And, to be truthful, I didn't really mind their condescension. They seemed to find me amusing—an occasionally entertaining younger brother, which was good enough for me at the time. Plus, I had the impression that they secretly enjoyed being stared at—that, down deep, they were still just show-offs, the only changes being in what they were showing off.

This time he showed up for the holidays just before Christmas. He arrived home with young John MacMaster from Long Point, and my mother didn't seem to mind that he had what she calls "a little Brannigan" on. Very cheerful all through the visit.

For Christmas I gave him the usual flat-fifty of Players, even though I think smoking is probably a bad idea for someone with questionable lungs. In fact, I read in a recent paper that a French-Vietnamese doctor has proven beyond any doubt that one of the ingredients in cigarettes causes cancer. The good news, according to this doctor's findings, is that the cancer-causing ingredient can be filtered out. So I figure that a flat-fifty full of filtered cigarettes will be a healthy improvement over the unfiltered smokes he rolls for himself.

Predictably, he was gone right after New Year. But, to my surprise, he was home again in February. The Port Hastings notes in the *Bulletin* reported that "D.R. MacIntyre is home on business from Newfoundland, where he is currently employed."

That was different. Business? What business? There was really only one, and it was sitting idle, almost invisible under the heavy snowdrifts. Perhaps the sawmill could be resuscitated after all.

"So what brings you home?"

"Time off for good behaviour!"

Always the clever answer that tells you nothing.

He was around for about a week, and there were many quiet conversations in the kitchen and some business trips to town. I went with him to Troy one snowy day to visit Neil Red Rory, from whom he'd leased some lumber land. The conversation was intense, but with the Gaelic and a lot of long silences, I was lost most of the time.

Then he went away again.

I asked my mother what was going on. All she said was that there wasn't quite as much lumber in Neil Red Rory's woods as they'd expected.

Suddenly I remembered all the stories about the *buidseachd*.

Tilt Cove, from what he had to say, is about as far off the beaten track as anyone would want to get. You can't drive there. Most of the time you take a boat, but in winter, when the northeast coast of Newfoundland is packed with ice, you fly there in a small ski plane and land on a frozen pond. And this particular winter, 1956–57, was the worst in recorded history—nothing but snow and gales and Arctic temperatures. It was one time, he said, when it's a relief to be working underground.

Just getting to the cookhouse was a battle some days. A couple of the Inverness County miners in Tilt Cove took a dog team to visit friends in Shoe Cove, one of the small communities along the coast from there. My father, in particular, was alarmed at their bravado because it reminded him of the winter in St. Lawrence when two of his miner friends, both originally from here in Inverness County, volunteered to walk to Lamaline for the Christmas liquor. A storm blew up when they were on their way back. They got lost and froze to death.

"It was one of those guys who owned the skates you inherited," he told me.

"Really?"

The winter here was almost as bad and, after one storm, I actually borrowed snowshoes to get the papers around. It created a lot of comment among the customers. One of them, Lennie MacDonald, said I should get my picture in the paper for my dedication, getting the paper around in spite of the weather.

The ice on Long Pond was about a foot thick and smooth as glass, and on still, cold nights the older guys would set fire to rubber tires they scavenged from behind Morrison's Esso station. The pungent black smoke shot straight into the windless sky, blotting out entire galaxies of stars, and the flames hurled shadowy light for a hundred feet in all directions.

You could skate on Long Pond, it seemed, forever, but you knew the danger lurking beyond the probing firelight, near the shore where the ice was fissured from the rising of the tides, or in the channel where the water was so swift it never really froze. Away from the blazing fire you'd hear the startling sound of the shifting ice, like gunshots, and the rattle of the northern lights shuddering beyond the starry bulge of the horizon. You'd feel the chilly solitude of the universe, then turn away. Too vast. Too much like the future. The beckoning bonfire would lead you back.

And once, as I approached out of the gloom, I could see a lone shadow floating on the perimeter of the light, swooping and twirling, graceful as the ghost for which the nearby beach is named. Then tip-toed prancing movements, and the ghost would vanish into darkness but just as suddenly return, hands and arms extended, elegant as wings, floating soundless as a moth towards the flames on waves of music only she could hear.

I didn't have to see the face to know it was Mabel MacIver and that, in this moment, she was nurturing the dream she had shared with me during one of our long, serious walks. I watched her in silence, fighting the chill in my feet and the desperate infatuation in my heart.

And then she was floating in my direction.

"I bet you didn't know I could do that," she said gaily.

I just shook my head, imagining that there was nobody on the pond but us. Imagining that I was three or four or five years older. And that I had a car, something like Angus Walker's Monarch, with the chrome wheel stuck on the back and the fender skirts and the whip aerial. And that, after the skating, we'd go somewhere warm, like the comic-book places where teenagers gather to have sundaes and floats and all sorts of exotic concoctions, and flirt with the beautiful Veronicas and Bettys. Because of the cold, we'd probably have cocoa—

Then the rowdy sound of voices and the scrape of blades on ice, and a gang raced towards the bonfire, calling for a game of whiplash. And she pranced off in the direction of the voices, urging all of them to look at her and her figure-skating style.

"Watch me," she cried, rising on one toe and spinning with her elbows held just so.

And everybody was suddenly silent, imagining the day when we'd be paying cash to watch Mabel skating at the Ice Capades.

Now the spell was gone, replaced by the sad, lingering thought that those who dream intensely will, inevitably, disappear. Dreams are what drag us all away. We come back successful, or exhausted strangers.

And I wanted something more, something I could hang onto after we were carried off in different directions. But I knew the most that anyone can take away from anywhere is memory.

———

The talk at Mr. Clough's in April was that, finally, something was happening with the Trans-Canada Highway. Bids had been requested, according to the newspapers, for seventeen miles of new road from Glendale to the intersection of Number 4 and the Victoria Line in Port Hastings. For reasons I don't quite understand, it seemed the work would begin out back and proceed in this direction for some distance before they started breaking ground here.

The big question still was where, exactly, the road would go as it passed through the middle of the village. Everybody seemed to understand why the precise routing of the road had to be kept vague. There were quiet references to sharp operators who buy up property they know will be required for public purposes, and then hire smart lawyers to force the government to pay more than it's worth.

These are the kinds of people who, according to my mother, become successful in business. People with the instincts to jump ahead of others to get the lion's share of what's available ahead of everybody else. People you wouldn't even want to know, let alone become. The government was playing its cards close to its vest so far as the land required in Port Hastings village was concerned.

I'd get the occasional note from my father, sometimes with a deuce or a fiver folded inside. His letters were chatty and funny, and his news was usually about the weather and the food. I'd be waiting for some inquiries about the new road, or some clue to signal when he'd be coming home to take advantage of this new phase in the transformation of the place. But there was nothing to indicate that he had any interest in the road-building project, even though he still had a truck parked beside the barn.

———

From the window of the Big Room, I study the winter causeway and the cape, sharp angles and jagged surfaces smoothed by the furrowed waves of drifted snow, and I try to imagine the place before all this change began. How long ago? Less than sixty months? Strange how memory so quickly empties itself of images that contradict the present moment. It is already difficult to remember details of the strait before the digging and the blasting; I struggle to recall particulars of the constant roar, the incessant bang of piledrivers, and the terrifying ground-heaving explosions that collapsed ten million tons of granite from the ancient mountain. I search the memory. Did the Malones really live here for three years? And Old John. Did he? Really? Just last summer?

A line from my mother's precious Latin book surfaces in my mind: "Carthago delenda est."

At least that's the way it seems sometimes. Rome must erase Carthage. The future must erase the past. I have to admit it—the old village is becoming unrecognizable.

Maybe it's the nature of the winter. Winter creates a sense of uniformity in time and space. Winter returns the landscape to the originality of other winters. New features vanish under nature's timeless garment. And for a while we are comforted by familiarity, the sense of continuity. Snow covering up the damage men do in their surroundings, covering the stains of violence in the shifting gravel and the frozen ground below it.

The last time I stood in front of the staff house at the camp, there were snowdrifts covering the ground and roofs and evergreens, rounding corners, collapsing limbs of trees down upon the lower limbs. In past winters, the walkways around the camp and cookhouse and staff house would be shovelled, the doorsteps neatly swept. Old John would be furiously attacking the snow, heavy coat hanging open, heavy woollen cap with untied earlugs hanging down. Now, I thought, the snow has reclaimed the place, and there is no longer any trace of John.

Where was it I saw him last?

Sitting there. Working on the step. Looking underneath for something. That is what I saw.

He didn't speak.

He was busy.

What about the rifle?

You imagine you imagined it.

Oh.

You must. And it's suddenly so very easy with all the snow to cover up the scars and stains of yesterday.

The early winter darkness was gathering around me, the wind was groaning in the tall spruces. I looked down and, for an instant, Old John was sitting there, his bald head pale as the pristine snow. And in that instant there is no rifle, and when I speak he turns his head and smiles as if he's glad to see me. But, still, he doesn't answer me. He turns back to his chore.

Near the cookhouse new snow swirls, lifts, drifts off towards the trees like smoke. The place is silent, but for the moaning of wind in creaking trees. Something has been altered fundamentally, but the snow conceals the significance of change.

I walk away from the abandoned camp, knowing I will not return. There is nothing here.

"Carthago delenda est."

My mother says, "Excuse me! Helllooo."

A snap of fingers.

Where were we?

Yes. Machine guns in Africa.

———

George the Wheeler is staggering when he accosts me. I haven't seen him since my father built the little camp in Troy and hired George the Wheeler to cut logs there.

"Your old man is a crook," he sneers.

I can smell the yeastiness of cheap wine and, when he turns away, I see the bottle sloshing in the back pocket of his overalls.

"You can tell him that," he says over his shoulder.

I feel an odd paralysis and know that afterwards, after this confusion falls away, I'll feel the self-accusing anger. Why didn't you say . . . ? You should have . . . ?

What?

He called my father a crook!

The impulse rises. Lash out, punish the injustice of the charge. Stand up for your father even if there's half a chance that what the Wheeler says is true.

"You can tell him that," he repeats as he stumbles on his way. "Nothin' but a friggin' crook."

I want to say: I'll do us both a favour; I'll forget that this encounter ever happened.

I want to go after him . . . the way the Irish would.

My mother sighs. "He probably owes the Wheeler money."

"That doesn't make him a crook."

"The Wheeler was probably drunk."

"He was."

"He'll get his money," she says. "When we have it, he'll get it."

"Which is why he's in Tilt Cove?"

"Which is why he's in Tilt Cove."

———

In May I saw surveyors in Mrs. George's apple orchard. The orchard is just below the house where Harry and Rannie MacDonald live, across the Victoria Line from the church. Our field and house are directly above Harry and Rannie's. The sawmill is at the far side of the field, just up past the orchard. Nobody was quite sure what the surveyors were doing there.

Then one evening in mid-May, my mother announced that my Aunt Veronica had an interesting new boarder—all the way from South Korea. An engineer or engineering student.

"South Korea?"

"Yes. His name is Ted."

One of the things my Aunt Veronica does to survive is take in boarders. She had Mrs. Hennessey when she was teaching in the Little Room. She had two interesting men from Quebec when they were building the causeway—Camille and Marcel. Friendly guys, with hardly any English. We'd spend ages practising each other's language.

How do you say this? Or that? In English. In French.

Then they were gone.

Now she has a boarder from Korea. I remembered Jean Larter's kerchief, the one Joe brought her back from the war. And I tried to remember all I had read about the war. Korea. A peninsula. Split in two. Communists on top. United Nations. Lots of Americans. Syngman Rhee. A meaningless jumble.

His name wasn't really Ted, he explained. That was what they started calling him at Nova Scotia Tech, the university in Halifax where engineers are trained. He had one more year to go at Tech, and then he'd be a mechanical engineer and get to wear the little iron ring on his pinkie finger.

There was nothing in the world as impressive as that ring.

"So what's your real name?" I asked.

"Tae," he said. "Tae Man Chong."

But he liked Ted better. Easier to fit in being called Ted.

I figured him to be in his mid-twenties.

Then the story was going around the village that this Chinaman showed up one day at Morrison's Esso asking if this was Port Hastings. He'd just come off the causeway on a bus. Alistair MacDougall was working there.

"Yes," he said. "You're in Port Hastings."

"What's the population of Port Hastings?" the Chinaman asks.

"A hundred and fifteen," says Alistair.

"Well, now it's a hundred and sixteen," says the Chinaman.

"Korean," I say.

"What?"

"He's from Korea."

"No shit!"

And that was Ted. Number one hundred and sixteen. You could actually imagine that he planned to stay.

I never thought of people of other races being handsome, although my mother always says that women in Japan are the most beautiful in the world. Like little dolls, she says. But I find people of the Orient or Africa just too exotic to be described by words we use to evaluate other people like ourselves. Handsome or homely—what do these words really mean?

After I got used to his appearance, it crossed my mind that I'd like to be exactly like Ted. He was taller than I was, slim, but with wide shoulders. He had a broad, open face. His skin was darker and his almond eyes twinkled. And he had a smile that lit up the room. He liked nothing more than laughing, and he always seemed to be finding things to laugh about in our village. The thing that I quickly learned about Ted was that he wasn't different at all. He wasn't exotic. Everybody here was different. Everybody here was exotic. After I figured that out, it was fun to be around him. He made you feel interesting.

I also learned that nothing would bug him more than being mistaken for someone who is Chinese. Even I understood that much. After all, it was the Chinese Communists who were responsible for the mess in his country. I never told him that, when he first arrived, a lot of people here thought he came from China. Or that Miss Annie Christie loves the Chinese people.

Korea, I learned, is near Japan. And that Japan occupied Korea before World War II and that Ted attended Japanese school when he was a boy in Seoul, Korea. He remembered the terrible days when atomic bombs blew two Japanese cities apart. His father took him to Japan after the war just to see Hiroshima, one of the cities the atomic bomb destroyed. It was terrible, he said.

"But Japan was the enemy," I said.

"Yes," he said. "That's how it is in war. There has to be an enemy. But there's no war now, and if there ever is another, we'll all be friends."

"Okay. So what was it like in a Japanese school?"

The best part of attending Japanese school, he explained, was learning how to speak Japanese fluently, and also learning judo. Judo was on the curriculum.

"No kidding. Judo on the curriculum?"

He swore that it was true. And to prove he knew judo, he flipped me over his hip and dropped me gently onto the grass in front of my aunt's house.

I was amazed at how smoothly and how quickly he did it.

"Will you teach me that?" I asked.

"Maybe," he said. "We have all summer."

All summer. Strange how it sounds like such a long time when you say it and it's still spring and you've just turned fourteen.

You don't think that Billy Malone was here for three years. And Marcel and Camille from Quebec were here for a whole winter. Your father was around for the entire time they spent building the causeway. And Old John—he'll be here forever, but, still, he's gone just the same. They're all gone. And it was like a blink of an eye, the time you knew them. And now they're gone, maybe never to be seen again.

We have all summer, says Ted. And he's also going to teach me Japanese.

First word. *Arigato.*

"What's that?"

"Thank you."

"Arigato!"

"You're welcome."

He was going to teach me judo and Japanese. What could I do in exchange?

"Take me fishing," he said. "And introduce me to girls." He was serious. He even bought a second-hand car.

At first it was the judo I found important. I suppose I had realized for a long time that the world is full of perils, and most of them are in the form of people. Everywhere, it seems, people are preying on each other until the weaker ones are driven away or driven to some act of desperation. Once upon a time you never really paid attention. There was the odd whack on the nose or minor bullying by bigger guys like Angus L. Cameron. But the nose gets better and the bigger guys get mellower or move away. You slip back into a safe stupidity.

But gradually the picture changes, and you realize that the most important thing in life is to be able to take care of yourself. It's another form of freedom.

It was purely coincidence, but shortly before Ted showed up, I'd sent away for a book on jiu-jitsu. I'd never heard of it before, but it seemed to be something I should know when I saw it advertised on the back of a comic book. And in spite of my mother's warning that products advertised on the backs of comics are a whole lot less than they seem, this book was actually pretty good.

Ted didn't think very much of it, though. Put the book away, he advised.

Then he offered to teach me a little bit of judo—just enough to stay out of trouble. That's what it's all about, he said. Staying out of trouble or, if that becomes impossible, getting out of a scrape with minimal fuss. Disabling the enemy, preferably without doing too much harm. Hurting people, he figured, just makes them more dangerous.

It made a lot of sense and, as the weather got warmer and the ground drier, we'd practise on the grass in my aunt's yard. Ted gently disabled me by knocking me down or locking my arms behind me—simple, effortless stuff that never hurt.

"But what if you want to hurt someone?" I asked him once. "What if you have to hurt him?"

"You'll have only one chance," he said. "So you have to strike where there can be no quick recovery."

"His balls," I said.

"Oh no," he said, laughing. "You miss his balls, you're dead. And everybody has an instinct to protect his balls."

"What then, if not the balls?" I asked.

He looked at me very seriously for a moment.

Then he said: "The eyes."

"Show me," I said.

"No," he replied.

My father loved going fishing, but he rarely ever caught anything, so I hardly ever went fishing with him. He liked going to lakes and brooks in the woods. I preferred the strait or the cove, where you always caught something, even if it was only a useless perch. Sometimes you'd catch the ugliest creature in the world, a sculpin. Even a hungry cat won't eat a sculpin, they're so ugly. So you catch them and rub their stomach with a stick and, for some reason, they fill up with air like a football. Then you throw them back and watch them drift away, struggling to get back under the water where they belong.

But mostly you try to catch what you can eat—mackerel or smelt.

Ted was interested in trout, which meant I had to take him places where I knew my father fished. We'd end up walking for miles through the woods, only to come home empty handed. Just like me, he gradually lost interest in fishing.

———

Then my aunt had to go to the hospital. I'm not sure why. She announced one day that she was going to St. Joseph's in Glace Bay, and that she'd be gone for a while. And that meant Ted had to find another place to live, at least temporarily.

Sylvia Reynolds's mother, Anita, took in tourists overnight but agreed to take a boarder for a week or two, so Ted moved in there. I guess it's safe to say he developed another interest. Sylvia was almost seventeen.

One Friday evening when my aunt was in the hospital, Ted announced that we should go to visit her. Saturday morning, he said, he and I and my aunt's boys, Barry and Blaise, were going to Glace Bay to see her. Glace Bay is even farther away than Sydney, and you have to pass through Sydney to get there.

"Better still," he said. He wanted to see Sydney.

That was the thing about Ted. He wanted to see everything. He wanted to feel everything and eat everything. He wanted to go everywhere in the world. And he kept telling me about the parts of it he'd already seen. And the part he mostly wanted to see and experience was America.

"The States?"

"Yes," he said. "New York."

We'd go to the movies in town, and he'd sit in a trance, his eyes wide and this little smile on his face, watching the Americans with their cocktails and their cars and their cities and their wars. His excitement was catching.

He was in love, he said, with an American movie star. Jean Simmons.

"Who?"

"Jean Simmons."

"I never heard of Jean Simmons."

"You never heard of Jean Simmons? The most beautiful woman in the world?"

"Sorry."

On the way to Glace Bay, he took me and my two cousins, who saw even less of their father than I saw of mine, to a restaurant and insisted that we order something more interesting than the hot chicken sandwich.

"Like what?"

"How about Italian spaghetti?"

"What's it like?"

"Delicious."

And it was.

And, afterwards, we visited my Aunt Veronica, who looked pale and uncomfortable in the sickly smelling room, with nuns peeking in the door to examine the exotic strangers, and the smell of city on the breezes that were pushing starchy curtains up against us where we stood around the bed.

Something about the hospital made my stomach feel queasy. Or maybe it was the spaghetti. In any case, we weren't allowed to visit very long. The nuns eventually came in and shooed us out. And we were soon back in Ted's car, driving around like tourists and taking pictures of Glace Bay and Sydney. And then, when it was dark, Barry and Blaise fell asleep in the back seat, and he told me about the world as we drove the twisting road back home.

Next year, he said, maybe we would go together to see New York— the most interesting place in the world.

"Sure," I said.

"We'll drive there," he promised.

And we would eat Japanese food, which is the most delicious food anywhere.

Had I ever heard of sukiyaki?

"No."

"Oh, wow. Wait until you eat sukiyaki. Yum yum."

"How long will it take to drive to New York?" I asked.

"Oh, days and days. But you'll be helping with the driving."

"But I don't drive."

"Oh, but you'll learn by then," he said.

And I suddenly realized with a sinking heart: he doesn't even know how old I am. He doesn't realize that I'm just fourteen. I won't even be able to get a driver's licence for two more years. And where will Ted be by then?

———

Sylvia was probably the first girl I ever knew, apart from my sisters and Annie MacKinnon—Ian's sister. Sylvia was almost three years older than I was, so you'd notice her and pay attention. Even though she was a lot older, she always seemed to treat me as if I mattered, and I guess that made her special. Plus, she was pretty, and she'd started looking grown-up ahead of most of them.

It didn't surprise me that Ted liked Sylvia. She's very direct, without being forward, and likes to make you laugh. And it didn't surprise me that she liked him. He was good-looking and funny, and he always wanted to be going somewhere interesting and had a car. Cars are important here because everything is far away.

I'd drop by to see him when he was boarding at her place while my aunt was in the hospital, and they'd be carrying on and laughing. And soon Sylvia was going on drives with us, to movies or the beach. And afterwards, instead of saying good night and going right in, we sat out in Ted's car and talked and joked. Sylvia and I explained everything about the place to Ted, and there seemed to be no end to his curiosity.

Sometimes he told us about home, but never much. It was as though he didn't think where he was from was half as interesting as where he was at any given time—the exact opposite of most people here. No matter where you are, when you're from here, you just can't stop talking about home or longing to be there.

I got the impression that Ted's family was important and that his father was influential. I never really understood why it was important to see a disaster like Hiroshima. Only once, very briefly, he talked about it and what the atomic bomb did to all the people there.

And we were all quiet for a while, waiting for more of the story. But he wouldn't talk about it anymore, and I knew we shouldn't ask.

Ted usually loved to talk about everything. But as the summer advanced, I noticed that he enjoyed talking about Sylvia more than anything.

Near the end of June, he asked me if I'd go on a double date with him and Sylvia.

I wanted to tell him I'd never been on a date. The word made me uneasy. It was like driving—something I looked forward to, some day, when I was ready.

But, remembering his expectations based on assuming I was more grown up than I really am, I didn't want to disappoint him again.

"A date," I said, trying to sound casual.

"A double date. Two couples."

"Couples? Where to?"

"The prom."

The prom was in town—a dance for people leaving high school and moving on to jobs or higher education. Going to a prom wouldn't have ever crossed my mind even if I was graduating.

"I don't think—"

"Come on," he said. "It will be fun."

"And who will you be taking," I asked, as if I didn't know.

Sylvia lined me up with Alice McGowan, who, like Sylvia, was graduating from grade ten. Alice is the daughter of Mr. McGowan, the storekeeper. Mercifully Alice, even though she is older, was as green as I was, and we mostly spent the night watching Ted and Sylvia dancing up a storm.

———

One day he asked me if I knew how to get to Lake Horton.

"Of course I do."

"I hear there's trout in Lake Horton."

"Maybe."

"Let's go fishing in Lake Horton."

It's a couple of miles out back, and he wanted to walk. That's the other thing about Ted. He was always wanting to walk places, which I found peculiar for someone with a car. Ted was always talking about exercise and staying in shape and being healthy. Apparently walking is good for you.

"Okay. We'll walk."

It seemed to take forever and, after all the effort, we didn't even get a bite. I think it was on the way back that I noticed stakes driven in the ground along the side of the dirt road.

"I did that," he announced.

I remembered. He's working as a surveyor. Working on the new Trans-Canada.

"How long . . ." I asked. "How long before you're in the village?"

"It won't be long," he said.

We just walked on then in silence for a change.

———

Our biggest expedition was around the Cabot Trail. It's at the very north end of the island, a gravel road that crosses at least five different mountains and, in places, hovers dangerously over the sea. He heard about it in Halifax. And when he heard that we had a grandmother living almost on the trail, he wouldn't stop talking about it until my Aunt Veronica told him he should go and take me and Barry, and we could all stay at Grandma's.

Driving there, I was trying to imagine Grandma Donohue's reaction to her first Korean, and I guess I was surprised that she didn't seem to notice he was at all different from all the other people she knows. She was on the front verandah waving when we drove up her lane, glad as anything to see us. We were hardly out of the car before you could smell the cooking, and it was as though Ted had grown up there in Bay St. Lawrence, the smile that came over his face at Grandma's welcome and the aroma in her kitchen. Grandma Donohue is a wicked cook.

Of course she doesn't have electricity or indoor plumbing, and that was pretty fascinating for Ted, who, I was convinced, came from a pretty fancy upbringing back in his own country. It wasn't that he looked down on us for being poor. He just seemed genuinely interested in the fact that an old lady could live alone in a clean, tidy old house without being connected to any of the power lines and waterlines and pavement that people nowadays seem to think are necessary for survival.

And I was thinking: wait until I take him to the mountain; wait until he meets my other grandmother, if he thinks this is old fashioned.

He kept asking questions about the winter, and how much snow they get. And Grandma pointed out that she doesn't spend the winters down there anymore because she moves to Port Hastings to help out at our place now that my mother is teaching school. The fact is that she's been coming up for winters for years now, well before my mother went back to teaching. But Grandma is proud. She wouldn't want anybody thinking that a bit of snow would leave her helpless. Or that she stays at our place in the winter without being useful to the house. If anyone has any doubt about how proud she is, watch her at Mass sometime, standing through even the longest Gospels when other older folk are giving up and sitting down. Grandma makes a point of sitting near the front, and she'll stand and sit and kneel with the best of them—even standing through the entire Passion, which takes the priest forever to get through, on Palm Sunday. She'll stand there in her black coat, with her trim black hat on top of her head, straight as a soldier. That's what Grandma Donohue is like.

And after supper, when she lit the lamps, she explained to us how, when she was young, they had only candles for light, and how making candles out of tallow was one of the skills she learned when she was still a little girl. And that got her into the real old times—people struggling to keep food on the table day by day. And Ted sitting there, taking it all in as if he was at a movie.

Shortly after dark, we all went to bed. I had the lounge in the kitchen, underneath her clock, which has to be the loudest clock on earth. Or it just sounds that way because of the unusual silence in a house that doesn't have electricity running through wires or water running through pipes. The clock is like one of those piledrivers they used building the canal—pock, pock, pock—with nothing but pitch-black silence in between the pocks. Anyway, I couldn't get to sleep, so went out and sat on the verandah step for a while. It was just as noisy there, with the sound of crickets and other nighttime creatures squeaking and squawking in the darkness. Every now and then a dog or the rattle of a distant car. Then the black silence again, and underneath the darkness, like a thick blanket, the deep, deep rumble of the ocean rolling against the rocky shore half a mile away.

Eventually I got sleepy.

The next day, after breakfast, we toured around, and Ted loved looking at the sea. I explained that the next stop to the east of where we stood was Newfoundland, and after that, Ireland, where the Donohues all came from long ago. And he wanted to know how they got here, and I had to tell him I don't know for sure. It was because they were so poor they had to leave the Old Country, and, while they were still poor over here, at least they didn't have people persecuting them just because they were Irish.

He didn't think Grandma Donohue sounded Irish, and I had to admit I wasn't sure what she was. Her name, before she was a Donohue, was Capstick, and they came up from the States after the American Revolution. And Grandma Donohue was very partial to the States and worked there once when she was a girl. And she loves to talk about it. Something else they had in common, my grandmother and Ted—their affection for America.

Coming home in the evening, he noticed a contraption on the top of Money Point Mountain, and I told him I thought it was a radar base.

That got his interest, and he wasn't going to rest until we went up to look at it. So we drove up, but you couldn't get very close because of the high fences and the warnings about what would happen if you trespassed. So we had to head back, and Ted decided it would be boring to go back on the same road and we should find another way to go down the mountain. I said I thought the road looped around and connected to another road that goes down and comes out near Grandma's.

"Great," he said.

And sure enough, the road soon crested the top of the mountain, and you could see the countryside sprawled out below, all the little farms and the tall white church in the distance. And the ocean glittering, with the sun dropping towards the western horizon.

I guess we were hypnotized by the breathtaking view and didn't notice that the road had turned into something that resembled a plunging river bed. And it was suddenly so steep that the three of us were leaning back as far as possible to keep from falling forward. You couldn't stop and you couldn't turn and you couldn't back up.

Ted went very quiet. It's hard to imagine, but he actually got pale. And when you could smell smoke from the rubber on the brake shoes burning, little beads of sweat popped out on his forehead.

I actually started praying—silently, of course—which I'm inclined to do when things get tense. And they got increasingly tense as we slid down the mountainside, the wheels actually locked at times. Ted now chewed on his upper lip. For a while it seemed that the car would tumble end over end, and we'd all be in the ocean.

Once he looked in my direction and laughed. But it wasn't the laugh of someone having fun. It was the short hysterical cackle of someone who seems to have just realized that we are going to die.

But of course we didn't. The road became a road again, and Ted could take his foot off the brake. And we could all breathe again.

Barry said "Wow" and actually admitted that, for once in his life, he'd been scared.

Ted laughed and said scared was an understatement.

Grandma Donohue was horrified when she heard that we'd driven down the back road over Money Point Mountain. Nobody has used that road for years, she said. And there has never been a car on it before.

She was almost cross, looking at Ted as if he was out of his mind. And I could tell that he felt guilty for risking all our lives, even though he'd had no idea what we were getting into when we were getting into it. Which, I guess, is how a lot troubles happen.

I got the impression after our adventure that he was growing distant. Maybe he was embarrassed by our close call on Money Point Mountain, or maybe just bored by my company. I was always asking questions, plaguing him with trying to learn Japanese and judo almost overnight—things that, I know, take years to learn. But I was in a hurry because, somehow, I knew I didn't have a lot of time. He'd seemed happy giving me lists of words to learn and carefully writing down a simple version of the Japanese alphabet. He was less enthusiastic about the judo but could be persuaded to show me a trick from time to time.

I knew he was supposed to be studying to write an important exam when he got back to Halifax, but he could never seem to get motivated. Then one evening he announced that he was expecting a visitor, if we didn't mind.

He was back at my aunt's place then, and she asked who the visitor was.

"My girlfriend," he announced. "Dr. Kim."

"Dr. Kim?"

"From New York City."

My aunt said Dr. Kim was welcome and that she could have her own room. My aunt would sleep on the cot.

Now, suddenly, when I'd go over to my aunt's in the evenings for a visit, he'd be gone or up in his room lying on the bed, hands behind his head, staring at the ceiling—like someone in a mood.

Dr. Kim was as pretty as one of those Japanese dolls my mother was talking about. A very nice woman, always smiling and interested. You'd think Ted would be drooling over her, but he was just being his usual friendly self.

And then she went back to New York, and he didn't talk about her—which I found strange.

One evening as I was walking along the road, I saw his car pulling away from Sylvia's and heading off towards town. And I realized that the moods and the absences didn't have anything to do with me or Dr. Kim at all.

I felt relief knowing that I hadn't offended him or bored him. But I also felt something else that I now can identify as jealousy. After thinking about it for a while, I recognized the feeling as a natural frustration at being so much younger than all the people I wanted to be close to. It was, it seemed, the story of my life—almost everybody was too young or too old. With Billy Malone gone, there was hardly anybody close to my age except Ian MacKinnon and Jackie Nicholson.

One evening he asked me straight out: "How old are you anyway?"

"Fourteen," I said.

"Oh," he said, as if, somehow, I'd let him down.

I asked him what was wrong with being fourteen.

He just laughed and punched my shoulder. "Nothing," he said.

But later he told me that he'd heard from someone that people in the village were making comments about an older guy like him hanging around with a kid like me—which was why he was curious about my age.

"You seem older," he said.

And then I realized what was probably on his mind: our trip to New York. And the fact that I might be too young to go on that kind of an adventure. At least I'd be too young to help him with the driving.

So I tried to reassure him. "Sometimes you can get a driver's licence when you're fifteen," I said. "I guess I'll just have to start learning how to drive right away."

"Sure," he said.

But down deep I knew that the trip to New York City and the sukiyaki had become significantly less probable.

And then one day in the late summer I saw him working in the village. First I didn't recognize him in the boots and hard hat and working clothes. Then he took the hat off and wiped his forehead. He seemed totally absorbed in his work.

He was, in fact, just below the church, and he was peering through a transit. I followed his sightline until I noticed the two men holding up a pole in the far corner of Mrs. George's orchard. Following on past where they were standing, I realized that I was looking at my father's sawmill.

———

Sylvia turned seventeen, and her mother put on a surprise birthday party. It was for people who she went to school with. Ted wasn't there. We played music and danced around in sock feet and ate sandwiches and sweets and drank soft drinks. I kept secretly looking at Sylvia and wondering if she was half as serious about Ted as he was about her.

You just couldn't tell.

The party got mentioned in the village notes in the *Victoria-Inverness Bulletin*. How her mother put on the party, and who-all showed up—the usual crowd. Ian and Jackie and Neil, etc. And "the misses" Mabel MacIver, Isabel Fox, and Linda MacIntyre . . .

I'd have been humiliated, except that, by the time the story came out in the *Bulletin*, almost everyone was gone. Sylvia and Isabel and Mabel and Ann Fraser to the boarding school in Mabou. Neil MacIver to the academy in Port Hood. Ted back to Halifax for his final year at Nova Scotia Tech.

———

One day after school I heard a knock at the door at home, and when I went to check on who was there, I saw a man in a suit, carrying a briefcase in his hand.

I called my mother. She went out and, after a few words with the stranger, shut the door behind her.

They talked for a while, and then she opened the door to come back in, but, for just a moment, the conversation continued. I heard just phrases. "A sorry situation" was one phrase she used. Another was "a person's livelihood."

The man didn't look very happy and was actually trying to apologize as she closed the door on him.

"What was that about?" I asked.

"They're going to expropriate part of our field."

"Expropriate?"

"They're going to take it for the road."

"What part?"

"The part that has the sawmill on it."

So that was it. And it made sense. All you had to do was stand at the top of the causeway and look straight ahead, following the line the road was taking. The church was safe, but the mill was in the way. Likewise, before too long, all the houses below the road. Even the old Phemie MacKinnon place, which they've moved once already. And, I suppose, if you look farther ahead, you'll see a lot more disappearing. Roads have a way of ploughing through places that lie between important destinations. And that's possibly all this place will ever be—a minor location on a road to a destination. And if that turns out to be the case? You could see a situation where big new roads become like serpents, consuming a place entirely.

I had a hollow feeling thinking how my father would react to the road going through his sawmill. Somehow I knew that this would be the end of something important for him. This mill had been his last shot at becoming his own boss, living in his own place more or less on his own terms. This expropriation would cut the legs from under him. There would never be another sawmill.

I thought of Carthage. And then—I have to admit it—I felt something like relief.

———

Grade ten was incredibly tedious, partly because the work I was doing was, by then, so familiar to me—the result of having been five years sitting in the same room with the grade ten courses droning around me. There were two of us in the grade—I and a new girl named Louise Embree. I had one advantage over Louise, who had just moved to the village. All her education up till then had been in a little one-room schoolhouse in the country. But it was no piece of cake. I don't think that girl ever slept. Nothing on her mind but books, which, I thought, was a waste, seeing how womanly she was becoming.

Around the school, the air was heavy with the tang of burning evergreens and loud with the roar of machinery as they tore up the orchard and our field and the Green Path and MacKinnons' and Jack Reynolds's and even the big back field where we once made hay for Big Ian MacKinnon.

My parents managed to find a buyer for the sawmill, and one day I saw a truck leaving the field loaded down with all the various parts I'd watched my father so painstakingly assemble.

My mother was watching too, through the kitchen window. She did not look unhappy.

And wisely, I thought: What's past is past. No point looking back. It's over and done with now.

Time to look ahead.

You couldn't tell from the cryptic letters what the hard-rock miner thought.

————

Ted came back briefly in 1958. He was finished at Tech. He was an engineer, proud of the little iron ring on his pinkie finger. He was hearty with me, pumping my hand, remarking on my growth—which I realize people do when they still see you as a kid. No talk of travel, which was just as well since I had a summer job. I was being paid practically nothing, but it was enough for basic independence.

I had started learning how to drive, but he saw no special significance in that development. Just a bit more enthusiasm over how I was growing up at last.

Not a word, I noticed, about New York City.

He was greeted like a homecoming member of the family by my mother and my aunt and by Sylvia's mother. But it was Sylvia he was here to see. You just knew it. He couldn't wait to talk to her alone. And after they had been together in private for a while, he seemed disappointed. Down, even.

He left shortly after that, promising to return.

Sylvia told me afterwards that he wanted her to go away with him. Far away—all the way to Korea. Meet his folks.

I couldn't imagine someone saying no to an offer like that. But she said no.

"I'm only seventeen," she said. "Plus, I belong here."

About a month later I had a postcard from Tokyo. And nothing more.

By then I had decisions to make. I was facing a whole new phase of schooling. There is no high school in the village. I had to go some-where—town? a new county high school twenty miles away in Judique? the monastery?

What about the monastery? I was attempting to recapture the feel-ing of that sunlit day when we went there as a family and each wandered off into his own private place. But I kept seeing my father standing there with the monk, talking about logs and sawing and the optimistic look on his face. And I realized I wouldn't want to be remembering that scene every time I turned around when I was going through high school.

I knew what my mother thought, so I didn't bother raising it with her. My father tried to raise the subject when he'd been home the previous Christmas.

"What are your plans for next year?"

I didn't answer right away. Here, I thought, is a chance to test the water.

"Maybe I'll quit school for a while."

I've noticed that people never say they're going to quit school for good. It's always quitting "for a while." Taking a break. To put aside a little money. Or just to clear your head, or maybe grow up a little bit before going on with life. Here I was suggesting bailing out even before high school. "Maybe I'll follow my father's footsteps," I said.

He laughed briefly, then started rolling a cigarette.

"I see," he said. "Is that it?"

"Or maybe I'll take a trade. Carpentry or something."

"Uh huh. This is possible."

Then my mother came into the kitchen, and we changed the subject.

But it was a discussion I couldn't avoid indefinitely. And when it finally came up again, the issue was whether I was still interested in the monastery. She'd heard of a kid my age from town who was going. What did I think?

I had, by then, seriously mixed feelings.

"And by the way," she said, "we haven't heard much about the vocation to the priesthood lately."

"I'm still thinking about it," I said, suddenly surprised by a feeling of emptiness.

"You are?"

"Yes."

She seemed to be looking right through my eyes and into the secret closets in my brain.

"You know," she said finally, "nothing would make a mother happier than to see one of her own ordained."

Another pause.

"Tell me again what you had in mind."

"I want to be a missionary," I said. "I want to go off into the world and help people."

"Yes," she said. "You're very interested in the world, aren't you?"

"Very," I said, aware that I was sounding more enthusiastic.

"But you should know," she said, "that there are much easier ways of seeing the world than as a missionary priest. It isn't an easy life. And it would be a big mistake to go into it for the wrong reasons."

"I suppose."

"Think it over carefully," she said. "Whatever you decide, the important thing is to make your choices for the right reasons."

And it was as if a weight was lifted off my shoulders.

That evening I walked along the old route I used to follow searching for the cow, up by the old MacMillan place. Just walking, lost in thought. I was almost past the now abandoned Gorman camp before I realized. The windows were dark, mirroring the fading light. I'd heard that the buildings were going to be removed—hauled away or demolished. Already people were inquiring whether parts could be recycled into housing. I pulled the collar of my jacket higher around my neck and walked on. For a moment I tried to grasp a dark elusive thought, but it had slipped away. Or maybe it was just the shadow of a thought.

The dog was with me. We communicated in a way we hadn't for a long, long time. Not since before Old John and noticing the changes in the girls and making friends with Ted had I felt so close to what I now realized was the one constant in my life. The one friend who never asked for anything or expected anything more than basic kindness. The one friend who never went away. My dog.

On the way back, we turned in by the old cemetery that overlooks the strait, and I saw a little platform jutting above the high embankment overlooking the approach road to the causeway. It was a "Look Off," according to a sign. I sat on a bench. The dog sat by my foot, his head resting against my knee. Port Hawkesbury was a slight bulge in the distance, more or less looking as it always had. I imagined the small white ferry boats plying the choppy water, back and forth, day after day, year after year, until time blurred into a single image printed in a common memory. And just beyond, the old train ferry, smoke stacks billowing. No more. And I tried to imagine how all those people in their graves, just behind me and over on the point where the lighthouse used to be, would feel seeing what I could now see—the causeway to the other world. And how privileged I was to have seen it happen. At least one large dream fulfilled. And suddenly I realized just how rare that was—to be a witness to success when so much seems to be the product of our failures.

And, at least in that passing instant, everything was clear to me. One day I, too, will lie blindly in a grave, missing all the drama and excitement that flutters from the folds of time. But now I was here. Who knows why or for how long? Only knowing that being here, with time passing through my senses, was a gift I could not waste—no matter what.

And, briefly, I grieved for Old John Suto, in a grave just beyond a town he never heard of before he came here. And for my transient father working deep in the darkness of the cold, hard rock of the planet in a province and a place he never heard of when he was a boy dreaming unlimited dreams on a green and sunny mountain.

We just sat there in the descending evening, the dog and I, watching the cars coming and going and the big green bridge squatting over the canal, just waiting for the signal to move and make way to let another ship, another traveller from the wide, chaotic world, come through. The strait was clear.

The dog yawned, stuck his nose under my hand, then wriggled his head so my hand was resting on the soft fur between his ears. Then he stood and looked as if to say: Let's go home; it's suppertime.

And I realized we'd reached the end of something. The causeway, finally, has been done. Today and yesterday are done. There is just tomorrow. And then another, and another . . . tomorrows flowing endlessly towards an ocean called the future. And, in my mind at least, the future will be anything I want to make it.

And we went home together.

IN
THE SPRING
OF '69

9

HOME

Certain things happen, and it's like they're happening to someone else. And if you reflect for a moment, you might realize these are the moments that become big memories—these are moments without end. My wife says to me: "Of course you'll have to go home for this." And, unaccountably, I reply, "But we're broke." And she looks at me in disbelief.

"Broke," says she. "Nobody is that broke."

And then I remembered the envelope from the bank that I'd set aside carelessly, figuring it was just another gimmick. A little plastic card with my name on it and, in capital letters across the top: CHARGEX. The literature said it was a credit card. I could use it to buy things. Pay later.

"I could use that new credit card," I said, half to myself.

"Of course," she said. "That's what those things are for—emergencies."

Of course I had to go home. He was gone. Again. For good.

Checking in at the airport in Ottawa, I noticed that the man in front of me was Mr. G.I. Smith, the premier of Nova Scotia. We all call him Ike. When he had his boarding pass, he turned slightly to leave, but he noticed me standing there and smiled. We shook hands. He's shorter than I am, a small pale man with a sad expression.

"I suppose we're heading in the same direction," he said.

"Yes," I said.

"A little winter holiday?" he asked.

"No," I said. "A death in the family."

He studied me gravely for a moment, an expression of sympathy on his face. I knew it was sincere. People from the small provinces are like that. We're all related by something—blood, familiarity, or need.

"I'm sorry to hear that," he said.

"Yes. Thank you."

He shook my hand again.

"Someone close?"

"My father," I said.

"Oh my," said Premier Smith. "Oh dear."

And his grip on my hand tightened.

———

It happens at the oddest times. A stirring in the memory, just below the threshold of consciousness. Not quite tangible, but the voice of the subconscious is saying you'd better pay attention—this could be important. You might wake up in the middle of the night and hear the rain pounding, and right out of nowhere a phantom thought pops into your head. You're wide awake then. Did I leave the car windows open? Maybe you're in a hotel, and you'd have to get dressed and go all the way outside to check. And probably find, when you got there, that you didn't. And then be so annoyed that you can't get to sleep anymore anyway. And then you're stranded in a completely pointless mental exercise that turns into an agitated reflection on reflection—like standing between two mirrors. Infinite frustration.

———

I wept once. I was in the shower, with the water pouring over me, and I realized that, mingled in with the water streaming down my face, there were gushing tears. But I quickly stopped when I became conscious of the weeping and felt that my self-consciousness somehow cheapened the sorrow, made it false. Grief, considered, loses its integrity, I think. I could be wrong. But that's how I felt at the time. There was something phony about standing in the shower weeping—something theatrical.

The other time I nearly wept was when my mother was telling me how he became fond of shopping after he'd been living at home for a while.

"Shopping?"

"Yes," she said.

She'd arrive home from teaching school in town, and there would be groceries on the cupboard. The first time it happened, she couldn't imagine where they came from. It didn't occur to her that he'd just spontaneously go into McGowan's or the new shopping centre in town and buy groceries. He hadn't done that since they were first married and living in St. Lawrence, Newfoundland.

Of course, when she thought about it, it was like being newly married all over again after he got the new job with the Nova Scotia Water Resources Commission and was living at home all the time. Lots of men who spend a lot of time living exclusively among other men have a hard time with domesticity. But not him. He seemed to enjoy it— buying the groceries. He even quit smoking.

We laughed briefly at the irony. So much for quitting smoking.

It was talking about him enjoying shopping that caused the second sudden welling up. But I crimped it.

———

Driving to town, it was raining. Back at the house they'd all been talking about the wet winter. It was March, but not a trace of snow. Apparently it's been like this since January. Much the same in Ottawa, I was able to report. And then everybody was interested in Ottawa, but I found it difficult to talk about Ottawa. The city and the Parliament Buildings and the newspaper offices and everything I did there suddenly seemed unreal. Come to think of it, nothing was real anymore. It was like the day Old John Suto shot himself. It didn't happen, but it happened. It's as if you acquire something that's too big for the house, and it's stuck in the doorway. Eventually you stop struggling to take it inside. You just drift off into something else.

That's when the Cadillac popped into my head—something about a Cadillac suddenly seemed relevant. More than relevant actually. *Urgent.* Understanding something about a Cadillac might be the key to understanding everything about what was going on around me—maybe release me from this heaviness, open up those entrances that suddenly seemed too small.

It was probably the emblem on the back of the Cadillac in front of us that did it to me. What about the Cadillac emblem? I'm leaning forward, peering past the lazy, sweeping windshield wiper that leaves a filmy smear behind every pass. What is it about the Cadillac emblem? I sit back, close my eyes, do what I do back at the office when I'm having a hard time recovering some obscure piece of information. Focus.

The one thing I know is that it has something to do with the night we got loaded at the beginning of that wasted weekend. When was it? November? Just four months ago. Wow—only four months.

So I work back through what I can remember. He picked me up at the airport on the Friday night. Great cheer over the new job. All the good stuff he never had before—benefits and job security. And living at home. And how it was almost a self-assigning job, as we say in the newspaper business. It's your performance that's accountable, not the physical location of your flesh.

How rare it was, that conversation, even though, as I recall it, there was so much nonsense. The thing about the Cadillac must have fallen into that category. But I probably wasn't paying a whole lot of attention because it was the fact of the conversation itself that was so significant. You see, I don't think we ever had many conversations— father and son, looking each other in the eye and talking turkey. How things really are, and the whole point of it being that if things aren't really as copacetic as they seem to be, then two grown-up men with a special bond between them can certainly combine their strengths and work things out. That is what those types of conversations are about, I think.

I remember, when I got back, telling Michael Cassidy, the guy I work with who is extremely bright and a fabulous writer, how we got loaded and talked our heads off for the entire evening and part of the next day. And Cassidy saying what a great experience that must have been. Like me, he hardly got to know his dad, who, in addition to being very active politically and therefore preoccupied with universal matters, died when he was quite young.

"Harry Cassidy, you must have heard of him."

"Afraid not."

"One of the founders of the CCF."

"Oh, right. Himself and Wordsworth and . . ."

"Woodsworth."

"Right, right."

The Cadillac emblem is distinctive, like the coat of arms of some high-ranking nobleman in an important medieval family. Designed to impress, perhaps even to intimidate.

There was only one Cadillac around these parts when I was growing up, and it belonged to Gordon Walker. If I'm not mistaken, he got a new one almost every year, but it always looked exactly like the one he had the year before. I might be wrong about that, but I think I'm correct. Mr. Walker owned a bank. He'd be in the paper from time to time, and they'd always point that out. The only individual in the whole country to own his own bank.

What would that be like?

I know a little bit about banking now because, when I started at the job I'm in and confessed to Cassidy that I didn't have a clue about any aspect of the world of finance and economics—which was what we're supposed to be reporting on from the nation's capital—he told me the quickest way to learn would be to read the report of the Royal Commission on Banking and Finance.

And I tried.

Maybe Gordon Walker's name came up, and that's why I thought of a Cadillac.

This is the trouble after you've grown older and found some common ground on which to meet your parents as equals—or as equal as they can ever be considering the peculiar circumstances of how you became associated in the first place. By the time you're old enough to command their serious attention as another adult, you're living away from them, and the only opportunities that arise for a meeting of minds are ceremonial—birth, marriage, death. Or they're so rare that you don't want to risk the quality of the time available by venturing into unknown areas of substance. Hence, getting loaded, either to keep things light or to lubricate the sticky places. The problem is that sometimes you can't remember afterwards. You can't separate the substance from the lubrication.

And then, much later, you'll see something that triggers a memory that's inaccessible. And it makes you crazy.

What about the damned Cadillac?

I know we talked a lot, that night in November, and that was rare. There are people who say that's understandable. Your father is an itinerant—which means, rarely home. People like that are always visitors, and just how meaningful can a conversation ever be when it's with a casual visitor?

But no, I say. Sure, he was a visitor a lot of the time. But there were long stretches when he'd be around, as when they were building the causeway.

Sure, and what would he be doing during those long stretches when he wasn't a visitor?

He'd be working.

See?

We actually lived together, as men. Two summers in the same mining camps. But never talked.

When I went to university, I needed work for tuition money. First he got me on in Tilt Cove, in Newfoundland. Buck thirty an hour for underground labour—powder monkey for the miners in the drifts and raises and stopes and, when there was nothing else, down in the bottom of the shaft mucking out the sump or smashing large rocks on the grizzly with a sledgehammer.

We actually shared a room for a month or so before he moved over to the staff house. He was a boss. But he resisted living among the other bosses. He was always happier among the men in the bunkhouse. But then I moved in, and I guess he wanted me to have the room to myself. So he went over to the staff house.

Actually, it isn't true to say we never talked. It was in Tilt Cove that we had one of two real "father and son" sit-down serious chats that I can remember. Neither of us had a drink on board. He was all dressed up and ready to go out on vacation for a week or two. Going home. Anything I might need when he was coming back?

"Bring back the mail," I said, half joking.

It was after my sophomore year, and I was waiting for my marks at the time.

I figured that was going to be the extent of the conversation.

He seemed to be searching for words, and that was odd. Even though English was his second language, he was a really great talker. Lovely flow of language—and never a swear word I would hear.

"I want you to be careful," he instructed.

Right away I think he's talking about Itchy's little saloon up above the commissary, where a lot of the younger guys spent all their evenings and most of their money. I figure he suspects I'll be up there like a shot the minute his back is turned. And, actually, he isn't all that far off the mark.

But he said: "Just keep in mind that, as far as you're concerned, this is temporary."

I hadn't thought of it like that, and, as a matter of fact, I wasn't so sure it was going to be so temporary. There was something I actually liked about working underground—something about the isolation and the unnatural surroundings. Just going down the shaft and putting in your day and coming back up in one piece gave me a feeling of accomplishment.

And I discovered that I loved blowing things up and had a natural comfort level around explosives. Before my first day was finished, I was like all the old timers, sitting on a powder box smoking cigarettes.

"I had actually considered . . . if the marks are as bad as I expect . . ."

"Nope," he said. "This is temporary. You're only passing through. You've got better things in store. Don't risk them in a place like this."

"Which means?"

Long pause then. And he was fishing out the package of Export Plain, trying not to look at me.

"Don't do anything that doesn't feel right," he said at last.

"Okay."

"Somebody asks you to do something you're not sure about . . . don't do it."

Amazing, I thought. Here's a boss telling you that if another boss asks you to do something dangerous or foolish, you're supposed to tell him where to go.

I could have sworn that the hazel eyeballs kind of watered up, but they were quickly lost behind the cloud of smoke. Then he stood and grabbed the little travel bag he calls his grip.

"As Martin Angus says, 'I'll be back.'"

We both laughed then at the family reference to the weird cousin with the extraordinary brain and nothing else going for him.

"All brains and no common sense," they like to say about Martin Angus.

It was after he came back from the holiday that he moved into the staff house.

Then there was the next summer.

I was stranded in Seven Islands—*Sept Isles*, as we say in Ottawa—when I ran out of money trying to find a job for the summer. Got the job all right, working on a railway project, but when they found out I was just nineteen, they told me to hit the road. You had to be twenty-one—something about being bonded.

I wanted to say: I'm not into bondage yet, but I was too busy panicking.

I pointed out that I'd worked underground in Tilt Cove when I was still seventeen, which is technically against the law, and everything was fine. The answer I got was, That's their problem.

I pointed out that I'd been born in Newfoundland and that Newfoundlanders were supposed to be getting preference for jobs in Labrador.

The man doing the hiring studied me for a moment. "So call up Joey Smallwood and complain," he said.

So here I am in Seven Islands and the money gone. Actually, I had enough to get a phone call to a place called Bachelor Lake in northern Quebec, where the old fellow was a shift boss at the time. It's 1963. And he wired me enough money to get there. I went to work as an underground labourer, this time for a buck twenty-eight an hour.

Heading in the wrong direction, moneywise. But there wasn't much of an alternative. After I was there about a month, an older fellow, a Scot named Jackson, suggested that he and I team up and head for Tillsonburg to pick tobacco. Hard work, he said. He did it every summer. But the harder you work, the more you earn. Not like this shithole. Plus, it's nicer working in the fresh air.

I was rooming in the bunkhouse with my father. I told him about Jackson's plan, and he lit a cigarette slowly, the way he always did when he was thinking.

"Whatever you think yourself," he said, blowing out a match.

So I figured that was it. Tillsonburg, here I come. Fresh air, sunshine, and big bucks.

But shortly before the day, over a beer in Ikey's store, which also served as the beer hall, not unlike Itchy's back in Tilt Cove, he told me that he didn't think it was such a good idea, going off to pick tobacco. We were playing cribbage at the time.

"I'm not so sure about this joker Jackson," he said, studying his hand.

I found that shocking, because I'd never heard him critical of anybody, and of course I always figured there could be nothing bad from Scotland.

So I told him one of the reasons I wanted out was because I was having a problem with one of the other shift bosses, who seemed to have it in for me.

"Which one?"

"Charpentier," I said.

"That doesn't surprise me," he said.

"Why doesn't it surprise you?"

"Ah well," he said, staring at the ash on the end of a cigarette. "It's probably got more to do with me."

And then: "I'll have a little word with Charpentier."

That was the second time that we spoke man to man. And Jackson headed off to Tillsonburg alone. From then on, all Charpentier did was scowl at me.

Another thing that made working underground so interesting was that I found university a drag. The camps were the opposite of the campus. I was attending university in Antigonish, which was fairly close to home but another world entirely. It was a huge challenge. I was never sure whether I was bored most of the time or if I was just slow at catching on. Sitting through endless classes and not hearing a word the professor was saying—as though I was deaf. Barely scraping by in the quizzes. Flat broke all the time. Walking around among all the bright young students from Upper Canada and New England with the arse out of your pants half the time. It wasn't fun.

In the mines, you went over to the dry at the start of every shift and hauled down the basket where you stored your working clothes and, in five minutes flat, you were the same as everybody else. Rubber trousers, battery belt cinched at the waist, battery hooked on, and the lamp cable casually looped around your neck like the pros. After only a shift or two, I could smoothly attach the light to the bracket on the front of the hard hat without having to take the hat off, just like the old timers. One swift casual motion of the hand and the light was in place, as if you'd been doing it all your life. Sure, the older miners knew I wasn't really as strong or as skilled as they were, but it didn't matter. I was learning. Plus, I was Dan Rory MacIntyre's Boy and, as one of them told me at Itchy's one night the time he was out on his holiday, Dan Rory MacIntyre is the Best Goddamned Miner in Canada.

I was shocked that one of these hard, truculent outsiders would declare such a thing and that it might be true.

Maybe the sickly kid from the mountain had turned into something, after all.

But what good was that if you don't realize it or, in the long run, you don't care about having become good at something you do because you have to? Maybe it was there that I realized the most important goal in life is freedom. And the key to freedom is choice. And the key to choice is either birth or education. And very few of us are born free. Really.

This is kind of silly, but one of the reasons I got off on the wrong foot at university was that I went there feeling sour because of a mix-up over gender.

Here's what happened. Early summer, 1960, I applied to St. Francis Xavier University, which is where all the Catholics from home tend to go. It was only forty miles away, but I was going to have to live there. It was a long forty miles because the Trans-Canada hadn't yet been finished on the mainland. Forty miles of narrow, winding roads.

And I remember the day the reply came back. I was picking up the mail as usual. I was driving. We had a '58 Chev Belaire at the time. Very nice car—cobalt blue, lots of chrome. Among the bills and papers, there was the envelope from the university. I won't deny that I was nervous. I drove down to the new railway station, which is only about half the size of the old one they tore down after they built the causeway and changed all the tracks around. There was nobody around. I parked out back and tore open the letter.

To make a long story short: I was accepted.

I sighed a great sigh of relief. Then I read on. I had requested campus accommodations, and a room was reserved for me in a place called Immaculata Hall. I'd known university students and heard of Mockler

Dorm and Aquinas and MacDonald and MacPherson and Tompkins, but I'd never heard of this one. But, anyway, I kept on reading.

I was instructed that I was to bring clothing appropriate to a Catholic institution—dark stockings, modest dresses . . .

Dresses?

I went back to the top of the letter. It was addressed to Miss Linda MacIntyre.

The curse.

———

That night in November when we got loaded at the start of a wasted weekend, I remember trying to explain exactly what I do for a living. I was telling him about Cassidy and the royal commission report. And my friend Prinsky, who works for Dow Jones and the *Wall Street Journal*, and who was a big help when it came to figuring everything out.

I was explaining the way Cassidy and Prinsky wait around every Thursday afternoon for some obscure statistic from the Bank of Canada, talking away as if they were waiting for something important like the hockey standings. And then arguing about what it means that some number has changed by a percentage of a percentage point. Same thing with the balance of payments figures, and the unemployment rate.

I was beginning to get the hang of it, but, like somebody learning a foreign language, I wasn't yet ready for a conversation on deeper issues. So, mostly, I'd just listen to the experts. And if I ever did have an input, they'd hear me out respectfully, but then carry on as if I wasn't there. That was okay because I wasn't really there anyway.

So there we were, crossing Boularderie Island and heading for the Seal Island Bridge at the foot of Kelly's Mountain on a crisp November night, sipping on a quart of Demerara and talking as we never talked before— about Ottawa and finance and economics. A chance for me to practise my new language on somebody who knew less of it than even I did.

I was trying to explain fine points of public finance, treasury bills, and bonds—

Bonds?

I'm peering past the driver, through the smeared windshield, at that Cadillac emblem when it strikes me like a bolt of inspiration.

Bonds. That was it. I can finally relax. I remember the Cadillac connection and smile privately and turn to stare out the side window at the passing countryside. The rain is thickening to sleet.

He bought bonds. He subscribed to the latest issue of Canada Savings Bonds. But here's what he'd never told anyone before. When the bonds matured in a few years, he'd cash them in, and he was going to buy a Cadillac.

He would be in a position, with the bonds and some savings and maybe getting a trade-in on his Volkswagen bug, to liberate the ten or twelve thousand, or whatever it might be by then, to buy the Cadillac. The basic package. Three hundred and seventy-five horses. Turbo Hydramatic transmission. But, most of all, that emblem on the hood.

Coming down the other side of Kelly's Mountain, he confessed he'd always wanted to buy a Cadillac—the ultimate symbol of success. The declaration to everybody who ever knew him that he'd made it—that you could come down off MacIntyre's Mountain with nothing but the rags on your back and make it in the wider world. And you didn't have to be a banker or a Mason or kiss some politician's ass. All it took was hard work—that and a little bit of luck.

Of course he realized he hadn't made it. And probably wasn't going to make it now that he was fifty years old and settled into working for someone else in a civil service job.

But, you know what? He'd given it his absolutely best shot. And that was what really mattered when all was said and done. And just that fact alone was worth a Cadillac.

It all came back to me, just in time. The happy Friday night excursion, racing down Kelly's Mountain, veins throbbing from the rum and the companionship. Now the wind is blowing, lashing our little procession with a muddy, salty rain. The Cadillac in front is slowing down. Then the left turn-signal light flashes. The rain is getting heavier. The Cadillac comes almost to a full stop for the hairpin turn below the church, then it starts creeping up the hill. The church bell is ringing slowly.

The Cadillac comes to a gentle stop. Then there are burly men in black overcoats gathering around the rear doors, blocking my view of the emblem that looks like something on the coat of arms of some important nobleman in some important clan. Then a man with one hand flat on the top of his hat, face turned away from the slanting rain, hurries to the rear of the Cadillac, preparing to open the doors. The burly men in overcoats form two lines, like soldiers.

———

For all the evidence of recovered domesticity, I gather that his basic tastes didn't change much near the end. My boyhood friend Ian MacKinnon, who now works in the liquor store, was telling me that, once or twice a week, Dan Rory would show up for his little six-pack. Usually Olands or Schooner, never Moosehead. Moosehead gives him the "seann buinneach mhor," he'd say. That's Gaelic, literally meaning "old shit in large quantities." I asked my cousin John Dougald, who shares his obsession with trucks and cars, if he'd ever heard the scheme about the Cadillac. And Dougie said he never heard a thing. The only plan Dan Rory shared with him after he came home for good was the one about a dog. He always loved dogs. Swore, when our dog Skipper disappeared without a trace in 1961, he'd never have another. They just don't live long enough. But then, after he got the new job, he was talking about getting a little dog to keep him company when he was working. It was wicked quiet over by the lake, and the time dragged when the pumps were working well—which they were, mostly, since everything was almost new.

Ian saw him on the Tuesday afternoon at the liquor store, picking up his little six-pack of Schooner. And when he didn't show up for supper, my mother figured he'd gone out to visit his nephew Dougie or his brother, John Dan. He'd been grieving, in his own inscrutable way, ever since Peigeag passed away, just two weeks earlier.

I was in the Parliamentary Reading Room in early March when I found out. I felt weird afterwards, finding out in a newspaper that my Grandma had died. Mrs. Margaret MacIntyre—a very common name around home. I had to look twice. I'd never thought of her as Mrs. Margaret MacIntyre. But this was Mrs. Margaret MacIntyre of MacIntyre's Mountain. Widow of the late Dougald MacIntyre. Died February 24. Survived by . . . and of course my name was there among us. There must be some mistake. But there it is, in black and white, in the pages of the *Victoria-Inverness Bulletin*.

She was ninety-five—same age as Dougald. No coincidence there. She was actually two years younger than he was, but out of sheer stubbornness she lived exactly as long as he did. Hung on for two extra years after the old man died to get the same amount of time in. Ninety-five years—no more, no less. She was born in 1874, though you could never be too sure with those old people. The record keeping, back when they were born, wasn't exactly meticulous. There was never much made of birthdays. One of the only birthdays I ever heard referred to was Grandpa's eightieth. The day he turned eighty, St. Patrick's Day, 1952, he dropped in on John Dan's and probably had a *dileag* or two to celebrate the occasion. *Fun at Five* was on the radio and they played a fiddle tune, and the old man just spontaneously got out in the middle of the kitchen floor and started step dancing. Everybody was cheering him on and somebody shouted "suas e bhodag," which is the Gaelic for "drive 'er, old man." It's a very common expression. You hear it all the time, especially when somebody is dancing. But he took it in the nose—being called an old man. Walked out and went home in a snit. That was the story, anyway.

Mrs. Margaret MacIntyre dead?

You think, in all improbability, that they've made a mistake. She was always larger than life, seemingly immune to death. Once that I know of she got seriously ill—gangrene in her foot; started spreading up her leg. Finally she went to the hospital in Inverness, where they couldn't do anything to stop it. They sent her over to Antigonish, where doctors told her she'd have to lose the leg entirely.

When she found out what they were saying, she hit the roof.

Not a chance. She came into the world blessed with two good legs, and she was going out the same way. This was all in translation, but I think I got the gist of it.

The doctors basically told her that she was committing suicide— that without an amputation, the gangrene was going to kill her.

"Send me home," she said. And so they did.

The first thing she did when she got back to the mountain was send for the priest—Father John Angus Rankin. Father John Angus is a whole story all by himself. He's very serious about the supernatural. Allegedly communicates with dead people. Exorcises demons. Has the Power. Just like herself.

The two of them retired to a private place and did something. Prayed, I guess. Whatever they did, the gangrene went away, and she still had two completely functional legs the last time I saw her—at Grandpa's wake just about two years ago. The night she threw Domhnaill-Angie Stephan out into the snow for something he said to my grandfather's corpse.

Mrs. Margaret MacIntyre, dead? Highly unlikely. But there it is in the paper.

It was only as I was making my way back up to the press gallery hot room that it struck me as odd that nobody had bothered telling me when the old lady made her exit. Not a peep from home to tell me how or when. Very strange.

So, that evening, when I got home from work, I called, and he confirmed it. Passed away nearly ten days ago. Just went quietly—the flu or something. "The old people's friend," they call it around here. An easy way out when they figure it's time. And she probably did conclude that she'd lived long enough, thank you very much, after two years' living without the Old Man, as she called him. Sure enough, I can't imagine that she'd have died if she didn't want to.

"But anyway, how come nobody told me?"

Well, said he, they thought of me. But they knew how busy I am up there in Ottawa. And it was the winter, and travel is expensive and treacherous this time of year. And, after all, she was ninety-five. It wasn't exactly unexpected.

"I'm sure she'd understand."

But I'm not so sure. And what if she didn't understand? What if she took my absence in the nose?

It might help explain what happened fifteen days later.

The doctor said he probably never felt a thing. He was probably dead before he hit the floor.

Old Jim Sandy, who was standing there in front of him, said afterwards that all he remembered was Dan Rory saying, "I'm going," then turning slightly and falling down. Jim Sandy, who was loaded at the time, figured he'd just flaked out. It wouldn't have crossed his mind that a man could fall down for reasons other than being plastered.

Jim Sandy went to bed. They figure it was only about five in the afternoon.

Ian said it was around four when Dan Rory picked up his six-pack. And he remembered seeing Jim Sandy hanging around outside the liquor store at the time. Of course the old man knew Jim Sandy from the sawmill days and just generally from growing up out back. My theory is that Jim Sandy needed a ride home, and the old fellow told him to jump in.

———

On Wednesdays, Cassidy and I would be getting serious about the Friday deadline—getting realistic about what we could deliver by the end of the week. Mondays we'd be gung ho, promising the moon, bringing down the government. Tuesdays we'd be trying to get the list of promised stories down to a manageable size. Wednesdays we'd be backtracking.

There was a knock on the office door, which was strange to start with. Nobody ever knocked. It was even stranger, when I opened the door, to see my friend Father Lewis MacDonald there, wearing his black suit, topped off by the Roman collar. Lewis is part of the post-Vatican-Two crowd of young priests—into T-shirts and jeans and guitars on the altar. And he's from home, a brother of my friend Dennis. Their mother, Dolly, taught me in grade seven. Their father, Jock, was also a hard-rock miner and had died in the fall of '67. We were close.

"Can you come outside for a minute?" Lewis asked.

He hardly ever wore the black suit. And he hardly ever came downtown. He was teaching in a Catholic high school out in the west end and rarely needed to be anywhere near the Hill.

"Hey, what brings you . . ."

"I have to talk to you," he said.

"Well, come in . . ."

He caught the doorknob and pulled the door half shut and said to me in a quiet voice: "It's about your father."

"What about him?"

I thought suddenly about the perils of the mine and all the bad things that can happen to you when you're off in the middle of nowhere.

But, hang on, I think. He isn't in the mines anymore. He's home for good. He's working for the government.

"I'm afraid he's gone," Father Lewis said.

———

After the funeral and the burial, we were all sitting around the house kind of shell-shocked. All the neighbours were there. People who knew him from the lumber camps and sawmills and trucking and the mines. People coming in, the way they were for days. There was even a surprise visit from the MP, Allan MacEachen, who is federal minister of manpower and immigration—a big gesture for a Tory house. But then, of course, Dan Rory was pretty neutral when it came to politics.

"Sorry for your trouble . . ."

"Life is full of surprises . . ."

"Well, isn't that it."

At one point Roddie Cueball, who is really Roddie MacDonald but called Roddie Cueball because he was born bald and stayed that way—and who is also a talented pool player besides being the under-taker—took me aside and said, "Somebody has to sign this."

He handed me a piece of paper, and I saw immediately it was the death certificate.

Cause of death: coronary thrombosis.

"How do they know?" I asked.

He shrugged. "That's what the doctor figured."

I signed.

There were drinks then. After the crowd thinned out, my cousin Dougie produced a forty-ouncer.

Soon somebody was talking about Grandma. Sure enough, there was no way Peigeag was going to leave Dan Rory here without herself to look after him.

Everybody laughed, because everybody knew Peigeag and the way she was.

He took it hard when she went, somebody said. Standing behind him at the old woman's grave, they said you could see his shoulders jerk ever so slightly when they started lowering her down.

My mother was sitting quietly in the rocking chair by the stove. She seemed numb. It was the rocking chair Grandma Donohue always sat in before she died in 1964. Now my mother was sitting there, and it was a little bit disturbing.

During a quiet moment, I heard her say to nobody in particular: "I just realized that I'm a widow."

Nobody responded.

Later, Big Ian MacKinnon, who is the local member of the county council (for the Tories), took me aside and asked if there was anything he could do.

And it occurred to me on the spot: "I wonder if you could take me out to where it happened?"

———

That was how Father Lewis put it. Simply, "He's gone."

As often happens in such circumstances, I asked a stupid question. "Gone where?"

I now understand the phenomenon. You're seeking refuge in absurdity, knowing that the moment you embrace reality, everything will change. Knowledge grafted to your understanding changes it forever and ever and ever. "Per omnia saecula saeculorum. Amen."

"Get your coat," Father Lewis ordered.

Numbly, I complied.

Cassidy looked up from his typewriter, suddenly confused, seeing the red-headed fellow in the priest suit.

"I have to go," I said. I felt cold, heard my voice and it was shaky.

"What's up?" he asked.

"I have to go home," I said. "Something has happened."

———

Jim Sandy's house is up behind Grant's Pond, near Embree's Island, just outside Port Hawkesbury. A little white house in the middle of the woods. It was a neighbour who discovered that there was a dead man in the house on the Wednesday. Later, my sister Rosalind went to fetch his car. But by then the little Volkswagen wouldn't start, and when they checked, they found the battery was dead. They were figuring that Jim Sandy needed help getting into his house, and that Dan Rory left the engine running and the lights on. Eventually even a Volkswagen runs out of gas.

Jim Sandy was sitting at the kitchen table when Big Ian and I arrived. He seemed vague, and it wasn't clear whether he was genuinely confused about what had happened, or hungover and evasive, or feeling guilty. Or a combination of everything. I let Big Ian ask the questions. Basically, what could he remember?

"Hardly anything," he said.

Just that bit about Dan Rory saying "I'm going" or something like that.

Completely ambiguous. Meaning: I'm going home; or something a bit more ominous.

But the part about falling down? This is what I want to interject. Is it normal in this house for your visitors to collapse in front of you? Your visitors fall down on the floor and never move? And you go to bed?

But it quickly became clear to us that talking to Jim Sandy was pointless. Part of me thought I should be angry. But I couldn't quite work myself up to anything approaching so constructive an emotion. His time was up. If it wasn't here, it would have been somewhere else. Looking at old Jim Sandy there at his kitchen table, I could feel only a mixture of pity and sadness. Another fellow from out back who never had much luck.

What was the curse, I wonder, inflicted on this generation? Battered from birth by poverty and war. In their time, all the politics and economics turned upside down. Men like these became mere disposables, in war and in peace—units of productivity or destruction in the service of tycoons and generals and politicians. They were born at the end of the worst war in history and were kids during the roaring decade when the world felt reborn. And then progress stopped. Gangs of Nazis and Communists set out to dominate the world. Hungarians and Poles died to win freedom from the Nazis and the Communists. Koreans and Arabs and Jews struggled—everybody was struggling for something. It was all part of the unending human impulse to rise above this hopelessness. A struggle to achieve some elemental certainty about your fate. A struggle that always seems to start somewhere in the soul and to end, for most, like this—in terminal confusion.

But was it . . . is it . . . ever any different?

Big issues to discuss with Cassidy and Prinsky when I get back to Ottawa.

Passing through Jim Sandy's porch on the way out, I spotted a small cardboard box in the corner—a Schooner six-pack. I stopped and walked over, bent down, and picked up the little beer case. It was empty. But in the bottom of the box I saw the receipt from the liquor store. I put it in my pocket.

Later I made a note of the time and date on the damp little sales slip from the liquor store. The purchase was just before four in the afternoon, Tuesday, March 11.

As he'd have said himself: "Co dhiubh . . ." I'm glad someone got some pleasure out of it anyway.

And then someone was saying there was no way Peigeag would do anything to harm Dan Rory. No way she'd want to take him with her. He was always her favourite. And somebody else saying, Yes, but it's entirely possible she discovered that things are really better Over There . . . over where they both are now. She'd have wanted him to be a part of that. God have mercy on the both of them.

I suppose.

Or, I'm thinking, maybe she could see the future. Maybe she suddenly became aware of what I could clearly see from Ottawa, reading the papers, talking to the young draft dodgers and deserters who are part of the urban landscape now. She knows where the world is heading. She knows about the drugs and the promiscuity. The conflict. She knows that the murders of the Kennedys and Dr. King are just the tip of the iceberg, that the world is becoming more unstable and more violent. Everything is changing. All the certainties of their culture and their faith are about to fall apart. Dan Rory wasn't ready for it. So she took him home with her. Somewhere safe.

Maybe.

But I can't stop thinking that it's probably a lot simpler. Maybe if he had told me when she died, so I could have come home and paid my respects. I know she was hovering over the proceedings. Her own wake and funeral. I can see her standing in the doorway, shawl over the head, long skirts to the ground, hands hidden in the folds of a long sweater, making the list: who came to remark upon her life and on her powers . . . who drank what and how much of it . . . who stayed away and what were their excuses.

She'd have known I wasn't there and why. Nobody told me. She wouldn't have blamed me. Not Lindy. *M'eudail* Lindy . . . but, just the same. If I'd been there, maybe she'd have left him alone. Or maybe, in her new state of wisdom, she'd have learned about the *buidseachd* and probably been disposed to cancel it.

Maybe, if I'd come home. Maybe. It's possible. Anything is possible where she's concerned.

———

Much later I asked my mother: "How did he pull it off?" How, after so many years on the outside looking in, did he finally gain admission to that exclusive club? The Fraternal Brotherhood of the Locally Employed. It had occurred to me that Inverness County finally had a Tory representative in the provincial legislature, Dr. Jim MacLean. And that Dr. MacLean's mother was a MacIntyre whose roots were on MacIntyre's Mountain.

"You don't think . . . ?"

She just stared at me.

"Never. Not in a million years."

"You don't think he finally broke down and went to see . . . ?"

"If he did, he never said a word to me."

It was, I gather, tediously straightforward. No political intrigue at all. It seems the job was posted. He applied. Got an interview. Explained his background in mining and how pumps and pipes serve as the complex vascular system that keeps a mine alive. And that he understood pumps and pipelines as well as he understood the lines on the palms of his hands. They were suitably impressed by his intelligence, experience, and poise.

As my mother said: "You'd only have to talk to the man for a few minutes to realize that he was capable of any job he put his mind to."

And then I wondered: What about the *buidseachd?* What happened to that factor in his life?

But there's nobody left to ask about the *buidseachd.*

Father Lewis was waiting at the office door. I explained briefly to Cassidy, whose own father had died suddenly, and he got it right away. My father died.

"But can't you spare a moment to talk about what you're working on for Friday?" he said.

"No," I replied.

We were on the street when I remembered that Father Lewis had also lost his father suddenly and at an early age—just a year and a half ago. Jock was never sick. He went upstairs one day after lunch to take a nap. Shortly after that, Dolly, his wife, heard a thump. And, when she went to check, poor Jock was lying there on the floor.

There was a cold drizzle falling. Wellington Street was thick with cars. Important people were making their way home after another day running the country.

"I was just thinking about Jock," I said. "How he went. I remember us talking about it afterwards, just after you moved up here."

Lewis asked me where I was parked.

"Up behind the West Block," I said.

We crossed the street in front of the National Press Building and climbed a short flight of stairs with black wrought-iron railings. The dark Parliament Buildings loomed like gargoyles.

"Give me the keys," he said.

I dug them out and handed them over.

Near the car I stopped him, my friend the priest.

"I don't recognize anything," I said.

"Just lead the way," he said. "I think that's you over there."

He was pointing towards my Beaumont.

"No," I said. "I mean I don't recognize any of the feelings. What

354

am I supposed to feel? What did you feel like, last fall, when they told you about Jock?"

"It's okay," he said. "It's okay. We're going to get you home."

And I think the rain was coming down harder then. I think that it had suddenly become colder. And that we were in Ottawa on a Wednesday afternoon in March. And I think it was at that moment I realized, with a terrible finality, that Dan Rory MacIntyre was home where he belonged. A home where nothing ever changes. Back with his mother, the eternal Peigeag, for good.

And suddenly it hit me, on that rainy afternoon in Ottawa. The major difference between us was, despite the *buidseachd*, that he was luckier than I am.

He always knew where he was going, even when he didn't have a clue how he might get there. Home—where Father Lewis says he's taking me now. But here's my problem—I'm not sure where home is anymore.

EPILOGUE

Late in 1969, seven months after my father's sudden death, I gave up my job as Ottawa-based correspondent for the *Financial Times of Canada* and moved back to Cape Breton. I worked there for six years as resident correspondent for the *Chronicle Herald*, a daily newspaper based in Halifax, Nova Scotia.

In those years I immersed myself in the life of the island. In my journalism, I reported aggressively on the industrial forces that were shaping and reshaping the life and culture of the place. I became active in a movement to restore and rehabilitate the Gaelic language, and I worked hard to achieve familiarity, if not fluency, in the language that was the key to unlocking so many mysteries in my personal history and communal past. I studied that history intensively; explored the long, rich memories of my elders; sought out and attempted to revive long-lost ties with distant relatives on the Hebridean island of South Uist.

I finally left Cape Breton again in 1976, somehow more secure in my identity. In 1980 I moved to Toronto, where I have now lived for more than twenty-five years.

In those later years I travelled widely in the world, carrying with me a profound curiosity about how we are altered by transient forces that, while appearing to be random and inevitable, are the consequences of ambition—another word for dreams. People dream, then seek the means—the wealth, the might, the political consensus—to make their dreams reality. When they succeed, we call it progress.

I've learned how much of human history depends on the sanity of dreamers. And how much of reality is the product of delusions. And how progress doesn't always mean improvement.

Each year I return to Cape Breton. Each year, it seems, the visits grow longer. But each year I leave again.

For many years I'd leave still wondering, as I wondered on that rainy afternoon in Ottawa in 1969: Where is home? Here? Where I'm going now? Where I get my mail?

Each visit to Cape Breton brings a common set of questions from my friends who never left there: When did you come home? How long will you be home this time? Doesn't if feel great to be home again?

When I return to where I live and where I work, it seems I've gone away. Again.

I've spent years struggling to understand this phenomenon of identity—understanding who you are by knowing where you're from.

I think I've come to terms at last with my dilemma. There is no answer because, essentially, there is no question. Where is home? Mere words, an admission of confusion from deep in the memory. When did you come home? It isn't meant to be a question, but, basically, a statement of who they think I am. And I am comfortable with that.

The confusion of that sad, cold day in March 1969 eventually lifted. I have come to understand the insight best explored by the French ascetic and philosopher Simone Weil in her reflection on "The Need for Roots." "Every human being needs to have multiple roots. It is necessary for him to draw well nigh the whole of his moral, intellectual and spiritual life by way of the environment of which he forms a natural part."

I take all that to mean that roots are what we learn from everything around us, wherever we happen to be at any given moment. And that home is not so much a place as what we know, a concept that becomes our compass.

POSTSCRIPT

In the late sixties and early seventies, the economic boom, long predicted for the Strait of Canso, materialized with an expansion of the pulp and paper mill built by a Swedish multinational in the early sixties and by the construction of a new oil refinery, a heavy-water plant, and a supertanker docking terminal. The refinery and the heavy-water plant have since closed. Current expectations are that a long-awaited economic transformation will flow from the processing of natural gas from recent discoveries off the Atlantic coast of Nova Scotia.

Cape Porcupine has become one of Canada's largest stone and gravel quarries, producing, by the late nineties, two million metric tonnes of material annually for shipment throughout North America and the Caribbean. The quarry is owned and operated by a subsidiary of Martin Marietta Materials, the second-largest producer of industrial aggregates in the United States. Since the construction of the causeway, which required ten million tons of rock, Cape Porcupine has produced enough stone for several more causeways. The cape, today, looks battered, weary, depleted.

Optimistic predictions that Port Hawkesbury would become a city have not yet happened. The population of the town has, however, doubled, to about five thousand. The village of Port Hastings is now a bedroom community for several hundred people, most of whom are employed in jobs that have been created since construction of the causeway in Port Hawkesbury and Point Tupper. One of the few recognizable parts of the old village today is St. David's United Church. All traces of the old coal piers and wharf facilities are gone. The stores owned by Mr. Clough and Mr. McGowan are gone, as are the school, the railway station, Mr. Clough's house, and the house I grew up in. The houses the MacIvers and Sylvia Reynolds lived in are gone, as are all the buildings on the water side of the road leading through the old part of the village. The house Mr. Malone built for his family, and the house Jackie Nicholson and his grandmother moved to in the village, are both vacant. Proposed changes in traffic flow at the various highway intersections in the village will mean further demolitions.

The railroad through Port Hastings and the bridge across the Canso Canal are now privately owned by Railamerica Inc., a U.S.-based company with close to fifty short-haul rail services in Canada and the United States. The rail line once used by the Judique Flyer—the train driven by Ian MacKinnon's father and grandfather—has been abandoned and is now a recreation trail for hikers and all-terrain vehicles.

Jackie Nicholson died in an automobile accident in 1973 at the age of thirty-one. The historic lighthouse in which his grandmother laboured for many years, and which was destroyed during the causeway construction, has been replaced by a replica near the site of the original.

Ian MacKinnon—a lifelong teetotaller—retired after a long career with the Nova Scotia Liquor Commission. He is a stalwart in his church and chief of the community's volunteer fire department.

Tae Man Chong, after a brief stay in his homeland, South Korea, returned to Canada in the late fifties, changed his name to Tae Di Yong, and established his own highly successful engineering business. He is now living, and still working, in a community north of Toronto.

In August 2005, on the initiative of the Port Hastings Historical Society, the last resting place of John Suto, which had never been identified by a permanent grave marker, was relocated and restored. A new headstone records that he was a native of Hungary, that he worked at the Gorman camp during construction of the causeway, that he died on August 11, 1956, and was buried on August 13. At a small dedication service on August 8, 2005, the present parish priest, Father Bill Crispo, recalled and commended the brave and compassionate response to John Suto's suicide by the late Father Michael "Spotty" MacLaughlin. John Suto and my father, whose lives were, oddly, symmetrical, are buried in the same cemetery.

Alice Donohue MacIntyre, who is my mother, and her sister, Veronica MacNeil, continue to reside independently in their own homes, with their political opinions and Hibernian sensibilities undiminished by time. They philosophically recall the days before the causeway when, it seems, all things were possible by strength of will and sinew.

There are now three MacIntyre households on MacIntyre's Mountain.

The last Gaelic speaker on MacIntyre's Mountain died in 2004.

On the headstone marking my grandparents' graves, there is a Gaelic inscription: "An Cuid de Pháras dhaibh."

It means: "May they have their share of Paradise."

ACKNOWLEDGEMENTS

The inspiration to write a memoir was not mine. My friends and literary representatives, Don Sedgwick and Shaun Bradley, first raised the idea with me. My initial reaction was a profound lack of enthusiasm. I told them early on that I was suspicious of the genre, because while I have felt comfortable writing journalism and fiction, I felt uneasy about the extent to which a memoir—especially a boyhood memoir—must rely on the subjectivity of memory. I decided to proceed when I discovered that there were abundant sources, some of them objective records, against which I could test the accuracy of my recollection of events that occurred half a century ago. Without the assistance of these sources, I would not have dared to begin.

My cousin and friend, Archie MacIntyre, was unfailingly generous with time and reminiscence during a particularly crucial period of his own life—the final stages of a desperate battle with cancer. He never hesitated to make time available to me, spoke frankly on the basis of his own extraordinary capacity for remembered detail, offered valuable advice and even read a first draft of my manuscript. His memories of growing up on MacIntyre's Mountain and our shared reminiscences about our grandparents, Peigeag and Dougald, gave the project an element of pleasure that I hadn't anticipated.

Besides the many relatives and friends with whom I shared a

seemingly unusual childhood—being caught on the threshold of the future while the voices of history still rang loud and clear in our daily experience—I had access to important media and archival resources. The Gut of Canso Museum offered a profusion of relics, reminders and records; the Public Archives of Nova Scotia provided access to newspapers from the period. Of incalculable value were the microfilmed back issues of the *Victoria-Inverness Bulletin*.

The Bulletin, as we knew it, was part of a tradition of community journalism that is sadly rare in these complex times, since the lives of ordinary people and their communities are seldom deemed worthy of media attention. *The Bulletin* and its many anonymous correspondents faithfully recorded the comings and goings, sorrows and celebrations, of its readers. Today, viewed from a vast distance in time and space, these records constitute a priceless people's history and a benchmark against which we can measure our progress and our losses.

To friends, relatives, archivists, and the selfless volunteers at the museum in Port Hastings, my deepest gratitude and apologies for unavoidable errors and omissions.

Once launched on the project of remembering, I was fortunate to have the guidance and help of a remarkable team of professionals at HarperCollins Canada. I'm especially grateful to Jim Gifford, Noelle Zitzer, Katie Hearn, Debbie Gaudet, and Phyllis Bruce for editorial advice and reassurance that the stories of people who were largely invisible in the sweep of history are really timeless and, in their potential for inspiration, universal. Thanks also to Rosemary Shipton.

I am also grateful to my wife, Carol Off, for her forbearance as I wrestled with many ghosts in what was sometimes an emotionally challenging project.

Alistair MacLeod was kind enough to read a draft of the manuscript and to respond with timely encouragement, important suggestions, and warm reminiscences about the history and the heritage we hold in common.

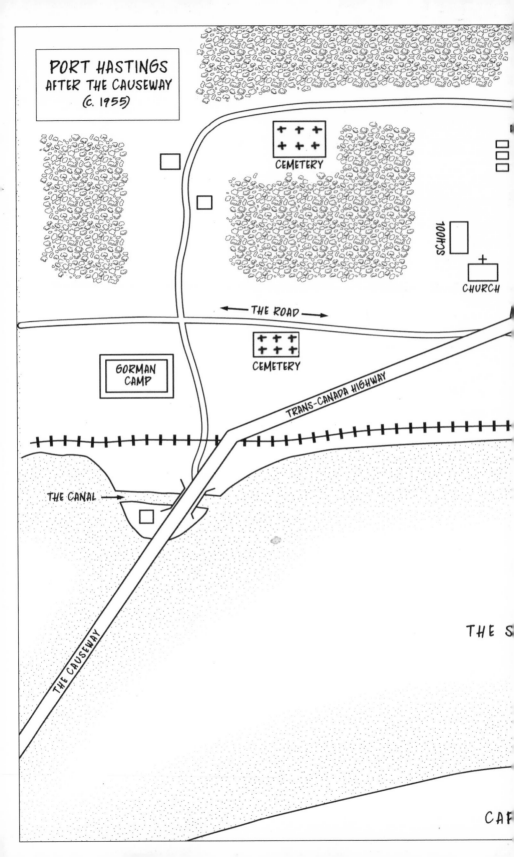

PORT HASTINGS
AFTER THE CAUSEWAY
(c. 1955)

CEMETERY

SCHOOL

CHURCH

THE ROAD

CEMETERY

GORMAN
CAMP

TRANS-CANADA HIGHWAY

THE CANAL

THE CAUSEWAY

THE S

CAF